African Americans
and American Indians
in the Revolutionary War

ALSO BY JACK DARRELL CROWDER

*Chaplains of the Revolutionary War:
Black Robed American Warriors*
(McFarland, 2017)

African Americans and American Indians in the Revolutionary War

JACK DARRELL CROWDER

McFarland & Company, Inc., Publishers
Jefferson, North Carolina

ISBN (print) 978-1-4766-7672-2
ISBN (ebook) 978-1-4766-3534-7

LIBRARY OF CONGRESS CATALOGUING-IN-PUBLICATION DATA

BRITISH LIBRARY CATALOGUING DATA ARE AVAILABLE

© 2019 Jack Darrell Crowder. All rights reserved

No part of this book may be reproduced or transmitted in any form or by any means, electronic or mechanical, including photocopying or recording, or by any information storage and retrieval system, without permission in writing from the publisher.

Front cover image of revolutionary war cannon and tents, the Grand Union flag and gun © 2019 Jennifer Griner/Stanislav Vostrikov/Shutterstock

Printed in the United States of America

*McFarland & Company, Inc., Publishers
Box 611, Jefferson, North Carolina 28640
www.mcfarlandpub.com*

For my father Jack, my son Christian,
and my grandsons Hunter,
Grayson, and Braydon

Table of Contents

Preface
1

I: African American Soldiers
3

II: Native American Soldiers
167

Bibliography
197

Index
205

Preface

While researching a book on chaplains who served in the American Revolution, I discovered many cases of slaves and freed slaves serving in the war. I became curious why a slave would fight for freedom that might not be granted at the end of the war. I also wanted to find out why, with such a large population of black people able to serve, the American government hesitated in using this manpower.

Most history books mention the exploits of a few black men that took part in the Revolution. The rest of the men that served are just footnotes in history, and their contributions are largely ignored. The purpose of this book is to give personal accounts of the men, mainly forgotten in history, that fought for liberty with the hope that they would achieve their freedom someday.

While researching the material for this book I discovered another group of people that fought and have been forgotten—Native Americans. Books and movies have been made about the Indian tribes being aligned with the British forces, while the importance of their contributions to the American cause has been overlooked. It is important that their service be remembered, and we not forget the treatment they received after the final victory was achieved.

Much of the information obtained on these men come from their own words in their pension applications. Their statements are the original wording and spelling, and they have not been changed. Some of the information is from sources written more than a hundred years ago and out of print. These sources provide a unique insight into the lives of these men.

At the end of each man's profile, some sources are given that contain specific information about the person. Full information about these sources may be found in the full *Bibliography* at the end of this book.

PART I
African American Soldiers

Introduction

> "All able-bodied men aged twenty-one and above are required to sign a declaration pledging hostilities against the British, with the exception of lunatics, idiots, and Blacks."—*Passed by the Committee of Safety in Windham, New Hampshire, April 12, 1776*

At the time of the Revolutionary War about 20 percent of the Colonial population of twenty-two million were black and the number of blacks that fought for the Americans was estimated to be over 5,000. By 1779, 15 percent of the army was black. These men served in an integrated army, which would be the last one until the Korean War.

When the Revolutionary War began, George Washington was opposed to the recruiting of black men, both free or slaves. In 1775 recruiting officers for the Continental Army were ordered not to enlist "any stroller, negro or vagabond." Black men already serving in the Continental Army could stay. This banishment from the regular army was done to appease the southern colonies and gain their support for the cause.

Slave owners, especially in the south, were concerned that training and arming black men could lead to a black uprising. A group of Carolina slave owners stated, "There must be great caution used [allowing blacks into the military] lest our slaves when armed might become our master."

Unlike the Continental Army, the Navy recruited both free blacks and slaves from the start of the war. They were desperate for sailors, and many blacks were already experienced sailors, having served in British and state navies, and sailed on merchant ships from both the north and south.

When the war began, the British saw an opportunity to further divide the colonies. Lord Dunmore the Royal Governor of Virginia offered freedom and wages to any slave who ran away to join British forces. The governor boasted he would have, "all the slaves on the side of the government." A British warning posted in the *New York Weekly Mercury* on July 5, 1779, said that any blacks captured with the rebel forces would be sold into slavery, regardless of their legal status. Many blacks saw more of an opportunity for a better life on the British side, so they joined with the British by the thousands.

This move by the British prompted many in the north to push for the abolishment of slavery. As the black population decreased in the north and the need for slaves lessened, abolition groups began to gain influence. By 1777, in Vermont where slavery was almost non-existent, they banned slavery outright. One historian noted, "The Revolution triggered the largest emancipation of American slaves outside the ultimate freedom won in the Civil War."

When fighting broke out in the north in 1775, patriots in New England needed every man they could gather. As a result black men were welcomed to serve in the militia units, but not in the Continental Army. In 1777 things began to go bad for the American Army. They had suffered huge losses, desertions, and recruitment began to dwindle as morale sank.

To meet the crisis, Congress called for eighty-eight new battalions from the colonies. Many of the colonies, particularly in the north, had trouble filling their quotas. This resulted in most states drafting soldiers, and they began to recruit black men. Some slave owners were given the option of freeing their slaves and sending them in place of members of their family. Slaves were guaranteed their freedom in exchange for service in the army. New England had the smallest black population of any region, and yet they provided the most black recruits. The southern colonies, with the exception of Maryland, still refused to send blacks to fight.

Some slave owners were reimbursed fair market value if they allowed their slaves to enlist. When the war spread into the south, the Continental Congress urged Georgia and South Carolina to raise slave battalions, and Congress would pay the slave owners $1,000. The slaves would receive no pay, but at the end of the war, the slaves would be given $50 and their freedom. Both states rejected the idea, and South Carolina threatened to leave the war if the plan went into force.

Slaves on the frontier were expected to help defend forts from Indian attacks. When they were killed in battle, their owners expected to be reimbursed by the colony for their loss of property. The following is a petition presented to the General Assembly of Virginia for such a loss.

> To the Hon. The General assembly of Virginia—The humble petition of Nathaniel Henderson Sheweth, that on or about the 11th day of September in defending fort Boon in present Boonesborough KY, 7–17 Sept. 1778 against an attempt of the Indians, your petitioner had a valuable Negro fellow killed. That the said Negro was ordered by the Commanding Officer to take a gun and place himself in a dangerous post and to keep watch & fire on the Indians which he accordingly did and was killed. The loss of so valuable a Slave together with the many other losses sustained by Your Petitioner in that country, distress him very much. Therefore hopes, that the Assembly will order a recompense and that the value of the said slave may be paid to your petitioner.

George Washington was in great need of soldiers, and he was aware of the British pursuing the black men as soldiers. He reversed his earlier decision about enlisting blacks and gave recruiting officers permission to enlist them. In January of 1778, the general gave his approval to Rhode Island raising an entire regiment of black slaves. This led to the formation of the 1st Rhode Island Regiment.

In July of 1778, a total of eighty-eight slaves and some free black men joined the regiment in the first four months. The regiment had a total of about 225 men, and less than 140 were black soldiers. It was the only regiment that had segregated companies of black soldiers. The regiment fought with honor at the Battles of Rhode Island and Yorktown.

This regiment was not the only army unit composed of black soldiers. Massachusetts had a company of black soldiers called the Bucks of America. It operated in the Boston area and may have been an auxiliary police or security service in the city during the war.

In May of 1780 when Charleston fell and many of the Virginia soldiers were taken prisoners, the situation was so serious for Virginia that the legislature began to debate arming and recruiting slaves. As the war shifted to the south, more southern black men were allowed to join. Georgia and South Carolina remained opposed to having blacks serve in the military. However, they did have a very small handful of blacks serving in the army. Other black men did manual labor in the army but were not considered soldiers. Some historians believe that if South Carolina and Georgia had allowed their slaves to fight it could have shortened the length of the war.

Prejudice was still present in the army, as many black soldiers were used as waiters for officers, wagon drivers, and laborers for building roads and fortifications. Yet, when given the chance, the black soldiers distinguished themselves on the battlefield. They proved to the white Americans that they could fight as well as anyone, and they did not run from danger. Unfortunately, they were not promoted in rank like their white counterparts. The highest rank any black soldier achieved in the integrated army was corporal by Sampson Coburn.

The Effects of the Revolution on the African Americans

In the northern colonies a large percent of African Americans had gained their freedom either through law or by service in the war. The northern colonies were slowly moving to use the courts to abolish slavery. Prejudice, however, remained in the north. The Massachusetts' legislature voted to bar interracial marriages and expel all blacks who were not citizens. White Philadelphians rioted against blacks around 1805 and drove them from Fourth of July celebrations on Independence Square. After that, black churches were burned.

In the southern colonies it was business as usual. Some black men had gained their freedom but many who had been promised freedom for their service were placed back into slavery. Eight slaves are known to have been granted freedom by the legislature for their service in the war.

The gains that African Americans had achieved in the military were erased after the war ended. In 1784 Connecticut and Massachusetts banned all blacks, free or slaves, from serving in the military. In 1792 the United States Congress excluded African Americans from military service, they allowed only free able-bodied white male citizens to serve.

By the end of the war, over 60,000 slaves had been freed in the United States. The 1790 Federal Census estimated that in the eight northern states there were still a little over 40,000 slaves, and almost half were in the state of New York. In the eight Southern states, it was estimated there were over 657,000 slaves.

In the early 1800s the north solved its own slavery problem by gradually emancipating the slaves and limiting the rights of its free black minority. The North was content by these actions and more than willing to share in the profits of the Southern plantations. They concentrated on keeping Southern blacks in the south and out of the north. For many the solution to the slave question was to ship the slaves out and place them in colonies far away.

The South was content to strengthen the slave culture and preserve the southern way of life. They continued to resent any talk, especially from the North, to discontinue the slave-based economy. For the next few decades both regions refused to acknowledge the "elephant in the room" and continued to put profits over morality.

What Became of the African Americans Who Supported the British During the Revolution?

Tens of thousands of African Americans sought refuge with the British, and only a few thousand served as soldiers. Some slaves were prevented from leaving with the British at southern ports. There were reports after the Siege of Charleston of slaves swimming out to boats, and the British hacking away at their arms with cutlasses and swords to keep them from following.

Some blacks were captured by the Americans and were returned to their owners or sold back into slavery. Many ended up as slaves in the Caribbean and working on sugar plantations. It is estimated that around 20,000 blacks left with the British and ended up in Canada, the West Indies, and in Europe. Over a thousand left for Sierra Leone, which was a colony established on the west coast of Africa for former slaves.

Revolutionary War Pensions

There is much information you can gather from a soldier's pension files. Age, marital information, birth and death dates, residence, and military service are the major items of information you can gather. The file may also include letters from other service personnel or friends about the soldier or his family.

On August 26, 1776, pension legislation was enacted. It provided for half pay for officers and enlisted men, and greater benefits if they were disabled in the service and incapable of earning a living.

The Continental Congress passed a resolution on May 15, 1778, which allowed half pay for all officers and a set gratuity of $80 to all enlisted men that stayed in the service until the end of the war. This was passed to encourage soldiers to serve for the entire war and also to encourage enlistments.

In 1818 Congress passed a pension law giving pensions to veterans who had not been disabled. Officers and enlisted men in need of assistance were eligible, if they served for nine months or until the end of the war. The applicant also had to provide a listing of property and its value to prove need of assistance. Names could be removed from pension rolls if it was proven that the veterans were not in need of assistance. If need was proven the pension was granted for life. In 1823 another act was passed that granted full pay for life to officers and enlisted men.

A major change took place with the passing of an act on June 7, 1832. If the soldier served for at least 2 years they received full pay for life. Those with service of less than two years but more than six months would not be granted full pay. In the act of 1836 some widows of veterans could apply for a pension depending upon when they were married. Those restrictions were removed by the act of 1853.

The soldier had to indicate in his pension application the time and place of service, names of units and officers, and engagements if any. Most of the men went to a courthouse and told their story to a clerk or court official who wrote the narrative down. In some rare cases the soldier wrote out the narrative themselves. A widow applying for a widow's pension would have to prove that she and the veteran were married and when they got married. For African American women, this could be very difficult because no marriage records were usually kept.

This author found that sometimes stricter requirements for a pension was required for people of color. At times a pension application for a person of color would be rejected, while given the similar circumstances it would be approved for a white person.

When the Civil War began any soldier or widow receiving a pension and living in the South, had their pension suspended. It would be reinstated after the war was over if the person could prove they did not support the South, and if they would sign a loyalty oath.

By 1867 most of the pensioners on the rolls were dead. The last soldier to die was Daniel R. Bakeman who died on April 15, 1869. The last widow on a pension to die was Ester S. Damon who died on November 11, 1905.

* * *

Philip Abbot

Phillip Abbot was from Andover, Massachusetts, and was the Negro servant of Nathan Abbot. He enlisted into the company of Captain Benjamin Ames under the command of Colonel James Frye. He was present at the Battle of Bunker Hill, and he served in the redoubt, where he was killed.

The Andover troops arrived too late for the Battle of Lexington. However, on June 16, 1775, they assembled on Cambridge Common and marched to Charlestown. Once at Charlestown they worked through the night and into the morning entrenching a redoubt on Breed's Hill, while under fire from the British ships and batteries in Boston.

At the Battle of Bunker Hill fought on June 17, 1775, the British advanced up the hill toward the American fortification. The British came under "heavy and severe fire" and retreated. British General Howe ordered them to attack again and they were met with the same result. The British launched a third attack and forced the Americans to retreat. Most of the Americans were out of ammunition, since they had only about fifteen shots each at the start of the battle. They also had run out of water by the start of the morning. In less than two hours the British had a victory but at the cost of 1,054 men killed or wounded. Phillip was one of 140 patriots killed during the battle, and he was buried on the battlefield.

Sources: 1. Bailey, *Historical Sketches of Andover*, pages 319, 325–6. **2.** Patrakis, *Andover Stories*, Andover Historical Society, February 17, 2011.

Adam Adams

Adam Adams, who was born c. 1763, at the time of his pension application was a free black citizen. He served in the 1st Maryland Regiment under Lieutenant John Mitchell in Captain Henry Gaither's Company from May 1777 until November 1783. He was married to Ann, and he received a monthly pension of $8 and fifty acres of land for his service.

Adam was probably induced to enlist with a ten dollar cash bonus, clothing, and the promise of fifty acres of land if he served for the duration of the war. The 1st Maryland Regiment had sixty black soldiers and took part in the following battles: Harlem Heights, Trenton, Princeton, Germantown, Brandywine, Monmouth, Camden, Guilford Court House, and Yorktown. The regiment disbanded on November 15, 1783.

Sources: **1.** National Archives Pension Application S34623. **2.** Grundset, *Forgotten Patriots, National Society of the D.A.R.,* page 455.

Thomas Addams

Thomas Addams was born a slave in Connecticut and he died there in 1810. His wife Abigale, who he married on July 10, 1764, filed for a widow's pension, and she gave the following statement:

> She was married to Thomas Addams who in the month of October or November 1775 enlisted in the grade of a private soldier into a company in Colonel William Richmond's Regiment commanded by Royzel Smith for one year. Soon after the expiration of the tour of duty he again enlisted for three months.

Thomas continued to serve short tours of duty and was in Spencer's Expedition and Sullivan's Expedition. He received a yearly pension of $40 for his service.

Sources: **1.** National Archives Pension Application W13615. **2.** Grundset, *Forgotten Patriots, National Society of the D.A.R.,* page 203.

Absalom Ailstock

Absalom Ailstock was born in Louisa County, Virginia, around 1764. He joined the militia and served under Colonel Nelson and Captain John Saunders. He applied for a pension in 1832 and stated,

> It being rumored that the British were about to land upon the Virginia Coast, he cannot state in what year this happened but believes it was in the year preceding Cornwallis's defeat [this would have been at Yorktown in October, 1781], and thinks he was about 17 years old, from the circumstance, that a short time previous to this, he was not capable of standing a draught for 18 months, not being 18 years of age; the age required by Law, and that in the summer following the first tour, he did stand a draught for a term of 18 months, but drew clear.
>
> He states that he marched from Louisa County in the beginning of the winter, to Hanover Courthouse, in this state, where he went under the command of Col. Fountaine, and Major Winston, Regular officers, and Col. Nelson returned home. thence proceeded to New Kent Courthouse. received orders (as this applicant thinks from the Governor, after remaining one week at New Kent Courthouse, and returned to Hanover Courthouse, there remained two or three weeks. When Adjutant Mayers (if this applicant recollects right, he being called by the soldiers Sandy Mayers) was sent to the Governor for further orders, who returned with directions to dismiss the men. And this applicant returned, after a service of 4 weeks.
>
> This applicant further states, that he was called out into the service of the United States, in the same manner as he was in his first tour, in the spring following, about the 1st of April in the year of Cornwallis's Defeat, and marched from said County under Capt William Harris of Louisa County, directly to Richmond, where he joined the 2nd Regiment, under Col Richardson and Major Armistead. The British he states had been at Manchester

on the opposite side of the river, and burned the Tobacco Ware houses, the ruins of which this applicant distinctly saw from the Richmond side. Thence marched down the River in Nelsons Brigade, how far he cannot say, but to a place called as he believes "Marben Hills" upon the river where the Brigade was stationed, for the reason as this applicant believes, that the British were in the habit of coming up the River as high as this place in two gun boats (little boats with a gun on each end) for the purpose of Plunder, whilst here Col. Richardson had a skirmish with these gun boats, two of which he took, and 17 men Prisoners, thence marched down the River about a days journey, thence across to Spotsylvania, where this applicants term of service expired, and he was discharged.

Here Absalom gives an account of the Siege of Yorktown,

> This applicant states that he served another tour of 3 months service, having been called out in the same manner as formerly, about the middle of July succeeding the last tour, and marched near old Williamsburg under Capt Benjamin Harris of Louisa County, where he joined Nelsons Brigade, Col Richardson was a field officer in this Brigade, and Major Martin had taken the place of Major Armistead, as this applicant believes. thence marched below Williamsburg, a short distance, where the Brigade encamped until Washingtons Troops came on from the north, in the rear of which, this Brigade fell and marched on to York. this applicant states that the Battle was commenced on Sunday morning, by the French at the Poplar Redoubt, and the next day, the regiment to which this applicant belonged, was transfered to this redoubt, for the purpose of changing it into a gun battery. This applicant states that he was occupied during the siege in digging intrenchments, and making sand baskets and facines for the intrenchments & Batteries. This applicant received his discharge, by order of General Lawson, from orderly Seargeant Shelton, which discharge he delivered to one of his mess mates, for safe keeping, and has never seen it since.

In 1810 he is listed in the census as head of a Botetourt County, Virginia, household of nine other free persons. In 1849 he applied for an increase of his pension, but it was refused and he remained receiving $22.78 for his service.

Sources: 1. National Archives Pension Application S6475. **2.** Grundset, *Forgotten Patriots, National Society of the D.A.R.*, page 513.

William Anderson

The War Department believed that William did serve, but they had to reject his pension claim because there was no proof. A note in his pension application states,

> His wounds have rendered him a cripple ever since he received them. Both legs or thighs appear to be broken, and his arm in one or two places. He is now, and has been for some years a public pauper, supported by the Township. He is rendered stupid by age and infirmities—he can scarcely recollect anything accurately. It seems to me that he is worthy of support from the government on account of the faithful services he has rendered.

William's pension application states,

> About twenty days after the Battle of Brandywine he enlisted as a private soldier under Captain Doberry who was attached to the sixth regiment of the Maryland troops on Continental

establishment. He was afterwards transferred to the artillery in which he continued eighteen months. He continued as a soldier in the continental army, being transferred to different parts of the army, until after the capture of Cornwallis, at which engagement he was present, and in which he was severely wounded.

Captain Jeremiah Collins stated in William's application,

> Jeremiah Collins who being duely sworn deposeth and saith that he the said Jeremiah Collins was a Captain of Horse belonging to the french troops who served in the American revolutionary war that during his service in the war aforesaid he knew William Anderson a black man that when he first knew the said William Anderson he was he believes a servant to Captain West who was killed at the battle of Brandywine that after the taking of the british garrison near little York in Virginia this deponent found the said William Anderson at a small distance from the garrison apparently dead but after some examination he was found to be still living and had received a severe wound in the left thigh this deponent procured the said William Anderson to be carried in to the American camp where his wound was dressed this deponent knew the said William Anderson for five years, that during the five years which this deponent knew the said William he was in the service part of the time with the American troops and part with the french troops this deponent has seen the said William in Battle and knows him to have been a soldier of undoubted courage.

Like many black soldiers, William was not found on the company's rolls so he was refused a pension. Even the letter supporting his service from Captain Collins was not enough proof.

Source: **1.** National Archives Pension Application R203.

James Anthony

James Anthony served in the army from March 14, 1777, until March 14, 1780. He stated in his pension application of 1818,

> I James Anthony now residing in Springfield Rhode Island state that in 1777, I enlisted in the 4 Regiment of the Massachusetts Line commanded by Colonel Shefford in Captain Staten Company and served in the Regiment three years.

James served under Colonel William Shepard and would have been at Valley Forge and the Battles of Saratoga in the fall of 1778, Monmouth on June 28, 1778, and Rhode Island on August 29, 1778. He received a monthly pension of $8 for his service.

Sources: **1.** National Archives Pension Application S38494. **2.** Grundset, *Forgotten Patriots, National Society of the D.A.R.*, page 100.

Jack Arabus

Jack Arabus was a slave owned by Thomas Ivers, who was a wealthy Connecticut merchant. It was very common for a person called to military service to pay someone to take their place. Sometimes the substitute would be paid in money or property. In the case of Jack Arabus, he was offered his freedom if he would serve in place of his master's son.

Arabus first enlisted in the 6th Connecticut Regiment under Captain David Humphreys and he was probably at the Battle of Stony Point. He later reenlisted in the 4th Connecticut Regiment, and he was discharged in 1783. When he returned home his owner had a change of heart and decided not to grant freedom to Jack.

Jack ran off and was soon captured and placed in jail. A Yale educated lawyer, Chauncey Goodrich, took his case and filed suit against Thomas Ivers. Goodrich based his case on the fact that there was an agreement between the slave and his owner, and that the owner failed to live up to his part of the agreement. The judge ruled that George Washington agreed to enlist freeman in the army. He further stated that if the owner of the slave allowed a slave to enlist, it amounted to freeing the slave so he could enlist as a freeman. This ruling allowed about 300 slaves, who served and returned to Connecticut as veterans to receive their freedom.

Sources: 1. Alexander, *Racism, African Americans, and Social Justice*. 2. Gregg and Hall, *America's Forgotten Founders*, 2nd edition.

Evans Archer

Evans Archer was born c. 1754 in Hertford County, North Carolina. At the age of twenty-five he was 5'4" tall with red hair and grey eyes. He enlisted for eighteen months on September 23, 1780, in a Virginia Regiment. He filed for a pension in 1823,

> The said Evans Archer enlisted as a Soldier for the term of eighteen months about the month of July 1780 at Portsmouth in the State of Virginia in the Company commanded by Captain John Anderson in the Regiment Commanded by Colonel _____ Campbell which this deponent believes to have been the first Regiment in the line of the State of Virginia on the Continental establishment, that he continued to serve in the said Corps or in the Service of the United States until sometime in the month of January in the year one thousand seven hundred eighty two when he was honorable discharged from the said Service (his time of enlistment having expired) in the town of Salisbury in the State of North Carolina, that he was in the Battle at Eutaw Springs South Carolina and at the Siege of ninety Six.

At the Battle of Eutaw Springs, on September 8, 1781, Evans served under Lt. Colonel Richard Campbell who commanded 350 men in two battalions. Evans was in the 1st Battalion in a company under Captain John Anderson. This was the last major battle in South Carolina and it broke the hold the British had in the South. A month later Lord Cornwallis surrendered to Washington at Yorktown.

Based on the 1790 Census Evens is listed as a "free Negro" living in Hertford County, North Carolina. He lived with his daughter Margaret, a single woman with a four-year-old child. He received a pension of $8 a month for his service.

Sources: 1. Heinegg, *Free African Americans of North Carolina, Virginia, and South Carolina Vol.*, page 62. **2.** National Archives Pension Application S41415.

James Arcules

James Arcules was born c. 1754 in Massachusetts, and he served in the Lexington Alarm from Medfield. He served at Bunker Hill in the company commanded by Captain Benjamin Bullard. He served for six years in the Continental Army. He stated in his pension application of 1818,

> Sometime in January 1777 I enlisted and served under Captain Moses Knapp in the 4th Massachusetts Regiment commanded by Col. William Shepard against the common enemy until June 1783.

James would have been at Valley Forge and the Battles of Saratoga in the fall of 1778, Monmouth on June 28, 1778, and Rhode Island on August 29, 1778. His regiment was disbanded at West Point on November 3, 1783. James was listed on a descriptive roll as 6 feet tall. He received a monthly pension of $8 for his service.

Sources: 1. National Archives Pension Application S32658. **2.** Grundset, *Forgotten Patriots, National Society of the D.A.R.*, page 100. **3.** Quintal, *Patriots of Color*, page 51.

James Armistead

James Armistead was born on December 10, 1760, as a slave owned by William Armistead in New Kent, Virginia. James was given permission to serve in the Continental Army by his master in 1781. He was employed by Lafayette as a spy to gather intelligence of British troop movements.

Lafayette was quartered near Richmond, Virginia, and the British under Lord Cornwallis were encamped near Portsmouth, Virginia, about ninety-five miles southeast of Richmond. In the spring of 1781 Lafayette sent James to spy on Cornwallis. He used the cover of an escaped slave from the Americans. James met Cornwallis who later recruited James to return to the American lines to spy on them.

Armistead, acting as a double agent, supplied Cornwallis with false information. Once James delivered a fake document to Cornwallis that was in a soiled and crumpled condition. He said he found the information it on the side of the road, and it contained information about a large number of replacement American troops on the way to Virginia. Cornwallis believed the fake report and kept his troops in a defensive position.

James later sent a report to Lafayette that 60 British ships were anchored in the York River, and that the British were fortifying downstream at Yorktown. This information led General Washington to send a French fleet to the mouth of the York River and blockade the British. The Americans were now able to lay siege to Yorktown which resulted in the surrender of Cornwallis. When Cornwallis later paid a courtesy call to Lafayette, he was surprised to see James Armistead who he thought was his servant and spy in the camp of the Americans.

In 1783 Virginia passed an act that gave freedom to slaves that served in the Revolution, but it did not grant freedom to those that served as spies. This injustice was not resolved until 1786 when Virginia passed a separate act granting freedom to James Lafayette (James had taken a new last name). In 1819 Virginia awarded James a yearly pension of $40.

Sources: 1. Metz, *I Was a Teenager in the American Revolution*. **2.** Reef, *African Americans in the Military* by, page 14. **3.** Mahoney and Mahoney, *Gallantry in Action: A Biographic Dictionary of Espionage in the American Revolutionary War*, page 59.

Gad Asher

Gad Asher served in the 7th Connecticut Regiment from July of 1780 until July of 1781. He then joined the 2nd Connecticut Regiment from July 1, 1781, until July 31, 1781. He was wounded while in the service. He stated in his pension application,

> I belonged to the company commanded by Captain Stephen Hall in the Regiment commanded by Colonel Herman Swift.

Gad died on November 28, 1835, and left no widow, but he did leave three children. He received a yearly pension of $80 for his service.

Sources: 1. National Archives Pension Application S17244. **2.** Grundset, *Forgotten Patriots, National Society of the D.A.R.*, page 271.

London Atis

London Atis was a slave owned by the Rev. William Lyons and served from 1779 until 1781 in the Massachusetts Artillery Corps. London was married to Eunice Foss on July 7, 1791. She received his yearly pension of $100 after he died in the summer of 1843. London stated in his pension application of 1832,

> He served in Col. John Allen's corps of Artillery in a company of Artillery under command of Lt. William Albe. He served until the end of the war. He was stationed at a small fort at Machias [Maine] except when detached for service in boats, in one of which he engaged in the taking of a British barge under the command of Lt. Street whom with his nine men they took prisoners. He served until Feb. 1781. I served about three months in the sloop

Winthrop commanded by Captain George Little whereby he obtained from prize money the price which his master had required for his freedom. He remembers his monthly pay was eight dollars.

The sloop *Winthrop* was employed on the Maine coast to protect coastal trade. The barge that was captured was taken in Penobscot Harbor in a daring raid at night. Fourteen men boarded the British ship and captured it without firing a shot.

Sources: **1.** National Archives Pension Application W23468. **2.** Grundset, *Forgotten Patriots, National Society of the D.A.R.*, pages 12 & 20. **3.** Hunt, *American Anecdotes: Original and Select Vol. 1.*

Ceasar Babcock

Ceasar was born around 1749 and was a slave owned by Hezekiah Babcock in Rhode Island. When Ceasar applied for a pension, Martha, the wife of Hezekiah, wrote a letter in his support.

> Ceasar was a slave to my said husband before the Revolutionary War and Ceasar served as a soldier in the militia for my said husband and went to the Island of Rhode Island with the army commanded by General Sullivan to act against the British.

Ceasar made the following statement in his pension application,

> In the year 1775 and 6 he served in the militia various tours of duty in guarding the shores of Narraganset sett Bay against the enemy ships commanded by __?__ Wallis.
> And again in 1778 in the same duty with the army then collecting under command of Genl. Sullivan. In the summer of that year was on the Island of Rhode Island where in an action with the enemy he saw a drummer by the name of Card killed by a shot in the breast while very near him __?__ another man wounded in the ankle.

Ceasar claimed that he served a total of one year and four months. He served in Sullivan's Expedition and the Battle of Rhode Island. Ceasar's application was rejected, so two black men that served with Ceasar wrote to the pension bureau saying that they served with Ceasar in the army during the time he stated.

The pastor of the Baptist Church of Newport wrote a letter in support of Ceasar's application and the two men that served with him. He stated,

> Being aware that the statements of "Negroes" we sometimes regard with a degree of suspicion where their character are not known, and supposing it very possible that the small degree of credit supposed to be due to Negro testimony might have operated to a great extent, in the rejection of Ceasar Babcock's claim confirmed as it appears to me, to be, by all the evidence which at this distance of time could reasonably be demanded.

The pastor explained that the two men were well known and were of high character. The pension bureau replied back that the rejection of the application would stand. The rejection was due to the fact that Ceasar could not prove that he served for the required six months. Ceasar was not on any army rolls, and no one could prove the dates of his service.

Sources: 1. National Archives Pension Application R339. **2.** Grundset, *Forgotten Patriots, National Society of the D.A.R.,* page 205.

Caesar Bailey

Caesar Bailey was born into slavery c. 1749 in Deerfield, Massachusetts. His owner, Nathaniel Dickerson was a Loyalist, yet he signed up Caesar to take his place in the militia. Caesar fought in the Battles of Lexington and Concord, and in June of 1775 he was at the Battle of Bunker Hill.

His wife Hagar filed for his pension in 1842. She stated that she did not know her age and that Caesar enlisted in Jonathan Brewer's Regiment in 1781, and that Caesar died shortly after that while in the service. Her pension application was rejected probably due to lack of proof of service or lack of marriage proof.

Sources: 1. Quintal, *Patriots of Color,* page 51. **2.** National Archives Pension Application R371.

Prince Bailey

Prince Bailey married Hannah Vineson after stating marriage intentions on October 12, 1780. He served for three years (1777–1780) in the 2nd Massachusetts Regiment. He filed for a pension in 1819 and stated,

> When I was about eight years of age I was stolen from Africa my native country, and brought to America, my original name was Prince Dunsick but on my arrival I was called my masters name which was Bailey.
>
> By the name of Prince Bailey I enlisted and served in the Revolutionary war and was discharged by the same name. In the month of March 1777 I enlisted into the army of the United States in the Continental establishment in the company commanded by Capt. Seth Drew in the regiment commanded by Colonel John Bailey in Genl. Learned's Brigade. My term of enlistment was three years.

At the Battle of Saratoga on October 7, 1777, Prince Bailey's regiment was in the center of the attack. During the Battle of Monmouth, Prince was in the heat of the battle on the left wing under the command of General William Alexander known as Lord Stirling. Prince spent the winter of 1777–78 at Valley Forge.

In 1823 he was required to show need of his pension and he filed his worth at $29. His property was listed as: one cow, one calf, and old house with old furniture, a coffee pot, tea pot, ax, shovel, and a hoe. He stated that his mother-in-law, Rhoda Woods age 77, lived with them. He said that his wife was in poor health and was inflicted with fits. Prince received a yearly pension of $80 for his service.

Sources: 1. National Archives Pension Application W17230. **2.** Grundset, *Forgotten Patriots, National Society of the D.A.R.*, page 101.

Jacob Banks

Jacob was born in August of 1754 in Goochland, Virginia, and he died on January 5, 1835. He received a yearly pension of $40. He stated in his pension application,

> He is a free man of color, that he was born in the County of Goochland in August 1754, that he has seen his Register and obtains the information from that source, that he always resided in the County of Goochland, and that whilst the Convention Troops under Burgoyne were stationed at the Albemarle Barracks he this affiant joined the American army by enlistment, being always free and went to the Albemarle Barracks and there remained as a *Wagoner* taking charge of one of the Wagons belonging to the American army & driving the same; that Martin Mims was Wagon master & Tho. Stanley Wagon Master General. This affiant further states that he continued in the service as a Wagoner & attended diligently to the duties as such at the Albemarle Barracks from the time he entered the service until the convention troops were marched from the Barracks time not now recollected, but this affiant well recollects that he remained in service at the Barracks 18 months. He continued in service as long as his service was required & returned home after the Barracks were broke up & the Wagons sent home.

A Wagon Department was created in 1777 under the control of the Quartermaster's Department. Sometimes supplies had to be shipped over great distances and across rugged trails. At times the wagons were attacked by enemy troops or by highwaymen. There were never enough drivers, and keeping them in the service was difficult. The life of a teamster was hard. Many times they drove the wagons for thirteen or fourteen hours a day in all types of weather. The roads were usually heavily rutted that would jar the spine of the driver.

Usually, the wagons had no seats, which allowed the wagons to carry more supplies. The wagoners would walk along side of the wagons and direct the teams. Some wagons had a "lazy board," a board that could be pulled out behind the left front wheels of the wagons to sit on. The lead horse and the driver were on the left of the wagons and they would stay to the right side of the road when passing approaching wagons. This is probably why we drive on the right side of the road in the United States.

Jacob had a very difficult job, since he was transporting supplies or baggage for the army. The enemy's goal was to cut the supply lines and capture the wagons. He also served as a fatigue man. This was a person that did not carry arms, but rather he worked on fortifications, carrying messages, or cutting roads.

Albemarle Barracks was a prison of war camp for British soldiers. Hundreds of British soldiers escaped from the barracks due to the lack of an adequate number of guards. The barracks were located outside of Charlottesville, Virginia. As the British army moved north from the Carolinas in the later part of 1780, the prisoners were moved to several places.

Sources: 1. Heinegg, *Free African Americans of North Carolina, Virginia, and South Carolina, Vol. 1.* **2.** National Archives Pension Application S8056. **3.** Frank, *American Revolution: People and Perspectives.*

John Banks

John Banks was born c. 1749, and he died on November 24, 1842, in Virginia. He married Sally in the summer of 1772, and she filed for and received a widow's pension of $80 a year. She also filed for land bounty at the age of 100. John stated in his pension application,

> The said John Banks enlisted in the company commanded by Capt. Holman Rice as a private soldier in the county of Goochland & State of Virginia about the year 1779 during the continuance of the convention troops in the State of Virginia and belonged to the Regiment commanded by Colo. Bland. That he continued to serve in the said corps or in the service of the United States for and during the term of upwards of two years that he was regularly discharged at the Barracks in the County of Albemarle in the said State of Virginia in May 1781 that he was in no battle during his service.

John registered as a free Negro in Goochland County on September 3, 1823, and he was described as about six feet high.

Sources: 1. Heinegg, *Free African Americans of North Carolina, Virginia, and South Carolina Vol. 1.* **2.** National Archives Pension Application S8056. **3.** McAllister, *Virginia Militia in the Revolutionary War*, page 32.

William Barber

William Barber was born on May 17, 1745, in Dinwiddie County, Virginia. He served in the army for six months and received a yearly pension of $20 for his service. He filed for his pension in 1833 and stated,

> He was drafted in the month of January in the year 1781 into the company of Virginia Militia commanded by Fleming Bates first Leut David Bates Sergeant John Pulliam. We rendevous'd at Cabbin Point below Petersburgh. they were cald into service the 15 Jan. they were at Bibbs Old Field when we joined & were commanded by Col. Dix. Our Object was to intersept the Traitor Arnold who was at or near Portsmouth. We were stationed near the Dismal Swamp 2 or 3 weeks. news was brot that the Brittish were Landing at Sleepy Hole. we raised our camp and marched across the Dismal in the night. We took up quarters & remained till my time of service was out. this tour was for three months.

When Benedict Arnold learned on September 23, 1780, that the British spy Major Andre had been captured with papers that exposed him as a traitor, he fled to West Point. Arnold rushed to the shore and ordered bargemen to row him to where the British ship *Vulture* was anchored. When he reached the ship it took him to New York. Meanwhile, Washington had sent men to West Point to capture Arnold, but they barely missed him.

> The following Sept. say year 1781 he was again Drafted into the company of Leut Jno Maxy. he thinks it was in the first days of Sept they rendevous'd at Boids Ferry on Dan River Our Col was Peter Rodgers. he thinks that General Butler commanded. Were marched to York-Town where we were under the comand of Gen Washington who besieged Cornwallis & took him. We had to guard 25 Tories up to Richmond. this tour was for three months.
>
> **Sources: 1.** Heinegg, *Free African Americans of North Carolina, Virginia, and South Carolina Vol. 1.* **2.** National Archives Pension Application S6572.

Charles Barnett

Charles Barnett was born c. 1765 in Albemarle, Virginia, and served for 18 months with the 7th Virginia Regiment. He received a yearly pension of $60 for his service. According to the size roll when he enlisted, Charles was 5'5" and a farmer. In the 1830 Federal Census he is listed as a free person of color.

> He entered the service of the United States in the War of the Revolution about the year 1780. At Charlottesville in the County of Albemarle as a soldier in the regular service by enlisting with Captain John Marks of the 7 Virginia Regiment, of whose company Ballard Smith was Lieutenant & William Quarles Ensign. that he marched thence to Richmond where the company was inspected by General Muhlenburg thence to Chesterfield Ct House where his company joined the Regiment commanded by Colonel William Davis from thence to Point of Fork on James River– thence to Cole's Ferry on our way to join Gen'l. Green but from some cause unknown to this declarant, the troops stopped at Cole's Ferry, & then returned to the siege of York where he continued until the Capture of Cornwallis. At York this declarant saw Gen'l. Washington, Steuben, Lincoln and Lafayette & other field officers. After the siege of York they marched to Powhatan Ct. House, where some troops were quartered. Before the expiration of his tour, he was sent to Philadelphia with baggage waggons and received his discharge at Philadelphia from Gen'l. Steuben.
>
> **Sources: 1.** 1830 Federal Census. **2.** National Archives Pension Application S8048.

Scipio Bartlett

Scipio Bartlett was born c. 1751 and died in Massachusetts on March 7, 1828. He married Kate Green on February 6, 1787, in Beverly, Massachusetts. Kate applied for her husband's monthly pension of $8 after his death, but her application was rejected. He stated the following when he applied for a pension,

> In the month of February in the year 1777, he enlisted in Capt. Samuel Page's Company, Colonel Ebenezer Francis Regiment and after his death Colonel Tupper in the Massachusetts Line and served as a Soldier three full years. Discharged at West Point February 1789.

I: African American Soldiers   Bates   21

> I further in oath declare that I was emancipated at the commencement of the Revolutionary War and was a free man during my whole term of service. I am a black man but free.

Scipio was a member of the 11th Massachusetts Regiment and he was at Valley Forge, the Battles of Hubbardton, Saratoga, and Monmouth. His regiment was disbanded on January 1, 1781.

Sources: 1. National Archives Pension Application R4010. **2.** Grundset, *Forgotten Patriots, National Society of the D.A.R.*, page 101. **3.** *Massachusetts Soldiers and Sailors in the Revolutionary War*, Vol. 1, page 721.

Caesar Bason

Caesar Bason was from Westford, Massachusetts, and may have been owned by Jason Burn. He first served at the Lexington Alarm in the company of Captain Jonathan Minot in Colonel William Prescott's Regiment. Caesar later enlisted for eight month's service in Captain Abijah Wyman's Company and Colonel Prescott's Regiment at the Battle of Bunker Hill.

According to the Rev. Edwin Hodgman's book Caesar found that his powder was nearly gone during the battle. When he put his last charge into his musket he said, "Now, Caesar, give 'em one more." He fired, was himself shot, and fell back into the trench dead.

Sources: 1. *Massachusetts Soldiers and Sailors of the Revolutionary War*, page 746. **2.** Hodgman, *History of the Town of Westford 1659–1883*, pages 112–13.

Caesar Basset

Caesar Basset married Flora Burhans on July 6, 1781. He served in the army for 22 months and three days and died on September 14, 1816. Flora filed an application for his pension and received a yearly pension of $73.66 for his service. Caesar served as a waiter for various officers during much of his service. She stated in her application,

> Caesar Basset volunteered for the military service of the State of New York under the command of General George Clinton, was part of the life guard of said General Clinton and remained in the service for two years or more.
>
> He entered again in the spring of the year 1781 in Captain Liningston's company inn Colonel Albert Pawlings Regiment for 8 or 9 months and stationed on the frontier of the county of Ulster County. He volunteered again in 1782 in the same company for 8 or 9 months.

Sources: 1. Grundset, *Forgotten Patriots, National Society of the D.A.R.*, page 331. **2.** National Archives Pension Application W16827.

Benoni Bates

Benoni Bates was a slave who enlisted into the 1st Rhode Island Regiment in 1780 about the age of twenty-one. He was listed at 5'7" tall and a laborer born in Newport, Rhode Island. He died in Cranston, Rhode Island, on January 23, 1838. He received a pension of $8 a year for his service.

> Benoni Bates, a man of color, on the 14th day of December, 1780 enlisted as a private to serve during the war into the regiment commanded by Col Christopher Greene. He served from enlistment until 15 June, 1783.

The 1st Rhode Island Regiment was also known as the "Black Regiment," because for the first time it had several companies of African American soldiers. The regiment's commander Colonel Greene was killed in a skirmish with Tories in New York. Benoni Bates probably took part in this skirmish.

Sources: **1.** National Archives Pension Application S38515. **2.** Grundset, *Forgotten Patriots, National Society of the D.A.R.,* page 205.

Shadrach Battles

Shadrach Battles was born in Albemarle County, Virginia, c. 1746. By 1752 he had moved to Louisa County on 191 acres of land purchased by his father. In 1775 his father sold the farm to a white farmer, John Duncan, and he moved further south. For the next two years Shadrach moved around working as a laborer and carpenter. In 1777 he enlisted in the army and served two eighteen month tours of duty in the 10th Virginia Regiment under the command of General George Weedon.

> On his oath declare that he served in the Revolutionary war as follows to wit; that he enlisted about the year 1777 or 1778 under Capt. Franklin of the tenth Virginia regiment attached to General Weedens Brigade, that he continued in in the said Corps or in the service of the United States for three years and upwards untill the close of the war when he was honourably discharged that he was in the battles of Brandywine, German Town, and Maunmouth Courthouse in New Jersey.

At the Battle of Brandywine, fought on September 11, 1777, Shadrach's regiment was to cover the road outside of town and hold off the British long enough for the Americans to retreat. By the time it grew dark they had held the British to a standstill, and the Americans were able to slip away under the cover of darkness.

The Battle of Germantown was fought on October 4, 1777, at Germantown, Pennsylvania. Shadrach was part of General Sullivan's Division that spearheaded the advance on the road to Germantown. They encountered the British pickets and chased them back to the town. Later, during the battle, Sullivan's Division advanced on the center of the British line.

After being defeated at both battles, Shadrach and the rest of the troops made winter quarters at Valley Forge. The next summer at the Battle of Monmouth on June 28, 1778, the temperatures reached over 100 degrees. Shadrach and his regiment was under the command of General Greene, and they attacked the British left flank. Lord Cornwallis personally led a failed British attack on Greene's right wing.

Archibald Stuart wrote to the Albemarle Court on the behalf of Shadrach, "Battles was the right hand man of Clough Shelton at the storming of Stony Point." Captain Clough Shelton led Virginia men at Stony Point. This was a battle fought on July 16, 1779, when a nighttime attack with highly trained select troops captured the British fort at Stony Point.

After Shadrach was discharged in 1780, he returned home and married Dolly Moss. In 1784 he got into trouble when Robert Murray, a free black, filed suit against Shadrach for trespassing, assault, and battery. Shadrach failed to appear in court and was ordered to pay court costs and enter into a bond to guarantee his good behavior for one year. Early in 1800 Shadrach fell deeply into debt and faced other troubles with the courts. When he applied for a pension in 1818 he appeared in court, carried on a stretcher, and in poor health. All he owned was an ax, an oven, and a handsaw.

Sources: 1. National Archives Pension Application S37713. **2.** Grundset, *Forgotten Patriots, National Society of the D.A.R.*, page 513. **3.** Heinegg, *Free African Americans of North Carolina, Virginia, and South Carolina. Vol.* 1. **4.** Von Daacke, *Freedom Has a Face: Race, Identity, and Community in Jefferson's Virginia*. **5.** Ervin and Markides, *Chasing Water: Elegy of an Olympian*, pages 313–14. **6.** Gilbert, *Black Patriots and Loyalist: Fighting for Emancipation in the War for Independence*.

Solomon Bibby

Solomon Bibby was born in North Carolina around 1764. In November of 1771, when he was around seven years old, he was ordered bound as an apprentice planter to Peter Goodwin. He married Charity Young on Christmas Day, 1789.

He served in the 10th North Carolina Regiment under Colonel Abraham Shepard and Captain Edward Yarbrough from May 17, 1780, until May of 1781. Some of the time in the army he served as a waiter to General Sumner. After the war when Solomon received his land bounty, [which was up to 640 acres for North Carolina privates] he sold it to Edward Sumner, the General's son. When someone told Edward that he got the land very cheap, Edward replied, "He [Solomon] would have fooled it away any how and I had as well have it as anybody else."

Solomon received a yearly pension of $80 and he stated in his application,

> That he joined the Army under Gen'l Sumner and Capts Ball, Armstrong, & Brickland others (whose names he cannot now recall) he entered the service in the Spring of the year

but what year he does not now recollect, he remained in the service three years from the time he entered as aforesaid as a volunteer. he was at the battles of Eutaw Springs Camden & Guilford Court House and attended most of his time to the care of the horses & as protector & guard to the baggage waggons; he was not engaged in any of the said battles,— he was a volunteer, & joined & continued as such whilst he was associated with the Army—He was well acquainted with Genl Gates, Greene, and also with Col. Washington & Malbry.

Sources: 1. National Archives Pension Application S6644. **2.** Heinegg, *Free African Americans of North Carolina, Virginia, and South Carolina Vol.1*, page 153. **3.** Hat, *Roster of Soldiers from North Carolina in the American Revolution*, page 110. **4.** Grundset, *Forgotten Patriots, National Society of the D.A.R.*, page 561.

John Biddie

John Biddie was born on July 17, 1762, in Lunenburg County, Virginia, and he died on October 14, 1841, in Alabama. He married Sarah Jones in 1810, and in the 1830 census they are listed as free. John received a yearly pension of $80 for his two year service in the 2nd Spartan Regiment of South Carolina.

> I entered the service under command of Lieut Hill in Union District, and marched to the Savannah River and joined the Regiment of Col Thomas under the command of Gen Williamson opposite to Augusta, where I remained about six weeks and was discharged. In October 1780 I again went into the service under Captain Saml Adisson [Samuel Otterson] in Colonel Brandons Regiment, in York district-in which service continued until the Battle of the Cowpens in which action I was engaged. I was employed afterwards in __?__ services and scouting tours until a very short time before the end of the war.

At the Battle of Cowpens on January 17, 1781, John was in Samuel Otterson's Company of the 2nd Spartan Regiment under the command of Colonel Thomas Brandon. British General Cornwallis had sent Lieutenant Colonel Banastre Tarleton to command the British troops. Tarleton had never been defeated and had little respect for the American army, especially the militia.

John Biddie and the rest of the South Carolina militia joined other militia groups and formed the center of the American line that was facing nearly 1,200 British regulars. Daniel Morgan, the American commander, knew that the militiamen had the reputation of running when facing a large number of British regulars. The night before the battle Morgan told the militiamen to fire two volleys at the British and then retreat and reform behind a hill. Behind the hill were Morgan's best troops, over 500 experienced soldiers. Morgan believed, and correctly that the British would run after the retreating militiamen into the waiting trap.

As the militia faced the British, General Morgan rode up and down the line telling them not to fire until the British got close. The militia fired their two or three shots, and as ordered retreated. The British charged the retreating

Americans and Tarleton thinking the battle was won, ordered his dragoons to charge the fleeing Americans. The retreating Americans led the British into a trap. The cream of Cornwallis' army was completely defeated. The final battle at the end of the movie *The Patriot* drew inspiration from this battle. General Cornwallis, present at the battle in the movie, was not at the battle.

Towards the end of the battle Lt. Colonel William Washington, cousin of George Washington, encountered Tarleton as he retreated. As Washington was about to attack Tarleton with his saber, he called out, "Where is now the boasting Tarleton?" Tarleton shot Washington's horse from under him and rode off.

After the war John moved to Alabama. On one of the letters in his pension file John signed his name. Most African Americans, especially in the south, could not write.

Sources: 1. (For the Washington Quote to Tarleton) *Historical Record of the 17th Regiment of Light Dragoons; Lancers: Containing an Account of the Formation of the Regiment in 1759 and Its Subsequent Service to 1841.* **2.** Heinegg, *Free African Americans of North Carolina, Virginia, and South Carolina Vol. 1.* **3.** Grundset, *Forgotten Patriots*, National Society of the D.A.R., page 591. **4.** National Archives Pension Application S10374.

Martin Black

Martin Black was freeborn c. 1751 in Craven County, North Carolina. He married Ann Moore on April 12, 1784, and they had at least two known children. He enlisted on May 16, 1777, in the 10th North Carolina Regiment for three years. He received a monthly pension for $8 for his service. He stated in his pension application,

> He enlisted as a Soldier in the Continental line of the State of North Carolina during the war of the Revolution. He enlisted at New bern and was marched with others under the Command of Colonel Ben Sheppard as a part of the tenth Regiment as he believes to Georgetown on the Potomack at which place the soldiers were inoculated for the small pox.

During the Revolutionary War the threat of smallpox was a major concern for the army. Most British soldiers had already been exposed and were immune. Unfortunately, the Colonial troops were not. Medics would create a small wound in the healthy soldiers' arms, and then they would rub some of the pus from the pox of the infected soldiers into those wounds. This would give them a slight case of the pox, and then they would be immune. This early method of inoculation had been learned from African slaves.

Since they had no way to control the dosage, there was danger involved. If you received too large a dose you could die. Washington estimated that as many as two percent of inoculated soldiers would die. Without the inoculation more than one third of the soldiers would die, and another third would be too ill to fight if an outbreak occurred. This would in effect destroy his army. By the end of March 1778 all the soldiers at Valley Forge had been inoculated. It has been estimated that around one in fifty of inoculated soldiers died from the pox at Valley Forge.

> From Georgetown he marched to Valley Forge in Pennsylvania where the American Army were encamped] under General Washington, while the enemy were in Philadelphia. He was in the battle at Monmouth at the Storming of Stoney point and at the capture of West point. from West point he went with the Army to Albany & marched thence in the Brigade of General Hogan to Charleston. He was a prisoner at Charleston with the army surrendered there but escaped on the seventh day & returned to New bern North Carolina. From his first enlisment as above mentioned to the return to Newbern, he served three years. After remaining at home a few days he enlisted as a soldier in Captain Benj. Colemans as an Eighteen months man in the Continental line of North Carolina, marched to Charleston where he remained with the army there encamped until the Peace, when the army entered the City as the British evacuated it & in a few weeks after was discharged. His discharge is long since lost. At Valley Forge (during the first term of service) the men were distributed to make up deficiencies in the regiment & he passed from the tenth to the second North Carolina Regiment, and from the Company Commanded by Silas Sears Stevenson to the Company Commanded by Captain Clem Hall.

The 10th North Carolina Regiment was depleted due to desertions and illness. The few members that made it to Valley Forge were disbanded and attached to the 1st and 2nd North Carolina Regiments. The 10th Regiment was officially disbanded effective on June 1, 1778, and never to be resurrected.

In 1811 the court minutes of Craven County, North Carolina, stated that Martin Black appeared in court. Two of his children had, without his knowledge and consent, been bound to Benjamin Borden. Martin told the court that the children were free and born in lawful wedlock. The court suspended the order, and it was settled out of court. Martin died in 1821 and in his will he left his son $10.

Sources: 1. *Minutes of the Court of Pleas and Quarter Sessions of Craven County, March 1811.* **2.** Heinegg, *Free African Americans of North Carolina, Virginia, and South Carolina Vol. 1*, page 131. **3.** National Archives Pension Application S41441.

Charles Bowles

Charles Bowles was born in 1761 in Boston. His father was African, and his mother was the daughter of Colonel Morgan a distinguished American army officer. At the age of twelve he was a servant for two years in the home of a Tory. When he turned fourteen, he joined in the Continental Army and served until the end of the war. He received a monthly pension of $8 and stated in his pension application,

In the month of January 1776 I enlisted for the term of one year in Captain Glenson's Company in Colonel John Nixon's Regiment in the Massachusetts line and served my time out and enlisted for two more months and served my time.

    Sometime in July 1777 I enlisted for four months. The later part of March or first part of April 1778 I enlisted (as I then supposed for two years) but being young and ignorant when my two years was out I applied for a discharge but was told I was enlisted for 3 years and I served the three years.

It was not unusual for an officer to trick a young boy, especially if they could not read, into serving extra time. After the first couple of years the war, it was not going well for the Americans and enlistments began to drop off. Besides the harsh conditions of war, many of the men were not being paid regularly or they were paid in worthless Continental money.

There was one story that a young boy accidently fired his musket in a foxhole, and he was reported to the officer in charge. The officer told him there was severe punishment for this offense, and he could avoid punishment if he extended his enlistment for a year. The boy agreed to extend his enlistment, and he was later told by some of the men that he was tricked by the officer.

Charles Bowles served in the 6th Massachusetts Regiment under the command of Colonel John Nixon. When Colonel Nixon was promoted to General, the regiment was commanded by his brother Thomas Nixon. The 6th Regiment saw action in the New York Campaign and in the Battles of Trenton, Princeton, and Saratoga. The regiment was disbanded on November 3, 1783.

After the war Charles moved to New Hampshire and became involved in farming, and he even went to sea for a short time. In 1808 he became a Baptist preacher. Being a black minister sometimes brought danger to Charles.

Once in Vermont a mob was planning to tie him to a wooden horse and throw him into a lake. Charles heard about it before the church service. Charles went ahead and conducted the service, and after the sermon he told the congregation that he had heard of the plot against him. He said he would make no resistance, and he requested that the group sing hymns as they carried him to the lake. The people were so overcome with his courage and conviction that they declined to carry out their plan. Later some of the troublemakers did meet Charles at the lake, not to throw Charles into the lake, but for him to baptize them.

He continued to lead revivals with participation of both races and both genders. Charles became known for his "noisy revival meetings" and "unblemished character and ability as a preacher."

Sources: **1.** National Archives Pension Application S44640. **2.** Morgan, *On This Day: 365 Amazing and Inspiring Stories about Saints, Martyrs, and Heroes*, July 24. **3.** Bittinger, *Vermont Women, Native Americans & African Americans: Out of the Shadows of History*. **4.** Duffy and Orth, *The Vermont Encyclopedia*, page 60. **5.** Stevenson, *God's Might Champions:*

Daily Devotions for Juniors, page 137. **6.** Neil, *The Colored Patriots of the American Revolution*, page 28. **7.** Grundset, *Forgotten Patriots, National Society of the D.A.R.*, page 103.

Jeffrey Brace

Jeffrey Brace was born c. 1742 in Africa, and he died on April 20, 1827, in Vermont. He was captured by slave traders at sixteen and was shipped to Barbados and sold. He was an enslaved sailor during the Seven Years War, which was fought between 1754 and 1763. After the war he was taken to Connecticut and sold again. In Connecticut he was sold three times, and the first time it was to a man by the name of Pridon. This man turned out to be a cruel person and Jeffrey wrote about him in his book *The Blind African Slave*. Although literate, he was blind in his later years, and he narrated the story of his life to an antislavery lawyer. He wrote of his first owner,

> Something was said by my master. He spoke so quick that I did not understand him, then immediately jumped up, and the first salutation knocked me down with his fist. As I went to get up he took up a chair and struck me on the side of the head near where I had been wounded in the first battle I was engaged in, and pealed up a piece of scalp about as big as my three fingers. I fell with the blow under a table, where he kicked and beat me until I became insensible.
>
> When I awoke in the morning I found myself in a most shocking situation. The blood had ran across the room and stood in a puddle in short, I was covered with wounds and poorly fitted for the service of the day; but work I must, as there was no charity to be found in my master's breast. I was ordered to go upstairs to get some corn, and while I was going to the pen to give it to the swine, there being a hole in the bottom of the basket, some of the ears dropped upon the ground. My Puritan master gave me two or three strokes with his whip.

Jeffrey was sold two more times, and the last time was to the widow Stiles. After four years she died and he was given "like real estate" to her son Benjamin Stiles. Jeffrey was drafted into the army, and it first entered his mind to go to Barbados to avenge himself and his country. Instead, he joined the army in Captain Granger's Company, in order to gain his freedom. Jeffrey wrote in his book, "I went into Capt. Granger's company, from hence I was drafted into Capt. Borker's company of light infantry, as they wanted six feet men. I then wanted but a quarter of an inch of being 6 feet 3 inches."

Jeffrey served in the army for five years in order to gain his freedom. He received a monthly pension of $8 for his service. He stated in his pension application,

> That said Jeffrey Brace enlisted in Woodbury in the state of Connecticut in the fall of the year but the year does not recollect but thinks it was in the year 1777 in the Company Commanded by Lt. Trowbridge afterwards commanded by Capt. Granger in Col. Megis Regiment in the Connecticut line afterwards was transferred to Capt. Bakers Company he

enlisted for three years as he thought but was returned for during the War that he continued in said Corps until the summer 1783 when he was discharged from said service in West Point by receiving an honorable discharge with a badge of Merit which discharge is lost that he was in the battles of White Plains at Stamford, West-Chester at Mud-Fort in New Jersey and received a Wound in his leg at the Capture of Mud-fort and retreated with the American Army to red Bank he says although he supposed he enlisted for three years yet he was returned for during the War he cheerfully served five years & nine months.

Jeffrey wrote in his book about his time in the army and the battles he served in. He joined the 6th Connecticut Regiment under the command of Colonel Return Jonathan Megis. Jeffrey claims to have fought at the Battles of White Plains, Monmouth, Princeton, Newark, Froggs-Point, and Horseneck.

This author does not believe he was at the Battles of White Plains, Froggs-Point, and Princeton because those battles were fought before Jeffrey enlisted. Also Colonel Megis was a British prisoner until January 10, 1777, and did not take command of the 6th Connecticut Regiment until May 12, 1777. Jeffrey may have later fought a skirmish in the area.

He said he fought at the Battle of Mud-Fort which was probably the Siege of Fort Mifflin, which is sometimes called the Siege of Mud Island and fought between September 26th and November 16, 1777. Jeffrey wrote in his book, "We proceeded to Mud-Fort, where we encamped until August. In the latter part of the month of August the Fort was attacked, and after every exertion we could possibly make, we were obliged to surrender to superior force; and we retreated to Kingsbridge."

The Connecticut Line wintered at West Point during the winter of 1777–78. While there they worked on various fortifications in the area. Jeffrey wrote of his time at the winter quarters at West Point,

> We marched to West Point, and took winter quarters. While we remained here the soldiers played many boyish pranks. One Samuel Shaw, a brave soldier, but as complete a petty thief as ever graced a camp. He with myself and some others from our camp, the day before we were to be reviewed, by his Excellency, Gen, George Washington, concluded we would have a soldier like frolick.
>
> Accordingly we secretly stole from the lines, went to a Farm not many miles distant, which was occupied by a Tory. From him we stole a shoat [a sheep-goat hybrid]. Shaw was the principle manager in this affair, and we got into camp just before day. We laid the Shoat in the middle of the camp, and in the language of gratitude, began conversing upon our success; but short was our confab.
>
> As we soon saw the frothing Tory coming for his Hog. We immediately covered ourselves with our blankets and effected to be asleep. He recognized his property; he went to the Col. To whose regiment we then belonged; and reported that we had stolen one of his shoats. Col. Megs, came immediately to our company, and with a contenance, that plainly bespoken a determination of punishing us if guilty. He asked how we came by that Shoat; I answered immediately that the owner had brought it for sale, but that manner of conservation

(knowing him to have been a tory) we unanimously suspected him to have come as a spy, and were determined to keep the Shoat until the officers might have an opportunity of being acquainted with his designs. My fellow soldiers were glad of the opportunity of confirming the truth of my assertion—which so completely satisfied the Col. Of our innocence, together with the circumstance of its lying in fair view, in the middle of the Camp—that he severely reprimanded the man for his insult on him and his soldiers. The man a little frighten at so unexpected a charge of guilt that he really had the appearance of a condemned culprit, and was glad to escape with his dead pig upon his back.

After the troops left winter quarters, they marched to Hackensack in New Jersey. While there the enemy stole some of their cattle from their camp. Captain Granger chose about twenty men, including Jeffrey, to go after the men and retrieve the cattle. The men split up and Jeffrey, Adam Waggonor, and Sergeant Ahiel Bradley searched a pasture for signs of the enemy. They came upon a small hill, and Jeffrey waited on one side of the hill and the other two men searched the other side on the hill.

While I stood there anxiously waiting for their return, I suddenly discovered a man riding up to me not more than eight rods distant on full speed with a pistol in his hand, and ordered me to lay down my arms. But not being so instructed by my officers you may well suppose that I did not. At first I thought he was a Jerseyman and was attempting to fool me, as they had played some such pranks before, upon some of the soldiers belonging to our line—therefore in return I demanded to whom I was to surrender and by what authority he demanded it.—he said I must surrender to him who demanded me in the name of the King his majesty of Great Britain. I then plainly told him that neither him or his King's majesty would get my arms unless he took them by force. He immediately cocked his pistol and fired; I fell flat upon the ground in order to dodge his ball, and did so effectually do it, that he missed me. I rose, he drew his sword and rode up to me so quick that I had no time to take aim before he struck my gun barrel with his cutlass, and cut it almost one third off—also cut off the bone of my middle finger on my hand, as he struck the horse jumped before he could wheal upon me, again altho' my gun barrel was cut. I fired and killed him, as he fell I caught his horse and sword.

He was a British light horseman in disguise.—I mounted immediately, and that instant discovered four men on horseback approaching me from different direction, I fled, passed one man, just before I came to a stone wall. Both of our horses were upon the full run he fired and missed me. My horse leaped the wall like a deer; they all pursued me. When we got into the road, they were joined by many more; and all with swords in hand pursued me in full career. I drove my horse as fast as possible, stabbed him with my sword and gun, kicked my heels in his side, but having no spurs, and not being so good a horseman they gained upon me. I looked forward and saw my Capt. in full view, almost a mile distant. This encouraged me, and the long shanked negro, soldier with a leather cap, mounted on an elegant english gelding light horse, made all whistle again. When I came in about twenty or thirty rods, I heard the Captain say, "there come one of our leather caps, and it is Jeffrey.—reserve your fire so as not to kill him; however the men fired, and three balls cut my garments, one struck my coat sleeve, the next hit my bayonet belt, and the third went through the back side of my leather-cap. They were so close upon me, that the same fire killed four of the British and five horses—and wounded some more; I did not stop for this salute, but pulled on for head quarters. When our men fired the enemy were within two or three jumps of me; but being so handsomely saluted upon surprise, as our men were conceled from their view, they made the best retreat possible.

There was a name problem with Jeffrey when he applied for a pension. His name could not be found on any company rolls. He had enlisted under the last name of Stiles which was his master's last name. He filed for a pension under the name Brace, which was his father's last name. This is the letter of explanation he sent to the pension bureau,

> On this 9 day of May 1820 personally appears Jeffrey Brace of the town of Georgia in said County aged between seventy & eighty years a man of Color who being by me first duly sworn according to law he was a slave to Benjamin Stiles of South bury in Connecticut that he went by the name of Jeffrey Stiles afterwards he altered his name to Jeffrey Brace he had the impression that he alterned his name at the time of his enlistment, but upon more mature reflection he thinks that he must have altered his name at the time of his discharge the reasons for altering his neme was that he was imported from Affrica when a lad that his Fathers name was Brace after he considered himself discharged from his master he concluded to take the name of his Father Brace was the reason of his altering his name.

Another soldier, Ansel Patterson wrote a letter to the pension bureau supporting Jeffrey's service,

> On this 3 day of March 1821 the deponent says that the Company of Negroes was generally paraded on the right of the sixth Company this deponent thinks he has a clear recollection of the name Jeffrey as belonging to the Negro Company this despondent in conversing with Jeffrey is well persuaded that he was a Soldier of Col. Butlers Regiment & belonged to the Negro Company from his narrating so many transactions which took place in the service which he could not have done had he not been there in the service he narrates the transaction of a mutiny in the Regiment the place where the Regiment lay the ring leader and especially of one Gaylor being hung as supposed to be one of the leaders the place of his execution he also narrates the execution of many tricks performed by a Negro boy necked named the Cat he also states many circumstances of the Negro boxing which the deponent recollects also the different movement of the regiment that I have no doubt in my mind but what he was a Soldier in said Regiment. After conversing with him & a first impression in my mind as to the name Stiles I think he may have gone by the name Jeffrey Stiles.

When Jeffrey was discharged from the army, he returned to his old master at Woodbury, and was told that since he was now free he could go where he pleased and seek his fortune. Jeffrey had heard good things about Vermont, so he left and moved there in 1784.

He met and married a widow Susannah Dublin, who was a native of Africa and they had two children. In Vermont there was still racism and the practice of taking black children from their parents. There was a feeling that Africans were incompetent parents and had no right to raise their own children.

Elizabeth Powell who was married to Martin Powell, a wealthy landowner in Vermont, filed to remove the two children of Susannah and Jeffrey. Elizabeth was successful and was given the two children to serve as indentured servants. Soon after Jeffrey and Susannah began to have their own children. By 1790 the census indicated that they had at least three.

Jeffrey and his wife bought a farm, and around 1807 they moved to a farm in Georgia. Susannah fell ill and on March 19, 1807, she died. In 1810 Jeffrey was blind and in his late 60s, he narrated his life story to an antislavery lawyer Benjamin Prentiss. Jeffrey received a monthly pension of $8 until his death on April 20, 1827.

Sources: **1.** Prentiss, *The Blind African Slave or Memories of Boyrereau Brinch, Nick-Named Jeffrey Brace*, 1810. **2.** National Archives Pension Application S41461.

Joseph Brown

Joseph Brown was born on November 18, 1749, in North Kingston, Rhode Island. He was a slave owned by Beriah Brown, the sheriff of King's County, Rhode Island. Joseph was married to Lucretia Thomas on January 5, 1794, in Massachusetts. Joseph died on April 1, 1834, and he received a yearly pension of $35.53 for his service.

Joseph enlisted in the militia as a substitute of Christopher Brown, who was the son of Beriah Brown. Joseph stated in his pension application,

> I was the substitute of Christopher Brown his Master's son about the middle of the Revolutionary War & served ten months & twenty days. The company I served of about sixty men under command of Capt. Dyer & Cable Allen Lieut. Kept guard from a place called Boston Neck to Greewich on Naragunset Bay.
>
> He was promised his liberty if he served. He can recollect that towards the last of the time of his service, he & the rest of the troops were under General Stuben, that the British burnt Bristol during this time.

On May 25, 1778, a British landing party raided Bristol and destroyed twenty-two houses and a church.

Sources: **1.** Grundset, *Forgotten Patriots, National Society of the D.A.R.,* page 207. **2.** National Archives Pension Application W1543.

Marlin Brown (Roorback)

Marlin was a slave born in c. 1750. He served in the army as a waiter for Colonel Fischer from October 1776 until June of 1778. He stated in his pension application,

> Applicant served all the time of his enlistment as a waiter or servant of Colonel Fisher but his name was on the muster roll of the regiment & he drew the pay of a soldier of the line. Once too on muster day he took his station in the ranks with his musket & answered to his name.
>
> He was pursuit in attendance in Colonel Fisher at the battle of Stillwater where Bur-

goyne was taken prisoner. General Gates was in command and General Arnold was wounded wither in or just before the battle. The main battle was fought on Friday beginning about noon & continuing till near midnight. There were other battles & skirmishes afterwards before the surrender.

When he first entered the service he was stationed at Albany for a short time. He then went to Ticonderoga where he remained till the spring of 1777 when the army retreated before Burgoyne. In one to the skirmishes on the retreat Colonel Hendrick or Henry __?__ was severely wounded in the thigh by a musket or grape shot. After the surrender of Burgoyne applicate came to Albany where he remained through the winter until his discharge.

Applicant was the slave of John Roorback of Mallkill then Ulster state of New York at the time he entered the service. About the beginning of June 1778 he was to be transferred to Frederick Roorback the brother of his former master. He enlisted with the permission of his master John Roorback during all the time he was to have remained in his service.

Marlin's pension was rejected for two reasons. First, the pension bureau could find no Colonel John Fischer on any army rolls. Second, Marlin enlisted as a slave. At the time of his enlistment slaves were not allowed to enlist. They had to be freed first by their masters, which Marlin was not. Because of a shortage of manpower it is very probable that the enlistment officer took Marlin knowing he was a slave. To fill the ranks they took men over the age of enlistment and boys under the age of enlistment.

Sources: 1. National Archives Pension Application R6978. **2.** Grundset, *Forgotten Patriots, National Society of the D.A.R.,* page 335.

Scipio Brown

Scipio Brown was born c. 1756 in North Kingston, Rhode Island. He was a 5'2" tall slave owned by Beriah Brown and served in the 1st Rhode Island Regiment. He participated as a drummer at the Battle of Rhode Island on August 29, 1778, and the Siege of Yorktown in October of 1781. Scipio received a monthly pension of $8 for his five years of service.

Young boys were recruited to act as drummers. The drums played an important part in communicating on the battlefield. The various drum roles signaled different commands from the officers to the troops. At times the boys were treated as mascots by the adult soldiers. Sometimes the youngest boys received no pay but were given money by the officers. About 200 drummers served in the Revolution. The average age was around twenty with only a few below the age of fourteen.

They would sometimes have other duties during the day. They might serve or wait upon an officer, chop wood, or help the surgeon during sick call. At times they would march out with the fifes in front of the regiment and play a tune before the battle began.

Scipio stated in his pension application,

> On the first day of May 1778 I enlisted to serve during the war, into Colonel Christopher Green's Regiment in the Rhode Island line. He served in said Regiment and afterwards commanded by Colonel Olney until the 15 day of June 1783.

In 1778 Rhode Island was having problems recruiting enough white soldiers to meet their troop quotas set by congress. They began to enlist slaves for the 1st Rhode Island Regiment in order to meet the quota. In February of 1778 the Rhode Island Assembly voted to enlist slaves for Colonel Christopher Greene. The owners of slaves that enlisted were to be compensated by the assembly in an amount equal to the market value of the slave. After serving the slaves would be granted their freedom. A total of eighty-eight slaves enlisted over the next four months.

Beriah Brown had three slaves serve in the Revolutionary War. Joseph, also in this book, served as a substitute for Beriah's son, so the master received no compensation. Scipio and Thomas enlisted, and their master Beriah would receive compensation. Thomas also served as a drummer for the duration of the war, but he did not apply for a pension.

Sources: 1. National Archives Pension Application S38584. Grundset, *Forgotten Patriots*, National Society of the D.A.R., page 272.

John Browne

According to one history book about black men in the Marine Corps, there were at least three black men in the ranks of the Continental Marines and ten others who served as Marines on ships of the Connecticut, Massachusetts, and Pennsylvania Navies.

John Browne's name appears on a list of applicants for an invalid pension, which was returned by the District Court for the District of Philadelphia submitted to the House of Representatives by the Secretary of War on April 25, 1794, and printed in the American State Papers, class g, page 98.

RANK: 1st Lieutenant, Marines
DISABILITY: wounded in his hip and the small of back by a large chest giving way out of the wardroom.
WHEN & WHERE DISABLED: May 28, 1777, frigate called the Boston
TO WHAT PENSION ENTITLED: half.
Source: 1. National Archives Pension Application.

Bristol Budd

Bristol Budd was born c. 1763 probably in Connecticut, and he died in 1848 in Pennsylvania. He married Phoebe Perkins in the spring of 1826. He served in the 6th and 7th Connecticut Regiments from 1777 until the end of the war in 1783. He received a monthly pension of $8 for his service. He filed for a pension in December of 1820 and stated,

> The said Bristol Budd alias Bristol Sampson enlisted as a soldier in the company of Capt. Stephen Betts in the regiment commanded by Col. Charles Webb on the ____ day of March in the year 1777 for the term of & during the war. He was discharged in the year 1783.
>
> He was detached in the light infantry for a time in the company of Capt. VonEyke of regiment commanded by Col. Meigs for a time as a waiter. He was in the battles of Saratoga, White Marsh, Monmouth, capture of Stoney Point.

Bristol stated in his application that he had no income, land, and only one hen turkey valued at $1. He said that he lived with his father-in-law who was a poor black man. He also said,

> I have labored for my living—I have been blind for six years—during that time I have lived entirely on the charity of the people—I performed a journey of seven hundred miles last fall on foot, led by my little son by a string to obtain the certificates hereinto annexed. My family consist of only myself & little guide—my son William aged 14 years.

Sources: **1.** National Archives Pension Application W253054. **2.** Grundset, *Forgotten Patriots, National Society of the D.A.R.*, page 272.

Silas Burdoo

Silas Burdoo was born on February 14, 1748, in Lexington, Massachusetts. His father Philip was from Africa and had probably gained his freedom by 1745. Silas first worked as a laborer and earned enough money to buy a farm on his own land. He had purchased land in New Hampshire but continued to live in Lexington. He received a yearly pension of $36.66 for his service.

He gave a detailed account of his service in his pension application,

> He volunteered in the service of the United States on the 19th day of April 1775 in Capt. Boardman's Company and was in the Battle at Lexington on the same day, and after the following the British forces back from Lexington to Boston, was dismissed.

The militia was summoned to meet on the Lexington Green, and at two in the morning on the 19th of April Captain John Parker called roll and about 130 men answered to their names. By day break the British troops were near Lexington, when they were spotted by a patriot who rode to warn Captain Parker. The militia had earlier sent out several patrols, but they had been captured by the British.

When the news of the advancing British reached Captain Parker, he ordered alarm guns to be fired and the drum beat to arms. In a matter of minutes the British would be in Lexington. Soon Silas Burdoo and about seventy of the militiamen stood with their muskets on Lexington Green ready to face the British. There were also some thirty or forty spectators standing nearby and a few with muskets. Around five in the morning these seventy ill-trained citizen soldiers were facing about 400 of the finest trained soldiers in the world.

Captain John Parker ordered his men, "Do not fire unless fired upon." One of the men present said years later that Parker's order was, "Stand your ground. Don't fire unless fired upon, but if they mean to have a war, let it began here." Paul Revere recalled the order as having been, "Let the soldiers pass by. Do not molest them without they begin first." Regardless what was the correct order given, it was clear that Captain Parker did not want to have the Americans fire the first shot.

When the British entered Lexington Green their commander told his men to hold their fire. He then shouted to the Americans, "Disperse, ye rebels; lay down your arms and disperse!" The Americans stood their ground. The British officer repeated his order with a curse. Some accounts say that the officer then ordered his men to fire upon the rebels. Most accounts say that some unknown person fired the first shot.

When the mysterious shot was fired many of the British opened fired. None of the Americans were hit, and they believed that the first British volley was just powder with no shot. When the British fired a second volley, however, some Americans began to fall. The Americans broke and ran leaving their wounded behind. The British marched on to Concord where they were met by a superior force of Americans. Shots were exchanged and the British began to retreat.

As the British retreated back to Boston, the Americans hid behind trees, fences, and buildings and fired as the British marched in retreat. The numbers of militiamen continued to grow and shoot at the British. When the British finally made it back to Boston, they had 300 wounded and seventy-three killed. The militia surrounded Boston with 15,000 troops and laid siege to the British Army. The road back to Boston became known as "Battle Road." Silas stated in his pension application,

> He enlisted in the Army of the United States, in May, 1775 at Cambridge with Capt. Wood and served in the Regiment of the Mass Line under Col. Gerrish, Major Febiger, who commanded the Regt. after Gerrish was broken. Rendezvoused at Cambridge common until the 17th June next following his enlistment when the Regiment took a line of march for Bunker Hill in Charlestown, and Capt. Wood's Company to which he belonged proceeded as far as Charlestown common in plain sight of Bunker Hill where the battle was then raging.
>
> At Charlestown common, they received several volleys of common & grape shot from the enemy and after the American troops were driven from Bunker Hill, he returned in Wood's Company to Cambridge where he stood guard during the night. The Americans were entrenching and fortifying the place.

Silas enlisted in the 9th Massachusetts' Regiment. He stated that Colonel Samuel Gerrish was "broken," which meant that he was court-martialed for failing to repel an attack on Sewall's Point. He was previously been accused of acting in a cowardly manner at the Battle of Bunker Hill. During the later stages of the battle he panicked his men by shouting, "Retreat! Retreat! Or you'll all be cut off!"

> I occasionally guarded at Innman's Point in Cambridge, and the remainder of the time, until Gen. Washington took the command, encamped on Prospect Hill. After Gen Washington arrived and took command of the Army he was in Capt. Wood's company to Medford and was occupied as a guard at that place.
>
> That whilst at Medford he once stood guard at General Sullivan's quarters, at the Bishop house, so called at the time, from it being owned by a man by the name of Bishop. I was discharged at Cambridge in January.

Silas declined to enlist again, and instead he lived as a civilian before enlisting again in 1781. He stated in his pension application,

> In 1781, the town of Lexington was required to furnish eight militia men, to join the Army of the United States at Gallows Hill on the bank of Hudson River south of West Point to serve three months.
>
> I volunteered and started from Lexington in the fore part of Sept, 1781 in company with William Diamond, and arrived in about eight days. He enlisted under Major Porter. I was for a while employed on fatigue [working] in making and repairing roads, he volunteered with about ten of fifteen others, to go to Danbury in the state of Connecticut and receive 105 head of cattle to be driven to the American Army the command of Gen. Washington then besieging Cornwallis. The party took charge of said cattle at Danbury crossed the Hudson River at King's Ferry, landed the cattle on the Jersey Shore, and proceeded with them to Morristown in the state of New Jersey, when he returned to Gallows Hill. That while at Kings Ferry he saw Capt. Calender of the regular troops, whom he knew and who commanded a company of artillery at the battle of Bunker Hill in 1775.
>
> That he remained at Gallows Hill but a few days only, when he was stationed at the Barracks in Fishkill, where he remained the remainder of the three months for which he volunteered. That he was in Fishkill on the day of general rejoicing for the taking of Cornwallis.

Silas served a total of eleven months of service. He was one of the few black soldiers that signed his name to the pension application. Years after the war he moved to Vermont and married Phebe who died in 1818, and then he married Rosanna who died in 1836.

Sources: 1. Phinney, *History of the Battle of Lexington: on the Morning of the 19th April 1775*, pages 10–22. **2.** Hudson, *History of Lexington*, pages 140–154. **3.** Ketchum, *The Battle of Bunker Hill*, page 126. **4.** Grundset, *Forgotten Patriots, National Society of the D.A.R.*, page 272. National Archives Pension Application S21099. **5.** Knoblock, *African American Historic Burial Grounds and Gravesites of New England*, page 259.

Seymour (Simo) Burr

Seymour Burr was born c. 1756, but the location of his birth is in question. Some sources say he was born in Connecticut, and others report he was born in Guinea, Africa when he was captured at the age of seven. He was owned by Seymour Burr, who was the brother of Colonel Aaron Burr.

Seymour was treated well by his master, but he longed for his freedom. He and several friends decided to steal a boat and escape to the British army. The British had promised that any slaves that joined the army would gain their freedom. The boat with the escaping slaves was captured by their masters and the slaves were returned home. Instead of punishment, Seymour's master showed sympathy for the slave's desire for freedom. He felt that Seymour would try again to escape to gain his freedom so he made him a proposition.

The master told Seymour that if he would give him the bounty money and enlist in the American army he would, at the end of the war, be a free man. Seymour agreed and on April 5, 1781, he enlisted for two years in the 7th Massachusetts Regiment. Seymour stated in his pension application:

> I served as a private in the war of the American Revolution in the Massachusetts Line in the company of Captain Coburns [the 8th company] and in the Regiment commanded by his Excellency John Brooks and afterwards in the company commanded by Captain Turner and in the regiment commanded by Colonel Jackson. I entered the service in the beginning of the year 1781 and was discharged on the 31st day of December in the year 1783.

Seymour was present at the Siege of Fort Catskill, and endured much suffering from starvation and cold. After some skirmishing, the army was relieved by the arrival of General Washington, who, as witnessed by Seymour, shed tears of joy on finding them safe.

After the war Seymour gained his freedom, and in 1805 married a widow named Mary Will, who was part Native American of the Ponkapoag tribe. He inherited six acres of land in Canton, Massachusetts, owned by Mary's previous husband. Seymour died on February 17, 1837, and his obituary was printed in the *Liberator* in Boston Massachusetts, page 35, on February 25, 1837, "DIED— In Canton, 17th inst. Mr. Semore Burr, a colored man, age 98. He was a soldier during the whole of the Revolutionary war. His widow died in 1852 at the age of 101." He received a monthly pension of $8 for his service.

Sources: 1. Grundset, *Forgotten Patriots, National Society of the D.A.R.*, page 104. **2.** Guthrie, *Camp-fires of the Afro-American: or, the Colored Man as a Patriot* by, page 175. **3.** Huntoon, *History of the Town of Canton, Norfolk County, Massachusetts*, Chapter II. **4.** Nell, *The Colored Patriots of the American Revolution*, pages 21–22, 1855. **5.** National Archives Pension Application W23726.

Jim Capers

Jim Capers was born on September 23, 1742, and died in the spring of 1852. He became a free man. However, he married a slave woman named Milley around 1826. Jim received a yearly pension of $96 for his service. His wife applied for a widow's pension after his death, but it was denied because she was a slave. He stated in his pension application,

> He enlisted in the army of the United States in the year AD 1775 and served in the 4th Regiment of the Continental line as Drum Major under the following named officers, to wit, Col John Brown, & Lieutenant Col. John Jeffrey, Major John Pearcey, Major William Sabb, with Captains Samuel White, & William Brown & Peter Maybrook his Orderly Sergeant; That said Jim Capers Enlisted during the War & served Eight years drum Major; That he resided in Christ Church Parish (opposite Bulls Island) in the State of South Carolina when he entered the service The Affiant further states that he was in the battle at Savannah Georgia, St. Helena, Pt. Royal, Charleston, Georgetown, Camden, Biggins Church & the Eutaw Springs: That in the last mentioned Battle, affiant was wounded, in four Different places, one on the head & two on the face with a sword and one on the left side with a ball. Killing the drummer Immediately behind him, whose name was Paul Ram Lee, that the name of the Physician who dressed his wounds received in said Battle to the best of his Recollection was Dr. John Gardner; Soon after the battle of the Eutaw Springs affiant was marched to the State of Virginia and was present at the surrendering of Lord Corn Wallace, and his Army, that after the surrender affiant was shipped to Philadelphia, and from thence he sailed to Charleston and was discharged six months after.

Jim claimed in an earlier letter in his pension application that he served with General Marion in 1775. Jim's memory may have been a little weak, when he applied for a pension. Francis Marion was a captain in the 2nd South Carolina Regiment in 1775. He later led his men in guerrilla warfare. Jim also said he was in the 4th South Carolina Regiment, but this was a regiment of artillery commanded by Lt. Colonel Roberts and Colonel Beeckman. It is very likely that Jim may have been passed around various regiments and companies during his tour of duty.

Sources: 1. National Archives Pension Application R1669. 2. Grundset, *Forgotten Patriots, National Society of the D.A.R.*, page 591.

Thomas Carney

Thomas Carney was born in 1754 and probably in Queen Anne's County, Maryland. He was a farmer that was born free. In 1810 he married Anna Winter and they had two sons.

In late August of 1777 a British fleet of 260 ships landed troops of British General Howe near the Maryland-Delaware border. Washington requested that Maryland, Pennsylvania, and Delaware provide 2,500 volunteer militia to back up the Continental Army. Thomas enlisted in a Maryland militia unit in early September of 1777.

> He enlisted & served as a private soldier in the Fifth Maryland Regiment of the Maryland line, where of William Richardson was Colonel, in the company of which John Hawkins was Captain, & served about three years under Col. Richardson & Captain Hawkins & continued to serve in that Regiment to the end of the revolutionary war, which at different times was commanded by Colonel John E. Howard, Col. Thomas Woolford & Colonel John Stewart, & in the said company also, which was commanded by different persons, after the resignation of Captain Hawkins; he was in the battle of Brandywine; Germantown; White Plains, Monmouth, Gates Defeat at Camden, at Camden under General Greene Guilford court house, Ninety Six & Eutaw Springs; he entered the service when the said Regiment was raised about the year 1776 enlisted first for three years, & then during the war, he left the service at the end of the war at the City of Annapolis in Maryland where he was discharged on furlough.

After Thomas participated in the Battles of Brandywine and Germantown, he spent the winter quartered at a bend in the Delaware River near Wilmington. Most of the troops stayed in homes leased from the civilian owners, and they spent their time on guard duty or gathering supplies for Washington's Army at Valley Forge.

In the spring of 1778 Thomas enlisted in the 5th Maryland Regiment of the Continental Line. He stood out in his unit due to the fact that he was over six feet tall and had great strength. Thomas claimed to have fought at the Battle of White Plains. This battle took place on October 28, 1776, which was before he enlisted.

The 7th Regiment was assigned to the 1st Maryland Brigade at the Battle at Guilford Court House. Thomas, according to his obituary, bayoneted seven of the enemy at this battle. His regiment was referred to by one British historian as the "finest regiment in the American army."

At the Battle of Ninety-Six Thomas carried his wounded captain, Perry Benson, on his shoulders some distance to the surgeon's tent, and when he laid the man down Thomas fainted from fatigue and heat. Captain Benson survived the battle, and the two men developed a lasting friendship.

After the war ended in January of 1783, Thomas remained in the army until November. He returned to Caroline County, Maryland, and received a monthly pension of $8. The state of Maryland introduced a bill in the legislature to give Thomas an additional pension. The bill passed in 1813 by a unanimous vote. Whenever Captain Benson, who lived in a neighboring county, visited near the home of Thomas he would visit him. Benson was a general in the local militia, and on muster days he kept Thomas with him "mounted on a horse at his side."

Sources: 1. Grundset, *Forgotten Patriots, National Society of the D.A.R.*, page 467. **2.** Sohlosser, *Remembering Greensboro*. **3.** D.A.R., *African American and American Indian Patriots of the Revolutionary War.*, page 121. **4.** National Archives Pension Application S35203.

John Chavis

John Chavis was born c. 1763 in the West Indies, Virginia, or North Carolina. He was a free African American who worked for James Milner a Virginia attorney. John was the first African American to graduate from a college or university in the United States. He later served as a minister and a teacher.

In 1778 he enlisted in the 5th Virginia Regiment and may have been at the Siege of Charleston. After the war he married Sarah Frances Anderson and moved to New Jersey to attend Princeton University. He was licensed to preach in the Presbyterian Church of Lexington, Virginia, in the fall of 1799.

After Nat Turner led the slave rebellion in August of 1831, both Virginia and North Carolina passed laws restricting free African Americans freedom of movement, and it barred their education. He was a vocal supporter of the abolitionist movement, and foul play may have caused his mysterious death on June 15, 1838. Local stories say that Chavis may have been beaten to death in his home by local whites that did not want him educating blacks.

Sources: **1.** Othow, *John Chavis: African American Patriot, Teacher, and Mentor*. **2.** Simmons, *Preaching with Sacred Fire: an Anthology of African American Sermons, 1750 to the Present*, page 21.

Cuff Chambers

Cuff Chambers was born c. 1738 in Massachusetts, and he died on June 8, 1818, in Maine. He and his wife Bette were married by Samuel Phillips on September 16, 1762, in Andover, Massachusetts. Before the war Cuff was a slave owned by Samuel Blanchard. At that time Cuff used the last name of his master, and when he gained his freedom he took the last name of Chambers to honor his mother.

After the Battles of Lexington and Concord his master promised Cuff his freedom if he would enlist. Cuff joined for eight months in the Andover Company of Captain Charles Furbush in the 27th Massachusetts Regiment of Colonel Ebenezer Bridge. Cuff was one of at least five African American men in the company. The regiment went to Breed's Hill on the night of June 16, 1775, in order to build the redoubt that many Americans died in the next day. Captain Furbush was wounded in the battle and had to be carried off.

After the war Cuff was, as promised, given his freedom. He later moved his wife and their five children to Leeds, Maine. By 1814 his children were grown, and Cuff and his wife were so poor that they had to receive assistance from friends. Cuff died in 1818 and his wife died in 1839. In 1849 Cuff's only surviving child, Elizabeth Roberts, filed for his pension and received a yearly amount of $33. She stated, "Her father was a soldier of the revolution. She heard her parents say he served eight months and was in the Battle at Bunker Hill."

Sources: **1.** National Archives Pension Application W23810. **2.** Quintal, *Patriots of Color.* pages 79–80. **3.** National Park Service, *Biographies of Patriots of Color at the Battle of Bunker Hill,* page 13.

Sampson Coburn

Sampson Coburn joined the militia for eight months in the company of Captain Oliver Parker in Colonel William Prescott's Regiment in Massachusetts. He served in the redoubt at the Battle of Bunker Hill. The day after the battle he was listed on an order "for cartridge boxes dated Camp at Cambridge." This would indicate his participation in the battle.

On June 22, 1775, he served as a guard under Colonel Loammi Baldwin, and in August of 1775 he is on the roll of the company commanded by Captain Ephraim Corey. In October of 1775 his name was on an order for bounty coat or its equivalent in money dated the Camp at Cambridge. He was listed as reaching the rank of Corporal, which was the highest rank given to African American soldiers.

A bounty coat was used in Massachusetts as an incentive for men to enlist in the army. It began nearly two weeks after the Battle of Bunker Hill. A total of 13,000 bounty coats were provided.

Sources: **1.** National Park Service, *Biographies of Patriots of Color at the Battle of Bunker Hill,* page 7. **2.** Quintal, *Patriots of Color,* page 85.

Primus Colburn

I enlisted at Abington in the county of Plymouth in the State of Massachusetts in the summer of the year 1780, marched with other recruits to West Point in the State of New York and muster in the company of Captain Miller of the first company, in the first regiment of the First Brigade in the Massachusetts Line then stationed at that post for the term of three years.

He was slightly wounded in the leg at a place called "Morris Sena" [this was probably the skirmish at Morrisania on January 22, 1781] below King's ferry on the North River, while on picket guard.

I was frequently on guard at "Tataway" [Tappan?] where Major Andre was imprisoned. I was present when the Regiment was drawn up and surrounded him at his execution at said place.

Major Andre was executed on October 2, 1780, in the Dutch village of Tappan, Orangetown. He was executed near the center of the camp of the

American Army. There was an exterior guard, which Primus was probably a member of, consisting of five hundred Infantry that surrounded the area. There was also an inner guard, under the command of a Captain. None were allowed within this inner square except the officers on duty and the Assistants of the Provost Marshal.

> The Regiment to which he was attached were authorized at the time of discharge to wear as a badge of honor, on the left arm, something resembling a "V." That the wound he received was literally broken out and at one time the surgeons were about to amputate his leg, but has since got so much better as to enable him to work, but not to gain comfortable subsistence by manual labor.

Primus signed his name to this statement, and he received a monthly pension of $8.

Many of the Revolutionary War doctors believed that amputation was "the antibiotic of the day." They thought that if a body part was severely damaged by a musket ball, then the only way to stop the effect on the rest of the body was to amputate. There was no anesthesia or sterilization, so it was a painful and deadly procedure. Officers would be given rum or brandy, if available to dull the pain. Since Primus was an enlisted man he would have been given a wood stick to bite down on. Less than 35 percent of the patients survived.

Sources: 1. National Archives Pension Application S34703. **2.** Grundset, *Forgotten Patriots, National Society of the D.A.R.,* page 106.

Abraham Cook

Abraham Cook was born on April 23, 1749, in Cumberland, Rhode Island. He served as a minute man, serving under Captain Elisha Waterman, and in the militia for one year and twenty-six days. He received a yearly pension of $42.89 for his service.

> I enlisted in said company of Minute men continually exposed to be called on, I had myself ready to turn out at a Minutes warning—being called out as a company once a fortnight for the same purpose doing all the duty required of a soldier in such a corps till the Spring of 1778. A term of three years.
>
> The business of the corps to which I belong sent to guard the sea board towns and other exposed places in the State of Rhode Island. During all the time aforesaid we were so much on our own that we had very little time to do anything to profit on our farms at home. Whenever we were called out we were required to carry with us three days provisions.
>
> After my term of enlistment as a minute man had expired I enlisted with the militia of Rhode Island and served in Providence and places in that vicinity. About three months I was dismissed.

Sources: 1. National Archives Pension Application S5019. **2.** Grundset, *Forgotten Patriots, National Society of the D.A.R.,* page 211.

Oliver Cromwell

Oliver Cromwell was born c. 1752 and probably was a free black man in Black Horse, New Jersey. He was raised a farmer by the family of John Hutchin. He was of mixed descent and may have been part Indian.

He enlisted in his mid-twenties as a drummer in the 2nd New Jersey Regiment from 1777 until June 5, 1783, under the command of Colonel Israel Shreve. He stated in his pension application,

> I enlisted at the beginning of the war in the company of Captain Lowrey—Second New Jersey Regiment. Lowrey was wounded and the Regiment was commanded by Captain Bowman. I served six years.

Captain Lowery was wounded and taken prisoner at the Battle of Short Hill on June 26, 1777. He was a Quaker who was disowned by the Chesterfield Monthly Meeting for joining the military. Lowrey died on the prison ship *New Jersey* in New York on July 10, 1777.

Cromwell was present at the battles of Trenton, Princeton, Brandywine, Monmouth, Springfield, and Yorktown. He also spent the winter of 1777–78 at Valley Forge. After the Battle of Princeton, Cromwell later remarked that Washington's men, "knocked the British about lively." At the Battle of Yorktown he claimed to have seen the last man die. At the Battle of Springfield he said he saw the house of Mrs. Caldwell burning.

The Rev. James Caldwell was an active supporter of the patriot cause. At the Battle of Springfield the British raided several towns in the area, which included Caldwell's home in Connecticut Farms. His wife Hannah soon became alarmed, when she began to see smoke rising in the distance and the screams of frightened women and children running through the streets. She began to straighten up her house and put on one of her best dresses as she remarked, "to receive the British as a lady." She also took the time to lower some of their valuables into the well.

She took her baby into the bedroom, and as she gave the child to her nurse Katy, Hannah noticed a British soldier climbing over the fence and heading toward the house. She began saying to herself, "they will respect a mother, they will respect a mother." She was not aware that she was in plain sight of the window.

The soldier walked by the window and looked in and realized that this was the wife of the "Rebel Priest" James Caldwell. He raised the musket to the glass and fired. Mrs. Caldwell was hit in the heart and fell to the floor dead. The soldiers then entered the house and searched through Hannah's dress looking for valuables. They then torched the house and dragged her body outside and into the street where it laid for several hours. A neighbor later moved the body into one of the few buildings left standing.

General Washington had great affection for Oliver Cromwell, and after the war he personally wrote and signed Cromwell's discharge papers. Some years after retirement Cromwell applied for a pension. He was unable to read or write, so local lawyers, judges, and politicians aided him. He was granted a yearly pension of $96 for his service. He used part of the money to purchase a 100 acre farm for his wife and fourteen children.

Sources: **1.** National Archives Pension Application S34613. **2.** Headley, *The Chaplains and Clergy of the Revolution,* 1864, pages 217–232. **3.** D.A.R. Lineage Book, Vol. 2, page 61. **4.** Thompson, *From Its European Antecedents to 1791 — The United States Army Chaplaincy,* Thompson, pages 195–196. **5.** Mitnick, *New Jersey in the American Revolution,* page 129. **6.** Reef, *African Americans in the Military,* pages 64–65. **7.** Trenton Evening Times, April 11, 1905, page 5.

Tobias Cutler

Tobias Cutler was born c. 1758 in Rindge, New Hampshire, and he died in August 1827. He married Dorothy Paul, and they had five children. He received a monthly pension of $8 for his service.

Cutler was a slave of lawyer Enoch Hale. Hale told Tobias he would free him, if he served in the army in his place. In the latter part of 1780 Tobias enlisted for three years in a company commanded by David McGregor in the 2nd New Hampshire Regiment, which was under the command of Lt. Colonel George Reid. Some of the soldiers of the 2nd Regiment served at Yorktown in 1781, and after the American victory the regiment returned north. The regiment was disbanded on January 1, 1784.

After he gained his freedom, Tobias married and purchased almost two acres of farm land from his wife's white grandfather. He agreed to pay for it by working on it for three years. He signed a contract with Mr. Paul that would allow him to keep half the produce and pay half the taxes. At the end of three years the farm would be his.

The connections with the Paul family gave Tobias access to the white society of the area. He became involved in various activities, and some were rather dubious in nature. He gained a reputation as a shrewd and successful trader which was due to education provided by his lawyer master. As a result Tobias was not well liked by many members of the white population.

In 1798 a group of five men destroyed Cutler's house, and they were sued for $160 in damages. The court ruled that he could only collect $59, because that was what the house was worth. This marked the beginning of trouble for Tobias.

In 1806 Tobias served as the lawyer on behalf of his sister-in-law, Harriet Paul. Harriet brought suit against a Mr. Frazier for breach of promise of marriage.

Tobias won the suit for Harriet, and she promised to pay him even if she, "had to go out washing to earn the money." Apparently Harriet decided against a career in washing, because Tobias sued her for $70 in expenses and a gold watch she promised to him in payment. Tobias recovered his full amount after an appeal. This action did not make Tobias a favorite in the Paul family.

For the next few years Tobias was involved with the Paul family in several lawsuits. Tobias was removed from his house by one of the Paul relatives, and he was forced to leave his family with relatives. To supplement his meager income Tobias began to sell rum without a license. He was brought to court on this in 1817, and later he obtained a license to sell rum. In 1820 he applied for a pension claiming that he was unable to work to support himself due to "lameness in his fingers." He was able to work the system to his own advantage, and at the time of his death he left his wife more than $55 and considerable property.

Sources: **1.** National Archives Pension Application S45710. **2.** Dixon, *Freedom Earned, Equality Denied: Evolving Race Relations in Exeter and Vicinity, 1776–1876*, pages 18, 22, & 23. **3.** Stearns, *History of the Town of Rindge, New Hampshire*, 1875, pages 7 & 169. **4.** Bell, *History of the Town of Exeter, New Hampshire*, page 398.

Austin Dabney

Austin Dabney was born about 1765 in Wake County, North Carolina, and he died around 1830. He was a slave and belonged to Richard Aycock. They moved to Wilkes County, Georgia. When Richard was drafted into the militia, Richard sent Austin as his substitute. To avoid any problems because Austin was a slave, Richard claimed that Austin was born free.

Austin enlisted in August of 1778 and served in the Virginia militia under Captain Samuel Campbell. He first marched to Jarrett's Fort in Greenbrier, Virginia, and during this time he did service at Jarrett's Fort and at Benhive's Fort. About nine miles separated the two forts. Most of the time he served at these two forts defending them against Indian attacks.

After he was discharged Austin returned home and soon enlisted in the militia again. On this tour he was under the command of Captain Trigg, and he marched to Petersburg, Virginia, and then to Cabin Point. At Cabin Point he was under the command of Colonel Meriwether and joined the army of General Muhlenberg. The army marched to Dismal Swamp and was engaged there in a skirmish with British troops. From there they marched to Gregory's Camp and then to Tan Yards where Austin was discharged. He served again under Captain Trigg which totaled twelve months of service.

Austin obtained his freedom after the war and received a yearly pension of $60. For about ten years after the Revolution, Austin was Captain of a company of militia in Bedford County, Virginia. He was banned from participating in the land lottery open to Revolutionary War veterans in 1819, but the legislature granted him acreage in Washington in 1821.

Georgia Governor Gilmer made the following observations of Austin Dabney,

> In the Beginning of the Revolutionary conflict, a man by the name of Aycock removed to Wilkes County, having in his possession a mulatto boy, who passed for and was treated as his slave. The boy had been called Austin, to which the Captain to whose company he was attached added Dabney.
>
> Dabney proved himself a good soldier. In many a skirmish with the British and Tories, he acted a conspicuous part. He was with Colonel Elijah Clarke in the battle at Kettle Creek, and was severely wounded by a rifle-ball passing through his thigh, by which he was made a cripple for life. He was unable to do further military duty, and was without means to procure due attention to his wound which threatened his life. In this suffering condition he was taken into the house of Mr. Harris, where he was kindly cared for until he recovered. He afterwards labored for Harris and his family more faithfully than any slave could have been made to do.

The Battle of Kettle Creek was fought on February 14, 1779, between 300 to 400 Tories and around 500 militiamen. The Americans defeated the enemy and scattered the Tories. The battle was called "the hardest ever fought in Georgia." Dabney may have been the only African American in the battle.

Giles Harris was a white soldier who lived in the area and cared for the wounded Austin in his home. The two men formed a close life-long bond. In gratitude Dabney worked for the Harris family, and out of his own pocket he sent his rescuer's oldest son through college and then arranged for his legal training.

> At the close of the war, when prosperous times came, Austin Dabney acquired property. In the year 18___ he removed to Madison County, carrying with him his benefactor and family. Here he became noted for his great fondness for horses and the turf. He attended all the races in the neighboring counties, and betted to the extent of his means. His courteous behavior and good temper always secured him gentlemen backers. His means were aided by a pension which he received from the United States.
>
> In the distribution of the public lands by lottery among the people of Georgia the Legislature gave to Dabney a lot of land in the county of Walton. The Hon. Mr. Upson, then a representative from Oglethorpe, was the member who moved the passage of the law, giving him the lot of land.
>
> At the election for members of the Legislature the year after, the County of Madison was distracted by the animosity and strife of an Austin Dabney and an Anti-Austin Dabney party. Many of the people were highly incensed that a mulatto Negro should receive a gift of the land which belonged to the freemen of Georgia. Dabney soon after removed to the land given him by the state and carried with him the family of Harris, and continued to labor for them, and appropriated whatever he made for their support, except what was necessary for his coarse clothing and food. Upon his death, he left them all his property. The eldest son of his benefactor he sent to Franklin College, and afterwards supported him

whilst he studied law with Mr. Upson, in Lexington. When Harris was undergoing his examination, Austin was standing outside of the bar, exhibiting great anxiety in his countenance; and when his young protégé was sworn in, he burst into a flood of tears. He understood his situation very well, and never was guilty of impertinence, He was one of the best chroniclers of the events of the Revolutionary War in Georgia.

Judge Dooly thought much of him, for he had served under his father, Colonel Dooly. It was Dabney's custom to be at the public house at Madison, where the judge stopped during court, and he took much pains in seeing his horse well attended to. He frequently came into the room where the judges and lawyers were assembled on the evening before the court, and seated himself upon a stool or some low place, where he would commence a parley with anyone who chose to talk with him.

He drew his pension in Savannah, where he went once a year for this purpose. On one occasion he went to Savannah in company with his neighbor, Colonel Wyley Pope. They travelled together on the most familiar terms, until they arrived in the streets of the town. Then the Colonel observed to Austin that he was a man of sense, and knew that it was not suitable for him to be seen riding side by side with a colored man through the streets of Savannah; to which Austin replied that he understood that matter very well. Accordingly, when they came to the principle street, Austin checked his horse and fell behind. They had not gone very far before Colonel Pope passed by the house of General James Jackson, who was the governor of the state. Upon looking back, he saw the governor run out of the house, seize Austin's hand, shake it as if he had been his long absent brother, draw him off his horse, and carry him into his house, where they stayed whilst in town. Colonel Pope used to tell this anecdote with much glee, adding that he felt chagrined when he ascertained that whilst he passed his time at a tavern, unknown and uncared for, Austin was the honored guest of the Governor.

Sources: 1. National Archives Pension papers W3007. **2.** Burns, *Record of Abstracts of Pension Papers Concerning Soldiers of the Revolutionary War, War of 1812 and Indian Wars Who Settled in Wayne County, Kentucky*. **3.** Tombstone **4.** Knight, *Georgia's Landmarks, Memorials and Legends, Vol. II*. **5.** Hicks, *African Americans in the Military* by Catherine Reef. 6. *Revolutionary War Amid Southern Chaos*.

Dolphin Dart

Dolphin Dart served for three years in the 3rd Connecticut Regiment and probably participated in the New York and New Jersey Campaigns in the spring of 1777. He received a monthly pension of $8 for his service.

> I enlisted in the war of the revolution in the Spring of the year 1777 during the war in the company commanded by Captain Edward Ellis in the Regiment commanded by Colonel Samuel Willys in the Connecticut Line. I served as a soldier until the 10th December 1780 at which time I became lame and was afflicted with Epileptic fits and on said 10th day of December John R. Martin the surgeon gave me a certificate delivered to Captain Robert Warner that I being frequently attended with Epileptic fits together with a lameness I had, was rendered entirely unfit for military duty.

Dolphin was given a 30 day medical leave. When he returned he still had the fits and was discharged.

Sources: 1. National Archives Pension Application S36456. **2.** Grundset, *Forgotten Patriots, National Society of the D.A.R.*, page 275.

Francis Dewitt

Francis Dewitt, born c. 1750, may have been owned at one time by Jacob Dewitt. In 1836 Francis filed for a pension.

> That in May in the third year of the revolution he entered the service of the United States as a Ranger under Captain Jacob Dewitt then of Ulster County [New York].

He served in the company of Rangers for about three years. Their duty was to scout on the back frontier then occupied by the Indians and Tories."

> In that year 1777 a fort was built of pickets around Dewitt's house to protect the neighborhood from the incursion of the Indians and tories, and Captain Dewitts Rangers when not called out were engaged in protecting and defending this fort and other forts of similar kind.
> In 1778 Fort Dewitt was attacked by the Indians & tories while I was stationed there. I was wounded in the leg with a bullet at this attack.
> When the Rangers were at the fort, they were ordered out frequently in squads of 10 to 15 as scouts and spies to look out for and follow the tracks of the Indians. And I was sent out very often as one knowing the woods. In 1779 Capt. Wood commanded Fort Dewitt & the troops there. The company of Rangers was broke up and the men turned into other companies in the month of Oct. I went into a militia company and served in that.

To support the pension claim, two men that served with Francis wrote letters to the pension bureau to support his service. The first letter was from Benjamin DeFry, and the second letter was from James Tennilliger.

> Francis lived at Fort De fry till October 1778 when it was burnt by the tories and Indians and our people retreated to Fort Dewitt. They attacked Fort Dewitt and the said Francis Dewitt there as a soldier and fighting bravely the whole time.
> Francis Dewitt rescued a man from the Indians and also saved the life of Esther Van Aukan from the Indians and tories with great hazard when Fort Dewitt was attacked in 1778.

Francis received a pension for his service. When he died on December 14, 1837, his wife Harriett applied for a widow's pension. It was rejected with no reason given. One of the common causes for a rejection was a lack of proof of marriage. Without a certificate or letters from people that knew the couple as man and wife, the pension would not be granted.

Sources: 1. National Archives Pension Application R2919. **2.** Grundset, *Forgotten Patriots, National Society of the D.A.R.*, page 333.

Prince Estabrook

Prince Estabrook, a tall man at 5'11", was born c. 1740 in Massachusetts and he died c. 1830. He was owned by the family of Benjamin Estabrook. Prince was present in Lexington on April 19, 1775, when eighty-seven other militia men under the command of Captain John Parker stood waiting for the British troops. When the British arrived and fired upon the militia Prince was wounded and he was helped home by his owner's son Joseph.

Early in 1776 the call went out for reinforcements to aid the American army after the attack in Canada failed. Prince joined Captain Charles Miles' Company in the regiment commanded by Colonel Jonathan Reed. Prince served with the unit at Fort Ticonderoga, when the American fleet was defeated at Lake Champlain in October of 1776. On February 16, 1777, Prince left Fort Ticonderoga and returned home.

On November 6, 1777, he enlisted for five months in Captain Simon Hunt's Company of the regiment commanded by Colonel Eleazer Brooks. On July 28th he enlisted for six months in Colonel John Greaton's 3rd Massachusetts Regiment. Prince also served at various times in 1780, and on June 11, 1781, he received a bounty from Lexington to enlist in the army for three years. During this time he served in Colonel John Greaton's Regiment and Colonel Michael Jackson's Regiment. Prince was discharged on October 14, 1783.

After Prince's service to the army Benjamin gave him his freedom. Because Benjamin had treated him with dignity and respect, Prince chose to remain with the Estabrook family and also did odd jobs around town.

Sources: 1. Lanning, *African Americans in the Revolutionary War*, page 5. **2.** Hinkle, *Prince Estabrook: Slave and Soldier*. **3.** Quintal, *Patriots of Color*, pages 97–98.

Andrew Ferguson

Andrew Ferguson was born free from free parents in July 1765 in Dinwiddie County, Virginia, and he died on October 1, 1855, in Monroe County, Indiana. He received a yearly pension of $20 and stated in his pension application,

> I am a colored man. I was born in Dunwidie County Virginia Free and was seventy-three years old in July last and at fifteen years of age I was drafted into the service of the United States by General Green who was at that time (the first of January 1780) in Dinwiddie County Virginia. Two weeks previous to my being drafted and in company with my father (Andrew Perley as he was called) was taken prisoner by the British under John and James Cuglie. We ran away from them because they whipped us with the cat of nine tails and fell in with the American soldiers under Green. General Green toled us that if the British ever got us they would kill us and he had better draft us and so we arrived out of a little hon black Tickets and he told us we should go with him and *must fight the British*. I was then put under the immediate command of Captain William Harris and Colonel William McCormick and stayed under their command and in this company during most of the time I was out. The first engagement I was at was the Battle at Allegany. Colonel Morgan was there Colonel McCormick and Captain Harris. The British commanders, who had taken us prisoners, were there also. Jack Head our drummer was with us all the time. I was well

acquainted with him but know not, what has become of him. The next place if I remember right was Kings Mountain away down in North Carolina. We got to that battle when it was partly over. We whipped the British badly who were commanded by Major Ferguson.

Major Patrick Ferguson was a Scottish officer in the British Army. He recruited Tories in the south and treated patriots harshly. At the Battle of Kings Mountain on October 7, 1780, he was shot from his horse, and with his foot caught in the stirrup he was dragged to the patriot's side. A patriot approached him for his surrender, and Patrick drew his pistol and shot the man. After the battle Patrick's body was found nude with eight musket holes in him.

> I do not recollect at this time the name of any of the American commanders except Colonel Campbell, Sevier and Cleveland. I saw at Kings Mountain a Tory they called Bill Cunningham kill an American in two hundred yards of us. He was on horseback and then rode off. This Battle was fought sometime in October 1780.

William "Bloody Bill" Cunningham was involved in several bloody massacres in the back country of South Carolina. He joined on the side of the British, when his mother was roughed up and his crippled brother John was killed by patriots.

> I was at Camden in South Carolina previous to the engagement at Kings Mountain, but was not in the action. Colonel Morgan was at Kings Mountain and after the battle he'd marched us down into South Carolina to the River Pacolet not far from the Cow-pens as he said to join Green but I did not see Green there. While we were at the River Pacolet, the British under Colonel Tarleton came upon us and Colonel Morgan marched us on towards the Cow Pens but before we got there we made a stand and whipped the British completely. This took place I think sometime in the month of January 1781.
>
> Immediately after this Battle we started back to North Carolina. I recollect of Marion and Colonel Washington being at the battle at Pacolet also Colonel William Howard and Colonel Pickens. On our route back through Carolina the British under Tarleton pursued us and was prevented from overtaking us by the high waters. At Guilford we fell in company with Green and Huger and then went on to Virginia across the Dan River sometime in February. We did not stay long in Virginia until we went back into North Carolina about ten or fifteen miles from Guilford at somebody's iron works on Troublesome Creek. From there we marched in about two miles of Guilford and there we had a battle with Cornwallis and after the battle was over we went back to the iron works. I was wounded in the head at Guilford and stayed about a month at the iron works. This battle was sometime in March 1781. I recollect that a man by the name of Auter Francis Franerse from Dinwiddie County was wounded at the battle of Guilford also. I was well acquainted with him. General Greene made a speech to us at Guilford. General Steven Lawson and Huger were there and Colonels Lee, Campbell and Washington.

At the Battle of Guilford Court House fought on March 15, 1781, Andrew and his Virginia militia were in the second line protecting the left flank. They were under heavy fire until they broke in the afternoon of the battle. Although, it was a British victory, Cornwallis lost 25 percent of his force. Another victory such as this, and he would lose the war.

> I was afterwards ordered back to South Carolina and we had another fight at the Cow Pens and stayed there a month or perhaps more and then we went to the Eutaw Springs and there we fought a last battle. Colonel Morgan was there. General Greene and my Captain and Colonel. This battle was sometime in September I think as well as I recollect. There we were discharged and General Greene said he would take all our names down and we should get our pay. He gave me some kind of a ticket or other which I have long ago lost. After I was discharged I went back to the iron works in North Carolina and my head got worse and I stayed there sometime and was attended on by Dr. Harris and Dr. Sidney and Mr. Furgison sent one of his sons for me and I got home again in the last of November 1781.

Sources: 1. National Archives Pension Application S32243. **2.** Tombstone. **3.** Monroe County Historical Society, West Virginia, website.

Cato Fiske

Cato Fiske was born in Massachusetts c. 1760. He was known as a fiddler in his hometown, and he enlisted as a drummer in the army. He received a monthly pension of $8 and stated in his application of 1818,

> I Cato Fisk, now of Deerfield in the County of Rockingham and State of New Hampshire testify and declare that I enlisted as a soldier in the company commanded by Capt. William Rowell of the second Regiment in the New Hampshire line of the American Army in the Revolutionary War in the year of our Lord one thousand seven hundred and seventy seven and served without any intermission from the time of my first enlistment to the seventh day of June in the year of our Lord one thousand seven hundred and eighty three at which time I was honorably discharged.

His wife Elsa applied for a widow's pension in 1827. Her statement and a letter from Sarah West provide an interesting insight into the marriage of Elsa and Cato.

> She [Elsa] declares that she was married to the said Cato Fiske by the Reverend Nathaniel Trask at Brentwood in New Hampshire in the month of March, as she believed in the year seventeen hundred and eighty three, but she knows that it was before the close of the revolutionary war because the said Cato Fiske was at the time of the marriage apart from the army on furlough and afterwards returned to it and served in it for sometime before the close of said revolutionary war.
>
> I Sarah West of Brentwood in the County of Rockingham and State of New Hampshire, aged seventy years and upwards, do testify, declare and say, that in the fall of the year 1780 I used to live with the late Rev. Nathaniel Trask of said Brentwood, and lived with him until I was out of my time, and made his house my home for several years, after I was out of my time and until I was married. Soon after I went to Mr. Trask's a colored woman came to line in the neighborhood of Mr. Trask's, not a quarter of a mile from his house—

she used to be called Aunt Sellars—a colored girl by the name of Else Huso used to live with her and was after at Mr. Trask's. I knew her well. She was courted by a colored man, Cato Fisk, and I remember her being published to Cato and I laughed at her about it. This was in the winter of 1782–3 and in the spring of 1783 the said Cato Fisk and Else Huso were married. I was not present at their wedding but I recollect on a Sunday after their publishment was out I heard Mr. Trask say that he was going over to Aunt Sellars to marry Cato and Else and after he returned the same evening—he spoke about the wedding of the colored couple. Jonathan Trask, a son of the minister was invited by Cato to attend the wedding and did attend it, and told me about it after he came home. The next day after they were married I went into Aunt Sellars, and wished Else joy of her marriage. Cato was there at the door cutting wood. Else continued some time at Brentwood after she was married and until Cato and her moved to Exeter which I think must have been the next fall or winter, but I don not remember the time. I several times saw here when she lived at Exeter where she was several years—she had no children until she had been married several years. I have been acquainted with Else ever since her first going to Brentwood and she had always borne a good character for truth and industry, and was much set by her neighbors wherever she lived.

Cato was not much in Brentwood after he was married until after he removed to Exeter. He was a drummer in the Army and a fiddler at home. He continued in the Army several months after he was married as I suppose, and until about the time he moved his wife to Exeter. I went to live with Mr. Trasks in the fall after the dark day, and Cato and Else were married a little more than two years afterwards in the spring and early in the spring, but I cannot remember the day of the month, nor the month with certainty, although I think it was the month of March.

Cato's daughter, Nancy Daley, wrote a letter to the pension bureau about the death of her father,

> He died, on about the twenty fourth day of March AD 1824. I remember that General McCleary died a few days after my father; and the next Sunday the minister preached a sermon on their deaths; I mentioned my father before he mentioned the General & some people in the Parish were offended at it. I went to church, and remember it was wet & sloppy walking. I was present at my father's death. He died on or about the day I moved. He died on Monday night, about eight o'clock.

Sources: 1. National Archives Pension Application W14719. **2.** Grundset, *Forgotten Patriots, National Society of the D.A.R.,* page 53.

William "Billy" Flora

William "Billy" Flora was a free-born African American from Virginia who served as a soldier in the revolution. In the American victory at the Battle of Great Bridge in December of 1775 Billy played a very important role. Billy took up a plank on the bridge that prevented the British from crossing the bridge. His commander Captain Thomas Nash wrote, "Flora, a colored man, was the last sentinel that came into the breastwork. He did not leave his post until he had fired several times. Billy had to cross a plank to get to the breastwork, and had fairly passed over it when he was seen to turn back, and deliberately take up the plank after him, amidst a shower of musket balls."

Source: 1. Lanning, *African Americans in the Revolutionary War*.

James Forten

James Forten was born on September 2, 1766, in Philadelphia, Pennsylvania, and he died on March 15, 1842. He was born free, and he started working at the age of seven after the death of his father in a boating accident. He attended the African School run by the Quaker abolitionist Anthony Benezet. By age nine James left school to work full time to help provide for his family.

At the age of fourteen James served on the privateer *Royal Louis*, which was commanded by Captain Stephen Decatur. Much of the time onboard he served as a powder boy. In 1781 his ship was captured by the British ship *Amphion* after a seven hour chase. James was concerned, because he knew that someone of his race would probably be sent to the West Indies and be a slave for the rest of his life.

Captain Bazely of the British ship had two sons on board and thought that James would make a fine companion for the boys. James and the Captain's sons would often play marbles, which James soon excelled in. One of the boys bragged to his father how well James played the game. At the insistence of the Captain, James demonstrated his skill and impressed the Captain. James soon found that he was given greater freedom than a prisoner usually experienced.

When the British ship sailed into New York to take on supplies and drop her prisoners off, the Captain made a surprising proposal to James. He wanted to take James to England with his sons, educate him, and let him experience freedom and equality. James declined the offer saying, "I signed up for the cause of liberty and I would not betray it."

James was transferred to the infamous prison ship *Jersey*. Captain Bazely gave James a letter to deliver to the prison commander. It requested that James should not be forgotten on the list of exchanges. James was then removed to the prison ship and became prisoner 4102.

The conditions on the ship were very harsh. Thousands of men were crammed below deck where there was little light, no fresh air, little sanitation, and sparse food to eat. In addition the prisoners were treated brutally, and as many as eight prisoners a day died. A total of 11,000 men died on the *Jersey*. It is estimated that 8,000 men died from combat during the war.

When the British surrendered at Yorktown, negotiation for the release of prisoners took a long time. First to be released would be prisoners that served in the army or navy, and the privateers were last. Seven months after being placed on the *Jersey*, James was finally released. He walked from New York to Trenton, New Jersey, in his bare feet. When he returned home to Philadelphia it was obvious from his appearance that he had suffered a great deal.

Once he recovered he signed on a merchant ship and sailed to London. He worked for more than a year in a London shipyard. He returned to Philadelphia in 1786 and became an apprenticed sail-maker for Robert Bridges. He learned quickly and was promoted to foreman. Eventually, he owned the business and employed more than forty workers.

On November 10, 1803, James married Martha Beatte at the African Episcopal Church of Saint Thomas. She died the following year, and he never again mentioned her. He married again December 10, 1805, to Charlotte Vandine.

By the 1820s James was one of the most influential black men in the country. Liberty for all people was important to him. He believed that this liberty should be gained without using violence. He spoke out against slavery and for equal rights for the rest of his life. He was one of the wealthiest Americans of his time, with holdings at over $100,000.

Sources: 1. Vallar, *Pirates and Privateers: The History of Maritime Piracy*, Cindy Vallar. **2.** Nell, *The Colored Patriots of the American Revolution, with Sketches of Several Distinguished Colored Persons*.

Jacob Francis

Jacob Francis was born on January 15, 1754, in Amwell, New Jersey, and he died on July 26, 1836, in Hunterdon County, New Jersey. He was bound to an Amwell farmer and resold several times by the age of thirteen. He was then purchased by Joseph Saxton who took him to New York, then to St. John in the Caribbean, and finally to Salem, Massachusetts. Jacob, at fifteen was then sold to Benjamin Deacon. Jacob's time as a servant expired on January 21, 1775, and he enlisted in the 16th Continental Regiment.

After the Battle of Trenton his enlistment was up and he returned home. His mother was in poor health, and while he was home she informed Jacob that his family name was Francis. After that he became known as Jacob Francis. After the war he purchased and married Mary at the home of her former master, Nathaniel Hunt, in September 1789.

Jacob served various times during the war and received a yearly pension of $80. He gave a detailed record of his service in his pension application,

> I enlisted as a soldier in the United States service for one year. I was told they were enlisting men to serve one year from the first of January, 1776, but I should receive pay from the time I enlisted, and I enlisted and entered the service about the last of October and received two months pay for my service up to 1 January 1776. I enlisted at Cambridge about four miles from Boston, under Captain John Wooley, or Worley, or Whorley, in colonel Paul

Dudley Sergeant's Regiment(Colonel Sergeant, I understood lived in Cape Ann. When I left New Jersey and went with Mr Saxon to St. John's, I did not know my family name, but called myself Jacob Gulick (or Hulic) after the Mr. Gulick I had lived with, and was enlisted by that name; but, after I returned to New Jersey, was informed by my mother that my family name was Francis, and after that time I went by the name of Jacob Francis. Captain Wooley was captain; his brother was lieutenant. His Christian name I forget, and he had two sons, one a sergeant and the other a drummer in the same company in which I enlisted. The major's name was Ashton or Aston; his Christian I don't recollect. At the time I enlisted the British army lay in Boston. After that, I remained with the regiment at Cambridge and in the neighbor of Boston until the British were driven out of Boston.

I recollect General Putman more particularly from a circumstance that occurred when the troops were engaged in throwing up a breastwork at Lechmere Point across the river, opposite Boston, between that and Cambridge. The men were at work digging, about 500 men on the fatigue at once. I was at work among them. They were divided into small squads of eight or ten together and a noncommissioned officer to oversee them. General Putnam came riding along in a uniform as an officer to look at the work. They had dug up a pretty large stone which lay on the side of the ditch. The General spoke to the corporal who was standing looking at the men at work and said to him, "My lad, throw that stone up on the middle of the breastwork.

The corporal, touching his hat with his hand, said to the general, "Sir, I am a corporal." "Oh," said the general, "I ask your pardon, sir," and immediately got off of his horse and took the stone and threw it up out of the breastwork himself and then mounted his horse and rode on, giving directions, etc. It was in the winter season, and the ground was froze.

In 1776, after the British had left Boston, the army, with our regiment and myself along with them, marched by way of Roxbury (that way we could go by land) over a causeway into Boston and lay over two or three days, then were ordered out to Bunker Hill. We marched out and encamped there and lay there for some time. Then our regiment was ordered to an island at that time called Castle William. The island contained about 10 acres. It was about three leagues, or nine miles from Boston. The channel for vessels passed close under it. The island had had a fortification in the shape of a half moon, but it was pretty much destroyed by the British before they left. The British fleet then lay about nine miles farther out. We lay on that island until about harvestime. Then we left the island and was ordered to New York from the island. We crossed the river, left Boston on our right hand, and marched to New London. There we took shipping and come to New York. Came down the east river; left Long Island on our left. The British was then on Long Island. At that time the people were culling oars. We stayed a day or two in New York. There were no other troops but our regiment with us. After a day or two we marched out to a place called Hell Gate [a tiny narrow tidal strait in the East River]. On the north side of the East River. There we threw up breastworks, and the British threw up breastworks on Long Island on the opposite side of the East River and used to fire across. We lay there for sometime.

While we lay there the battle of Long Island took place. There was a number of men detailed from our regiments, so many from each company, to go over and join the American army, perhaps two hundred men, I was one. We crossed the river at Hell Gate and marched on to the island in the direction we was ordered, but did not get to join the army till the battle had commence and our army was on the retreat. We had to cross a creek to get to our army, who had engaged the enemy on the other side, but before we got to the creek our army was repulsed and retreating, and many of them were driven into the creek and some drowned. The British came in sight, and the balls flew around us, and our officers, finding we could do no good, ordered us to retreat, which we did under the fire of the enemy. We retreated back to Hell Gate and recrossed to our fortifications. Soon after that we had orders to leave that place and marched to Westchester by way of Kingsbridge.

We lay for some time, and every night we had a guard stationed out two or three miles from where the regiment lay at a place called Morrisania. I mounted guard there every time it came to my turn. There was an island near there. The tide made up around it. The British had a station on the island, and a British ship lay there. In an attack on the Island one night, Colonel Jackson was wounded. After some time we were ordered to march to the White Plains. We marched there and there joined General Washington's army.

We lay for some time at the White Plains. While we lay there, the British land and attacked some of our troops and had a brush there. Our regiment and I with them marched by general Washington's orders toward a hill where the engagement was, but the British got possession of the hill, and we retreated back to the camp. The British established a garrison on that hill. I stood sentinel that night in a thicket between the American camp and the hill, so near the British lines that I could hear the Hessians in the garrison, which was between one-quarter and one-half mile from me. The British lay there awhile and then left that place, and our regiments marched after them about three or four miles farther east. Then we received orders and marched to Peekskill on the North River. We halted a day and night a little distance from the river and there crossed at Peekskill to the west side of the river. From thence we marched on, and I do not recollect the names of the places we passed through till we got to Morristown, New Jersey. We lay there one night, and then marched down near to Baskingridge and lay there the next night. That night General Lee was taken in or about Baskingridge. I heard the guns firing. The next morning we continued our march across Jersey to the Delaware and crossed over to Easton. From thence we marched down the Pennsylvania side into Bucks County.

It was then cold weather, and we were billeted about the houses. Our company lay off from the river a few miles below Coryell's Ferry and above Howell's Ferry. We lay there a week or two; then we received orders to march and, Christmas night, crossed the river and marched down to Trenton early in the morning. Our regiment marched down the River Road and wintered the west end of the town, general Washington with the rest of the army crossed at McKonkey's Ferry, four miles above Howell's and marched down the Scotch Road and came into the north end of the town. We marched down the street from the River Road into the town in the corner where it crosses the street running up towards the Scotch Road and turned up that street. General Washington was at the head of that street coming down towards us and some of the Hessians between us and them. We had the fight.... After about half an hour the firing ceased, and some officers, among whom I recollect was General Lord Stirling, rode up to Colonel Sergeant and conversed with him. Then we were ordered to follow them, and with these officers, and Colonel Sergeant at our head, we marched down through the town toward Assanpink and up the Assanpink on the north side of it and to the east of town where we formed in the line and the view of the Hessians, who were paraded on the south side of the Assapink and grounded their arms and left them there and marched down the old ferry below the Assanpink, between Trenton and Lamberton.

Soon after that a number of men from our regiment were detailed to go down and ferry the Hessians across to Pennsylvania. I went as one, and about noon it began to rain and rained very hard. We were engaged all the afternoon ferrying them across till it was quite dark, when we quit. [The captured Hessians were sent to Philadelphia, later to Lancaster, and in 1777 they were moved to Virginia.] I slept that night in an old millhouse above the ferry on Pennsylvania side. The next morning I joined the regiment where I had left them the day before up the Assanpink, east of Trenton. We lay there a day or two, and then the time of the year's men was out, and our regiment received part of their pay and were permitted to return home. I did not get a discharge. At that time I had seven and a half month's pay due to me, and I believe others had the same. I received three months pay, and all the rest of the regiment the same, and we were ordered to come to Peekskill on the North river, and then we should receive our pay and get our discharges.

After I came home, I was enrolled in the militia in Capt. Philip Snook's company. The next spring I was called out in the militia in the month's service. The militia took turns, one part went one month, and then the other part went out a month and relieved them, and then those that were out on the first month went again, so that one-half the militia in this part of New Jersey was out at one time. I always went out when it came to my turn to the end of the war as one of the militia and went out once as a substitute for a person who was to go but could not and gave me seventy-five dollars Continental money to take his place, and I did and served the month.

I was out another month under Capt. Philip Snook. We marched that time to Newark and stayed a month. We lay in a building in Newark called an academy or schoolhouse. At that time the British and Hessians lay on Staten Island. An alarm came that there was an attack on the militia in Elizabethtown, and our company marched on toward Elizabeth two miles or more along the road till we came to a piece of rising ground, where the British came in sight. When we saw their numbers, we fired on them and then retreated. A piece of low ground covered with bushes lay on the west side of the road. We turned into that. The Hessians I think came foremost. There was three columns, blue coats, green coats, and red coats and, when they got on the rising ground fired on us.

After we got off some distance, some of us concluded to cross back toward the road and get a shot at them. One Joseph Johnson belonging to the company and myself went. We separated, and I crept along among the bushes till I got almost within gunshot, when I heard a noise behind me and looked round, and there was three Hessians near me that belonged to a flanking party and had got between me and the company. They took me prisoner, Johnson was some distance from me and was taken prisoner by another party. I was taken by the Hessians that took me out to the road to the British army and marched with them under guard through Newark and was carried some distance up the river called Second River. Night came on and sometime in the night we came to a creek that ran down into the river. Some of our militia, but I don't know who, expecting the British, had placed themselves in some buses on the left side of the road near the creek and fired on the British as we came up. This created some confusion and broke the ranks, and the most of them left the road and turned off to the right toward the river. There was four men that had me under guard. They turned in the alarm and left me. I stood near a steep bank that ran down into some bushes toward the creek. Finding the men was a little ways from me, I stepped down the bank into the bushes and laid down. The militia that had fired retreated, and I saw nothing of them. The British stayed a few minutes. One of the captains was wounded. Then they formed in the road again and marched on. That same party marched on to Esopus and burnt Esopus at that time. I lay in the bushes some time till they were all gone, then came out and pushed back to Newark and joined Captain Snook's company there about two o'clock in the morning. I stayed my month out.

I was out afterwards and did a tour of duty of a month, in which we marched up to

Pompton, stayed there some time. We marched from Pomptom to Paramus; from that we marched down to Hackensack and stayed all night there. The next morning, marched down the river toward the British lines and Bergen a few miles to where there was an old guardhouse on the west side of the river that was unoccupied by the British. We went to the guardhouse on the west side of the river and stayed an hour or two. On the other side a, piece from the river, was rising ground. After waiting some time we saw some troops come over the rising ground at a distance and march down toward the river below us, where they were obscured from our sight by an intervening wood. There appeared to be a much larger number of men than we had, and the subalterns who were with us, apprehending they might cross the river below and come in on our rear, ordered us to retreat and not to fire. We had not proceeded up the river far when a considerable party of the British troops we had seen below us cane in sight and on the opposite side of the river and fired upon us. The subalterns took the lead in the retreat and ordered us to hurry on without firing. We marched a little way. The British kept firing, I was behind the rest of our party, and a bullet struck near me upon which I suddenly turned round and fired. Then our whole party turned and fired upon the British, upon which they retreated again. Our subaltern officers had pushed on ahead, and we saw no more of them. We marched on without them and joined the army at headquarters, and I joined my company.

I was out afterwards under Capt. Philip Snook. I think several times. I recollect particularly being out under him at the time of the Battle of Monmouth. We were in a regiment of the Jersey militia at that time commanded by Col. Joseph Phillips belonging to General Dickerson's brigade. Our regiment and myself with it was on the battleground and under arms all that day but stationed on a piece of ground a little to the northwest of where the heat of the battle was and were not actively engaged with the enemy. But our Captain Snook was permitted to go or went in the course of the day for some purpose, but what I am unable to recollect or state, to another part of the field and receive a wound from a musket shot through his thigh. After the battle was over, we were discharged and returned home.

I recollect other occasions when I was out, although I cannot state them exactly in their order of time. I was out in the militia at the time of the battle of Brandywine. I was at Newark at the time Lord Cornwallis was taken.

Sources: 1. National Archives Pension Application W459. **2.** Grundset, *Forgotten Patriots, National Society of the D.A.R.,* page 383. **3.** Yazawa, Henretts, & Fernlund, *Documents for America's History, Volume 1: To 1877,* page 145. 4. Dohla, *A Hessian Diary of the American Revolution,* page 48.

Chatham Freeman

Chatham Freeman was born c. 1750 in Africa, and he died on February 13, 1834, in Meriden, Connecticut. He received a monthly pension of $8. And he stated in his application,

On the end day of June 1777 I enlisted as a private in Capt. Leavenworth's Company in the fourth Regiment Connecticut Line, commanded by Col. Meigs. I continued faithfully to serve for three years.

Chatham was given his freedom for taking the place of his master's son in the army. Noah Yale, his master, still owned the sweetheart of Chatham named

Mercier. So Chatham agreed to work for Noah for seven more years to gain her freedom. Mercier along with her child was given her freedom on April 29, 1792. Chatham told Noah that he "wanted to be married just like white folks."

Sometime after the marriage had taken place Chatham came to Noah and said he wanted to be "unmarried as I never can stand it to be married to that woman." Chatham was told that it can't be undone and he must stay married. Chatham walked away and muttered, "Oh Massa what I gwine to do, what I gwine to do?" Things must have worked at well, because Chatham later became a land owner.

Sources: 1. National Archives Pension Application S36524. **2.** Franco, *Meriden*, page 56. **3.** Bancroft & Curtis, *An Historical and Pictorial Description of the Town of Meriden*, page 245. **4.** Raphael, *A People's History of the American Revolution*. **5.** Grundset, *Forgotten Patriots*, National Society of the D.A.R., page 277.

Jordan Freeman and Lambert Latham

Jordan Freeman was born on October 30, 1732, in Lyme, Connecticut. His parents were servants in the house of Richard Lord, Jr. In 1755 Jordan married Lilly who was a servant to Mary Prentice of New London. Jordan later became a servant to John Ledyard and was passed to John's son Colonel William Ledyard. Colonel Ledyard freed Jordan before the Revolutionary War began and the two men became close friends.

Lambert Latham was a slave who was working with his master Captain William Latham in a nearby field when the British invaded New London. He went with his master to defend the fort from the British.

On September 6, 1781, the Battle of Groton Heights or Battle of Fort Griswold took place. British General Benedict Arnold was ordered to raid New London in hopes of diverting General Washington from marching against Lord Cornwallis in Virginia. The Connecticut militia under the command of Colonel William Ledyard occupied Fort Griswold across the river from New London. Inside the fort, serving with the Colonel was his good friend Jordan Freeman. Lambert Latham was also there with his master Captain Latham.

The Americans ran out of ammunition, and as the British began to scale the walls of the fort the Americans fought with bayonets and pikes. British Major Montgomery led the attack on the fort and as he scaled the wall he was killed with a pike by Jordan Freeman. About the same time, Lambert Latham picked up the American flag which had been shot off of its pole, and he held it above his head. The British overpowered the remaining defenders of the fort.

A British officer asked the American prisoners, "Who commanded the fort?" Colonel Ledyard replied, "I did once. You do now." Ledyard then handed the British officer his sword as was the custom with a surrender. The officer took the sword and thrust it through Ledyard's body all the way to the hilt. This act was witnessed by the remaining Americans, including Lambert Latham.

Without hesitation Lambert took a bayonet and killed the British officer with it. In return, Lambert was bayonetted thirty-three times. The British, already angered that so many of their men were killed by so few Americans, slaughtered all the remaining Americans in the fort including Jordan Freeman.

Sources: 1. Garrison, *The Loyalty and Devotion of Colored Americans in the Revolution and War of 1812*, page 15. **2.** Nell, *The Colored Patriots of the American Revolution*, page 136. **3.** Reef, *African Americans in the Military*, pages 95–96. **4.** Burgan, *The Untold Story of the Black Regiment: Fighting in the Revolutionary War*, page 30.

Sampson Freeman

Sampson Freeman was born in 1765 in Ipswich, Massachusetts, and he died on March 28, 1843, in Waterville, Maine. He joined the navy at twelve and served as a waiter and later was a steward. He received a yearly pension of $48. After the war he married a widow, Venus, who owned a farm.

> In October 1777 I entered on board the United States Frigate Boston, Hector McNeil Esq. commander at Newburyport Massachusetts for one year. I entered as a waiter to Lt. ___?___ & as such sailed in the ship to Boston where we lay two or three months. That while at Boston I discovered that one McIntire, who was Captain of the stewards, was in the habit of stealing & carrying away from the ship, provisions & stores belonging to the officers.

The Captain of the Stewards was in charge of supplies and some equipment on the ship. He purchased and dispersed these supplies, and because this position was one of an officer he would have his own room on the ship.

> This I made know to Capt. McNeil who examined particularly into the facts & circumstances of the case & upon finding that I had been uncommonly vigilant & afterwards to my duty & for this particular act was deserving of reward immediately displaced said McIntire from his situation of Capt. Of the stewards & appointed me in his room. That said McIntire immediately left the ship & I have never since heard of him.
> I continued to serve on board said ship during her cruise in my last named capacity until her return to Boston in 1778 when I was discharged. Having served at least nine months as Captain of the Stewards as aforesaid.

Sampson sailed on the *Boston* under Captain McNeill. The ship sailed out of Boston on May 21, 1777, and cruised the North Atlantic with the USS *Hancock*. On June 7th they captured three prizes including the HMS *Fox*, which Sampson mentioned in one of his pension papers. The British captured the *Boston* when Charlestown fell and renamed her HMS *Charlestown*.

Source: 1. National Archives Pension Papers S17419.

Nathan Fry

Nathan Fry was born c. 1755 in Westmorland County, Virginia. He received a monthly pension of $8 for his service. He stated in his pension application on December 21, 1822,

> Nathan Fry, a man of Color, and native of Virginia, was born free in the County of Westmorland—enlisted in the minute Service under Dennis Duval of Henrico County in the year 1775—went to Savannah in Georgia and served under Col. Elbert against the Creek Indians in the capacity of a Drummer and return from Savannah and joined the Army at Valley Forge—was in the action at Monmouth—afterwards joined the Baron Steuben, and served under him as Bat man [servant] till after the Siege of Yorktown and the surrender of Lord Cornwallis—was then transferred by the Baron to the service of General St. Clair, by whom I was discharged in Winter of 1781 & 1782.

In June of 1823 Nathan submitted an additional document which added two battles he fought in, "That he was in the battles of Monmouth & Stony Point." In January of 1824 Nathan submitted additional information. He gave this information to John Marshall, Chief Justice of the Supreme Court who was also from Virginia and also served at Valley Forge,

> United States of America District of Virginia Nathan Fry a colored man, an inhabitant of the City of Richmond appeared before me John Marshall Chief Justice of the United States this first day of January in the year 1824 and being first duly sworn deposes and says That he enlisted in the town of Savannah in the year 1775 for the war in the company commanded by Capt. Mosby in Col. Elbert's Regiment. He is informed that in his former declaration the name of his Capt. was said to be Mosbury. This is a mistake in writing the name which was unknown to this deponent who is unable to read & who misunderstood the affidavit in this particular when it was read to him. He served as a drummer in this company until he was taken out of that to wait on Major Duval who was aid-de-camp or Brigade Major to General McIntosh [Lachlan McIntosh]. He attended the Major Duval in the capacity of a waiter until he accompanied General McIntosh to the Army under General Washington and remained with him until he was taken into the service of the Baron Steuben with whom he remained as a waiter or Batman until after the siege of York in Virginia. He was then transferred to General St. Clair by whom he was discharged in the course of the winter. His discharge is lost.

John Marshall was the fourth Chief Justice of the Supreme Court of the United States from 1801 to 1835. He was the longest serving Chief Justice and probably the most famous and influential in the history of the United States. In his early 20s he was a Captain in the 4th Virginia Regiment at Valley Forge.

Marshall was a slave owner and supported resettling freed slaves in Liberia, on the West coast of Africa. In his will he gave his elderly manservant the choice of either freedom or remaining a slave of one of Marshall's children.

Sources: 1. Beveridge, *The Life of John Marshall*, page 132. **2.** Smith, *John Marshal: Definer of a Nation*, page 64. **3.** National Archives Pension Application S39545.

Anthony Garnes

Anthony Garnes was born c. 1759 a freeman in Hertford County, North Carolina. He had a relative, Jeffery Garnes, that served in the same regiment during the war. Anthony received a monthly pension of $8 for his service.

> The said Anthony Garns enlisted for the term of three years early in the spring of 1778 in the State of North Carolina in the Company commanded by Capt Lemuel Eli, in the 7th North Carolina Regiment commanded by Colonel James Hogan in the line of the State of North Carolina, on the Continental establishment: and that during his said term of three years, he enlisted for during the War, & that he was transferred from the 7th to the 1st North Carolina Regiment, that he continued to serve in the said Corps, until the spring of 1782 when he was honorably disbanded from the said service at Murfreesborough in North Carolina. That he was in the battle of Brandywine under Capt Lemuel Eli, of the 7th Regiment, North Carolina Continental troops, in the battle of Monmouth under Capt Tilman Dickson of the first Regt No Carolina Continental troops and in the battle of Charleston where he was taken prisoner, under Capt Dickson.

At the Battle of Brandywine on September 11, 1777, the 7th North Carolina Regiment fought along Brandywine Creek near Chadd's Ford. The British suffered heavy losses before pushing the Americans back. At the Battle of Germantown on October 4, 1777, the 7th North Carolina Regiment was held in central reserve under the command of Lord Stirling.

After these two defeats the Americans took winter quarters at Valley Forge. The North Carolina Regiments were badly undermanned, and on June 1, 1778, at Valley Forge the 7th Regiment was disbanded and the men sent to other regiments. At this time Anthony joined the 1st North Carolina Regiment.

At the Battle of Monmouth on June 28, 1778, Anthony and the rest of the 1st North Carolina Regiment were under the command of General Nathanael Greene. They were on Washington's right flank. During the battle British General Cornwallis personally led a force of British and Hessians against the troops under General Greene. Accurate musket fire from the Continental regiments, and four of the six pound cannons on Comb's Hill repelled the enemy.

The 1st North Carolina Regiment arrived at Charlestown, South Carolina, in March of 1780. The British army lay siege to the city and captured it and 5,266 American troops.

Sources: 1. National Archives Pension Application S38723. **2.** Moss and Scoggins, *African-American Patriots in the Southern Campaign of the American Revolution*, pages 92–93. **3.** Grundset, *Forgotten Patriots, National Society of the D.A.R.*, page 562.

Anthony Gilman

Anthony Gilman was a free man from Massachusetts when he served as a fifer in the army. He received a monthly pension of $8 for his service. When he filed his pension application in 1818 he had no money, no property, and no family.

> In the latter part of December 1775 I enlisted as fifer in the army of the Revolutionary war for the term of one year; I immediately entered the service at that time in Capt. Gilman's Company, in Col. Nixon's Regiment of the Massachusetts line and served therein the whole time of one year.

Anthony served in the 6th Massachusetts Regiment under Colonel John Nixon and saw action at the Battle of Harlem Heights. This battle took place in northwest Manhattan Island during the New York and New Jersey campaign on September 16, 1776.

> When I again enlisted for during the war then without leaving the service entered in Capt. Hutchin's Company in Col. Joseph Cilley's Reg. of the New Hampshire line and served until when the late General Hull was sent in the command of a detachment of about 150 men to go to Morrisena in New York state to drive out the cowboys, or Refugees as they were called, the time I do not remember, but I was one of the men and was with about 40 more taken by the British & carried into New York & then kept a few weeks prisoner & then being a man of color was sold for a slave to one John Falkingham & was left as a slave for more than a year there, then sent to St. John's and to Anapolis-Royal from whence after about 6 or 7 months I made my Escape & came away. The war was over. I was in the battle of Harlem Heights & Monmouth.

Colonel Joseph Cilley commanded the 1st New Hampshire Regiment. Anthony was sent with other troops to drive out the cowboys in the Hudson River area of New York. The area below West Point and on the eastern border of the Hudson River was Westchester County. The county was considered neutral ground. The area south of the neutral ground was controlled by the Tories and the northern area controlled by the Patriots. The Tories would send raiding parties into the rich agricultural area of the neutral ground.

The most famous of the raiding groups was DeLancey's Cowboys. The raiders were organized by John DeLancey and acquired their nickname "cowboys," because they would steal the cows of families that were sympathetic to the patriot's cause. The raiders were dangerous and ruthless fighters.

Anthony Gilman was probably captured at the Battle of Morrisania on January 22, 1781. A Patriot force made a surprise attack on the Tory position at Morrisania, New York, near New York City. The Patriots burned the enemy's barracks and killed thirty Tories. Anthony was later taken to Annapolis Royal, a French settlement in Nova Scotia that was at the time under British control.

Sources: **1.** National Archives Pension Application S32729. **2.** Grundset, *Forgotten Patriots, National Society of the D.A.R.*, page 113. **3.** Mays, *Historical Dictionary of the American Revolution*, page 244. **4.** Greene & Pole, *A Companion to the American Revolution*, page 315.

Tobias Gilmore

Tobias Gilmore was born c. 1734 in coastal West Africa. He was an African prince by the name of Shibodee-Turry-Wurry, and he was captured by slave traders as he was gathering coconuts. He was shackled below deck on the slave ship *Dove* which was sailing to Virginia. Due to a storm the ship changed its course and landed in Rhode Island. Tobias was one of the slaves sold at auction to pay for repairs for the ship. He was purchased by Captain Gilmore of Taunton, Massachusetts.

Tobias enlisted in the military on December 8, 1776, in Captain Jonathan Shaw's Company in Colonel George Williams' 3rd Bristol County Regiment. He served three tours of duty and fought at the Battles of Fort Ticonderoga, Monmouth, Forts Clinton and Montgomery, White Plains, and West Point. He also was at Valley Forge in the winter of 1777–78.

There is some myth surrounding the service of Tobias. It was said that he rose through the ranks and became a bodyguard or servant to George Washington, and that he was the African-American in the painting *Washington Crossing the Delaware*. None of these statements have been proven true.

After the war Tobias returned to Raynham in December of 1781 as a free man. He married Rosanna Hackland they had eight children. He bought some land that had been confiscated from a Tory and auctioned off. Because Tobias was so popular few people bid against him. He was given an old cannon by his regiment after his discharge, and some claim it was given to him by George Washington. The cannon was nicknamed "Old Toby," and it was fired off by the town on Washington's Birthday, the Fourth of July, and other important days. Tobias Gilmore died on April 19, 1812.

Sources: 1. Greene, *Black Defenders of America, 1775–1973*, page 11. **2.** Rosenburg, *First in War: George Washington in the American Revolution*, page 57. **3.** *A Catalogue of the Portraits and other Objects of Historical Value Belonging to the Old Colony*, Historical Society, Taunton, Massachusetts, 1907, page 19.

Prince George

Prince George was one of sixty African-American troops in the 2nd Company and 4th Connecticut Regiment under Colonel Humphreys. The regiment was disbanded after the Invasion of Canada and reformed on September 16, 1776. Prince George was a drummer at the Battles of Brandywine, Germantown, and Monmouth.

Prince received a monthly pension of $8 for his six years of service. He stated in his pension application,

He the said Prince George Enlisted when he was thirteen years of age as a Drummer in the month of Mat in the year 1777 in the State of Connecticut. He continued in the service of the United States until the Eighth Day of June in the year 1783.

Sources: 1. Grundset, *Forgotten Patriots, National Society of the D.A.R.*, page 279. **2.** Anderson, *Life and Narrative of William J. Anderson Twenty-four Years a Slave*, pages 65–66. **3.** National Archives Pension Application S43594.

Jehu Grant

Jehu Grant was born a slave c. 1752 in Rhode Island, and he died on December 28, 1840. He escaped from his master, Elihu Champlen, who was a Tory and served for eight months in the wagon service. When Jehu was discovered to be a fugitive he was returned to his master, who later sold him to a man named Grant. With the assistance of Joshua Swann, his freedom was purchased from that master, and in return he agreed to work for Swann for a certain time. He stated in his pension application,

> That he entered the Service of the United States, under the following named officers and served as herein stated, That he was a slave to Elihu Champlen, Who resided at Narragansett, Rhode-Island, at the time he left him. his said Master was Called a Tory, and in a secret manner furnished the Enemy, Whose shipping lay near by, with sheep, cattle, chees &c, and received goods from them, And this applicant being afraid his said Master, would send him to the British ships, ran away some time in August 1777, as near as he can recollect, being the same summer that Danbury was burnt. that he went right to Danbury after he left his said Master and enlisted to Captain Giles Gates for eighteen month that according to the best of his memory General Huntington and General Meig's Brigades or a part of them were at that place, that he this Applicant was put to teaming with a team of Horses, and Waggon, drawing provision and various other loading for the Army, for three or four Months untill winter set in. then was taken as a servant to John Scidmore Waggon Master General (as he was called) and served with him as his Waiter untill spring, When the said troops went to the Hyghlands or near that place on the Hudson River, a little above the British lines. that this Applicant had Charge of the Teams as Waggoner and Carryed the said General Scidmores Bagage and Continued with him (and the said troops) as his Waggoner near the said lines untill some time in June, When his said Master either Sent or Came and this applicant was given up to his Master again, and he returned, after having served nine or ten month.

Grant's application was denied because he had remained, technically, a slave during his time of service. He was also denied, because his service as a teamster and waiter did not imply that he was a soldier bound to military duty. He wrote back on December 30, 1836, pleading that they reconsider, because he was eighty years old, blind, and very poor.

> Your servant begs leave to state that he forwarded to the War Department a declaration founded on the pension Act of June 1832 praying to be allowed a pension (If his memory serves him) for ten Months service in the American Army of the revolutionary war—that

he enlisted as a soldier but was put to the service of a teamster in the summer & a waiter in the winter. In April 1834 I received a writing from your Hon, informing me that my "Services while a fugitive from my Master's Service Was not imbraced in said Act." And that my "papers were placed on file." In my said declaration I just mentioned the Cause of leaving my Master as may be seen by a referance thereunto, And I now pray that I may be permitted to express my feelings more fully on that part of my said declaration. I was then grown to Manhood in the full Vigour and Strength of life and heard much about the Cruel and arbitary things done by the British, Their ships lay within a few miles of my Master's house which stood near the shore and I was confident that my Master traded with them, and I suffered much from fear that I should be sent aboard a ship of war, this I disliked But when I saw liberty poles & the people all engaged for the support of freedom, I could not but like & be pleased with such thing. (God forgive me if I sinned in so feeling) And living on the borders of Rhode Is. where whole companies of coloured people enlisted, it added to my fears and dread of being sold to the British These considerations induced me to enlist into the American Army where I served faithfull about 10 months. When my Master found and took me home, had I been taught to read or understand the precepts of the Gospel, "Servants obey your Masters" I might have done otherwise notwithstanding the songs of liberty that saluted my ear, thrilled through my heart. But feeling conscious that I have since compensated my Master for the Injury he sustained by my enlisting and that God has forgiven me for so doing and that I served my country faithfully and that they having enjoyed the benefits of my Service to an equal degree for the length time I served with those generally who are receiving the liberalities of the Government I cannot but feel it becoming me to pray Your Hon, to review my declaration on file and the papers herewith annexed. A few years after the war Joshua Swan Esqr of Stoningtown purchased me of my Master and agreed that after I had served him a length of time named faithfully I should be free, I served to his satisfaction& so obtained my freedom. He moved into the Town of Milton where I now reside about 48 years ago. After my time expired with Esqr Swan I Married a wife We have raised six children 5 are still living I must be upwards of 80 years of age and have been blind for many years and Notwithstanding the aid I receive from the honest Industry of my children We are still very needy and in part are supported from the benevolence of our friends, With these statements and the Testimony of my character herewith presented I humbly rest my claim upon the Well known liberality of Government.

Jehu never received a pension even though pensions were given to white soldiers who served as teamsters and waiters. The pension office was in the Southern dominated national capital and where they did not always look favorably on the pension requests of black men. Jehu's obituary appeared in the newspaper *Saratoga Whig* on January 5, 1841, "In Milton on the 26th, Jehu Grant, a colored man aged 112 years, a soldier of the Revolutionary, and for many years a member of the church."

Sources: 1. Kennedy & Bailey, *The American Spirit: United States History as Seen by Contemporaries, Vol. 1*, page 167–68. **2.** Dann, *The Revolution Remembered: Eyewitness Accounts of the War for Independence*, page 26–28. **3.** Kaplan & Kaplan, *The Black Presence in the Era of the American Revolution*, page 63. **4.** National Archives Pension Application R4197.

Ned Griffen

Ned Griffen was a slave owned in North Carolina by William Kitchen. William was a militiaman who deserted just before the Battle of Guilford Courthouse. Instead of returning to the battle he ordered his slave Ned to take his place. Ned, who was promised his freedom, joined the rest of the militiamen at the battle. When Ned returned home from the battle William refused to grant him his promised freedom. The issue was brought before the North Carolina Legislature and they passed legislation that gave Ned his freedom and the right to vote.

Sources: **1.** Neimeyer, *America Goes to War: A Social History of the Continental Army,* page 88. **2.** Crow, *The Black Experience in Revolutionary North Carolina,* page 100.

Jack Green

Jack Green was born in June of 1761 and married Tama. His owner enlisted him in May of 1777 and at the end of the war Jack received his freedom. He served in Captain Child's Company in Colonel Philip Bradley's 5th Connecticut Regiment. He was at the Battles of Germantown, Chestnut Hill, White Marsh, and Monmouth. After his three year enlistment was up, he joined Captain Benjamin Stevenson's New York Company. He received a monthly pension of $80 for his three years of service.

At the Battle of White Marsh, in early December of 1777, Jack fought on Chestnut Hill. During this fight, on the first day the Connecticut troops were fighting with the Pennsylvania militia. The Pennsylvania militia fired the first volley but were soon routed by the British. The Connecticut troops made a brief stand before retreating. The next day the Pennsylvania militia faced the British and again panicked and fled. The Connecticut regiments made a stand and fired between two and five rounds per man. They only retreated when the British got within fifteen to twenty yards.

Jack described an event in his pension application that occurred at the Battle of Germantown, "He was in the Battle of Germantown and in that detachment which surrounded a large stone house in which the British were lodged and captured three Field pieces together with the soldiers in said house."

Sources: **1.** National Archives Pension Application S43631 **2.** *Forgotten Patriots,* National Society of the D.A.R., page 279. **3.** Grundset, *Forgotten Patriots, National Society of the D.A.R.,* page 279.

Joseph Green

Joseph Green enlisted in Captain Adam Bailey's Company in Colonel Sprout's 2nd Massachusetts Regiment. While he was at Easton, Massachusetts, on furlough, he married Sarah Phillips on January 31, 1782. Sarah said in her application to receive a widow's pension that after they were married, she returned with him and joined the army and was discharged with him at the close of the war. The application does not give length of service or what she did while her husband was serving.

Some women were camp followers and accompanied their husbands or family members when they enlisted. Some of these women sought adventure or were in search of a living. Most were involved in cooking, nursing, or doing wash. Occasionally, they fought alongside the men and were usually dressed as men. Even though they were dressed as men, they did not pass themselves off as males.

Sarah stated in her application that her husband was hung for stealing on January 5, 1873, when she was seventy-two years old. No details were given of her husband's crime. Sarah was granted a yearly pension of $80.

Source: 1. National Archives Pension Application W27415. **2.** Grundset, *Forgotten Patriots*, *National Society of the D.A.R.*, page 114.

William Guy

William Guy was born c. 1763 in Brunswick County, Virginia, and he died on January 30, 1857. He married Abigail on June 12, 1780, in Virginia. She received a widow's pension of $40 a year for his service.

> That he was born in the County of Brunswick & State of Virginia, that he believes he is upwards of Seventy years of age, tho' upon this point he only speaks from tradition in his family, having no record of his age now in possession, nor never having had one—that he therefore cannot with certainty say in what year he was born—that he lived in Virginia in the counties of Brunswick & Mecklenburg in Va. both before & since the Revolution, until about thirty years ago, when he removed to this County & has resided here since that time—that he is a free man of color & was living in the said County of Mecklenburg, when he was called into service—that he entered the army of the United States in the Virginia Militia as a substitute for one Jack Goode at Mecklenburg Court house under Captain Reuben Vaughan, Leut. Whiting, Leut. John Holmes, & one William Halloway ensign—that his company marched to Granville Court House in N Carolina & joined a Regiment commanded by Colonel David Mason & Leut Colonel Burwell—that he believes it was in the Spring of the year 1779, when he joined the company under Captain Vaughan that he entered for a tour of six months—that his company after leaving Granville Court House, marched to Hillsborough, then to Salisbury, & then into South Carolina & joined the main army under Gen'l. [Benjamin] Lincoln, near a place called Ashley Ferry—then on the 19 or 20 of June, an engagement took place between the portion of our army & the British at Stono Ferry when our forces were driven back—that he served out the remainder of his tour of six months in that portion of S. Carolina surrounding the City of Charleston.
>
> After his return to Mecklenburg & in the next year, viz. 1780 he was drafted in the same County in a company commanded by Captain Stephen Mabry, for a tour of three months, to go to Portsmouth in Virginia—after getting as far as Dinwiddie Ct. House he

received a very severe wound from the bite of a dog, which prevented from doing duty in the ranks, & he received a furlough in consequence of his inability—& before he recovered from the wound his term of three months expired.

 He was again called out for three months towards the close of the Summer, or early in the Autumn of 1781 he is not able to say certainly which—by draft in Mecklenburg Va, under Capt Stephen Mabry & Leut Edward Pennington in a Regiment commanded by Colonel Lewis Burwell—They marched to the siege of York—and were stationed on the Gloucester side of the river—and was at that Place when Cornwallis surrendered—At the end of this three months he received his discharge at Gloucester.

 William stated that he was on the Gloucester side of the river at the Siege of Yorktown. Gloucester is across the York River from Yorktown. It is a point of land that juts out into the channel and narrows the river to half a mile. French Brigadier General Marquis de Choisy commanded French troops and 800 Virginia militia, which included William Guy. They faced 1,000 British troops under the command of Lt. Colonel's Thomas Dundas and Banastre Tarleton.

 Gloucester was the escape route from Yorktown for the British army. Cornwallis had decided to remove the majority of his troops from Yorktown and ferry them across the river at night to Gloucester. Once across the Americans and French troops would be greatly outnumbered and no match for the British. Cornwallis would then be able to escape into Virginia with most of his army intact.

 The escape was put into action on the night of October 16, 1781. British troops began to load onto boats very quietly, and the first wave of boats carried 1,000 troops across. As Cornwallis was preparing to leave in the second wave, he wrote a letter to Washington requesting that the General show mercy to the small detachment of British soldiers left behind in Yorktown.

 Then a miracle occurred, at least from the patriot point of view. Before the second wave of boats were launched a hard storm blew in, and it scattered boats downstream that were caught on the river. A hard windy rain fell until two in the morning. It was now impossible to move the British troops across. Lt. Colonel Banastre Tarleton wrote after the war, "Thus expired the last hope of the British army."

 The Americans had moved their cannons closer to the British positions at Yorktown, and Cornwallis had no choice but to surrender or face annihilation. On October 17, 1781, the British surrendered their army to General Washington.

Sources: **1.** National Archives Pension Application W17969. **2.** Grundset, *Forgotten Patriots, National Society of the D.A.R.,* page 519. **3.** Landers, *The Virginia Campaign and the Blockade and Siege of Yorktown* by Army War College Historical Section, page 202. **4.** Carrington, *Battles of the American Revolution, 1775–1781,* page 640. **5.** Greene, *The Guns of Independence: The Siege of Yorktown, 1781,* pages 38 & 75.

Jude Hall

Jude Hall was born c. 1747 in Exeter, New Hampshire, and he died there in August of 1827. He had a powerful physique standing six feet tall, and it is said that the parts of his ribs which are usually cartilaginous were of solid bone, so that his vital organs were encased in a bony case. People said that he could lift a cider barrel and drink from the tap.

He was enslaved as a farm worker to Philemon Blake of Kensington of New Hampshire, and he was sold to Nathaniel Healey. Jude soon ran away from his new master, and on May 10, 1775, he joined Captain Jacob Hinds' Company in Colonel James Reed's Regiment. Jude took part in the Battle of Bunker Hill on June 17, 1775. It was reported that during the battle he was "thrown headlong by a cannonball striking near him." He stated in his pension application,

> I Jude Hall of Exeter in the County of Rockingham and state of New Hampshire declare I was in the army in 1775, and that in the month of December 1775 I enlisted into a company commanded by Capt. Hinds in a regiment commanded by Col. James Reid, that in the month of December 1776 I enlisted for three years into a company commanded by Capt. Cloyes in the 2nd New Hampshire Regiment that in the month of December 1779 I again enlisted for and during the war into a company commanded by Capt. William Rowell second New Hampshire Line until the Peace and then was discharged.

Jude probably took part in the Battle of Trenton in 1776. In the winter of 1777–78 his regiment camped at Valley Forge and he stayed in Albany due to illness. On July 7, 1777, the British, in a surprise dawn attack, attacked American troops at Hubbardton, Vermont and captured many members of the 2nd New Hampshire.

In June of 1778 he fought with his regiment at the Battle of Monmouth, and during the battle he earned the nickname "Rock." In 1779 Jude and his regiment served in the Sullivan Expedition against the Indians in southwestern New York. Some of the members of the 2nd New Hampshire Regiment served under Lafayette at Yorktown in 1781. It is not known if Jude served at Yorktown. In one battle Jude took cover behind a tree and escaped unhurt. The next day he cut the tree down and obtained a basinful of bullets.

After the war Jude gained his freedom, and in 1785 he married Rhoda Paul and they had at least twelve children. Jude was a man of religion. According to one story about him he found a man washing out his cider barrels at the brook one Sunday morning. The man, who seemed ashamed of his Sabbath breaking, looked every way to see if anyone was coming. Jude asked the man, "Brother, did you look above?"

Jude and his family were free, however, three of his four sons were kidnapped and sold into slavery. James was kidnapped at the age of eighteen from the Hall home. David Wedgewood claimed that James owed him four dollars, and that he was justified in dragging him away from his mother. He was sold into slavery and never returned to Exeter. James was later seen by a man from Exeter in New Orleans chained up in the jail.

Aaron, another son was put to sea and signed a promissory note for $20 to pay for his sea clothes. When he returned the merchant demanded $200, and he was taken back to sea and never heard from again. The third son, William, also went to sea, and when he arrived in the West Indies he was sold there as a slave. After ten years he managed to escape and make his way to England. William's mother did hear from him after twenty years. Jude died in 1827 and never saw or heard from his sons again. Rhoda received a widow's pension of $80 a year.

Sources: **1.** Rimkunas, *Hidden History of Exeter,* Chapter IV. **2.** Grundset, *Forgotten Patriots, National Society of the D.A.R.,* page 518. **3.** National Archives Pension Application W23238. **4.** *History of Rockingham and Strafford Counties, New Hampshire,* page 360. **5.** *History of the Town of Exeter, New Hampshire,* pages 397–98. **6.** Kaplan & Kaplan, *The Black Presence in the Era of the American Revolution,* pages 60–61.

Pero Hall

Pero Hall, a small man at 5'4", was born c. 1720, and while in his 50s he joined Captain Jonathan Evans' Company in Colonel James Frye's Regiment. At 6 p.m. on the 16th of June 1775 Pero's regiment was part of 1,200 men ordered to set up positions from which artillery fire could be directed into Boston. They were also ordered to furnish themselves with packs, blankets, and provisions for twenty-four hours. During the battle the regiment defended the left flank on Breed's Hill. Most of the fighting took place on Breed's Hill, because it was closer to Boston and easier to defend than Bunker Hill.

On August 24, 1777, Pero enlisted in Captain John Noyes' Company in the 4th Massachusetts Regiment commanded by Colonel Samuel Johnson. The regiment served on the right flank under the command of General Benjamin Lincoln and played a very minor role in the Battle of Saratoga. Pero served at various times in 1778, 1779, and 1780. In 1781 he enlisted for three years in the Continental army.

Sources: **1.** Fronthingham, *History of the Siege of Boston and the Battles of Lexington, Concord, and Bunker Hill,* 1851, pages 121–132. **2.** Quintal, *Patriots of Color,* page 120. **3.** Grundset, *Forgotten Patriots, National Society of the D.A.R.,* page 114.

Primus (Trask) Hall

Primus Hall was born to a slave on February 29, 1756, in Boston, and he died there on March 22, 1842. He married three times: 1. Phebe Robson on May 2, 1786, and she died of consumption December 8, 1808. 2. Martha Garden on January 17, 1810, and she died of typhoid fever on January 20, 1817. 3. Ann Clark on October 29, 1817.

At the age of one month he was bound out to Ezra Trask a shoemaker in Essex County. Primus was given to Ezra with the understanding that he be taught the trade of shoemaking and then be given his freedom at the age of twenty-one. When it was determined by a doctor that this trade did not suit his health, Primus worked as a farmer and a truck man. At the age of fifteen Ezra gave him his "freedom with full liberty for me to transact any of all business of every kind."

At the age of nineteen Primus enlisted in the army. He stated in his pension application,

> That he the said Primus was born in the City of Boston on the twenty ninth day of February Anno Domini 1756 in the family of David Walker in Beacon Street in said Boston, and at the age of one month old was given to Mr Ezra Trask of Beverly in the County of Essex who subsequently removed to the town of Danvers in said County in whose family he continued to live until the commencement of the revolutionary War, and that forepart of the month of January in the year one thousand seven hundred and seventy six he the said Primus enlisted in the town of Cambridge in the county of Middlesex as a soldier in the army of the Revolution for the term of one year in a company commanded by Capt Joseph Butler of Concord in said County, of the fifth Massachusetts Regiment commanded by Colo Thomas Nixon. The Majors name was Scammell. The name of the Lieutenant was Silas Walker, and Ensign Potter, Gad Smith and Wheeler were Sergeants.

Lieutenant Colonel John Nixon served in the 6th Massachusetts Regiment, not the 5th Regiment. His brother Colonel John Nixon was the commander of the regiment from May 19, 1775, until August 9, 1776. John was promoted to Brigadier General, and his brother Thomas became the commander of the 6th Regiment.

> He the said Primus further testifies that he served the full period of one year, and at Trenton in New Jersey, at the earnest solicitation of General Washington he volunteered for a period of six weeks which he faithfully served, and at Morristown in New Jersey was honourably discharged by General Washington, after the taking of Princeton in said State. The foregoing term of time completed thirteen months and a half service. During his service as before stated he was at the following stations and in the following battles to wit, First at Winter Hill near Boston, the winter of 1776, where were also stationed on said Hill and the vicinity of the same several Regiments to wit, Colonel Hutchins, Colonel Glover's, Colonel Stark's, Graton's and others, and that he continued at said Station until after the British troops evacuated that City March 7th 1776. Thence he marched to New York with the Army, and was stationed in the Bowery and was employed for some time in erecting Fortifications near Byards Hill. About that time Colonel Nixon was at the place promoted to a Brigadier General and his brother, John Nixon who was Lieutenant Colonel assumed the command of the said fifth Regiment. After this period he was stationed on Governor's Island in the harbour of New York, but was ____?___ to evacuate the same, when the British took possession of the Island. He distinctly remembers that Major Walcott was Bearer of a flagg of truce demanding the surrender of the place which demand was disregarded and a cannonade

commenced—that two of the Vessels of the enemy came beating up the narrows and that by General Washington's orders they were taken off the Island and in passing over to New York the Cockswain was killed by a chain shott fired from the Asia Man of War belonging to the enemy. Said Primus was after this stationed at the grand Battery in New York, but soon joined the Maine Army at Rattle-snake hills, and there had an action. After the engagement retreated to Harlem Heights and there had a skirmish—thence to Miles Square and had another skirmish—thence to White Plains, and there had a Battle—thence crossed the Hudson River at Kings Ferry, and marched into New Jersey, and was under General Lee at the time that General was surprised at Basking Ridge and taken prisoner.

General Lee and his troops were supposed to join with Washington's men in Pennsylvania. Lee, however, chose to maintain a slow pace, and on December 12, 1776, while looking for a comfortable place to spend the night, he found White's Tavern at Basking Ridge. Lee and a few of his officers spent the night at the tavern which was several miles from his main army. The next morning a British patrol surrounded the tavern and demanded the surrender of Lee. While still in his dressing gown, Lee surrendered to the British. Lee was "bare-headed, in his slippers and blanket coat his collar open and his shirt very much soiled from several day's use." He asked that he be allowed to put on his uniform, but he was refused. He was later exchanged for a captured British General.

Then General Sullivan took command, and marched the troops to Pennsylvania, to a place called Bristol and after remaining at Bristol a few days recrossed the Delaware, and attacked the Hessians at Trenton & Burlington and took them prisoners, the Regiment to which said Primus belonged being station at the former place when his term of service of one year expired, but at the earnest request of General Washington he volunteered for the further term of six weeks, and during said service he was at the taking of Princetown, and soon thereafter marched to Morristown in New Jersey and there received an honorable discharge from the Army signed by General Washington and returned home to Danvers in the Spring of 1777.

He further testifies that he again enlisted in the fall of the 1777 in the town of Danvers for three months, into a Militia Company commanded by Capt. Samuel Flint of said town and Lieutenant Herrick of Beverly and Colonel Johnson of Andover, and marched to Saratoga to join the Army under General Gates, who was then acting against General Burgoyne; that he was in the second engagement between the two armies when the Hessian Brigade was together with eight pieces of British Artillery—that he distinctly recollects the death of Captain Flint who together with Lieutenant Herrick were both killed in said Battle. that he was standing near his Captain when he received his mortal wound, and caught him in his arms to prevent his falling, but on observing that bled profusely set him down against a tree when he expired immediately. This battle was fought in October 1777.

Primus joined the 4th Essex County Militia Regiment under the command of Colonel Samuel Johnson. During the Battle of Bemis Heights, which was fought on August 14, 1777, Primus witnessed the death of Captain Samuel Flint.

After the surrender of Burgoyne he with the Regiment marched to Albany crossed the river at that place to Greenbush, continued down the Hudson River on the east side till they arrived at a place called East Chester on the shore of Long Island Sound, when his term of three months service expired, and he was a second time discharged, again returned to the town of Danvers. He further testifies that in the year seventeen hundred and seventy eight he enlisted at Danvers for a further period of three months under Capt Woodbury of Cape Ann, and a Colonel whose name he has forgotten, but who was from Topsfield, and thence marched with the company to Rhode Island, and was stationed on the North part of said Island opposite Tiverton, and was employed in building a Fort and keeping ___?___ until his term had again expired and he was a third time discharged from service.

The French Fleet and Army under Count Rochambeau were at Rhode Island landed 11 Jul 1780, the French troops being stationed on land above New- Port on said Island at the time of his last tour above stated. that himself with another coloured man by the name of Manual were detached from Captain Woodbury's company and performed service with the French Corps of Sappers & Miners, and that the time he performed military duty in the three foregoing tours was nineteen months and a half.

He further testifies that in the years 1781 and 1782 he served twenty two months as Steward to and under Colonel Timothy Pickering of the United States Quarter Master department, and was with that Officer at Verplanck Point Philadelphia, Baltimore & other places, and was at Yorktown at the time that place surrendered to the American Army, under General Washington & the French forces and went into the British Garrison in said town with Colonel Pickering and there assisted him in taking an account of the enemy's specie deposited in the military chests in said Fort. that after the troops marched to the ___?___ and were stationed at or near a place called Rattle snake hill near Newburg in the State of New York he received a final discharge from the Army and in the month of December 1772 [this date is a mistake] he returned home to Danvers Massachusetts. He further testifies that while serving as Steward in the army aforesaid during the Revolutionary War at a place called Dumfries in the state of Virginia his pocket book was stolen from him containing his several discharges from the Army and he has not to this day heard any thing of them, and that he has also lost his last discharge.

In 1835 the Pension Bureau rejected the claim for a pension. Two questions were raised by the Pension Bureau. First, was Primus a free man or a slave? If he joined as a slave he might not be eligible for a pension. Second, was Primus a soldier or a servant to an officer? If he was a servant he might not be entitled to a pension. Several letters were written to the Pension Bureau by people that knew Primus that would answer those questions.

The following letter was sent to James L. Edwards, who in 1833 was the Commissioner of Pensioners and responsible for many of the pensions granted to applying Revolutionary War soldiers.

Boston, Massachusetts/ June 3d 1836 Sir Your letter of the 28th Ult'o, relating to the claim of Pension of Primus Hall is received, and handed to him for perusal, who expresses much disappointment at its Import—particularly of that clause, requiring "evidence whether he was freeborn or emancipated"?—especially as the laws of this Commonwealth have always recognized him since he arived at the age of 21 years, as one of her Citizens enjoying in common with other Inhabitants, all the rights and immunities granted by her laws, and paying his full share of Taxs, in support of her Government. I am instructed by mr. Hall to say that he was never a Slave—and that Mr Ezra Trask of Beverly, who brought him up never applied that appelation to him, but always considered his Guardianship as ending when his Ward should arive at lawful age—the same as any white person under like circumstances [see endnote] I am at a loss to conceive how that question can have any influence, or bearing on the case under consideration, provided the applicant was a free Citizen when the Act of 7th June 1832 passed, and became a Law. any other construction would be irreconcileable to the fact within my own knowledge of the many coloured persons who are now receiving the bounties of the United States, in the form of Pensions—but who at the time of their Enlistments, were slaves. [See endnote.] I presume that on receiving the foregoing explanation, the Dept. will reconsider the case in question, and no longer with hold from the worthy old Soldier the munificence of the National Government, which he so justly deserved. Please answer this communication and forw'd. the same to me at this place Very Respectfully sir I your Obedient Servant/ Reuben Baldwin

On June 13, 1836, Primus replied to the letter from James L. Edwards with additional information of his service,

I was born in Beacon St. in this City on the 29th day of February of the year 1756; and in the family of a Mr Walker—My Fathers name was Prince Hall, and he was a free man—my Mothers name was Delia Hall and she was a servant in the family of said Walker and at the age of one month old I was given to a Mr Ezra Trask of Danvers, with the express understanding that he the said Trask was to bring me up and learn me the Trade of Shomaker—as soon as I was old enough, and that at the age of Twenty one years I was to be free—the same as any white person.

And accordingly at the age of ten years or thereabouts I began to work at said trade—and from then untill I was fifteen—when it was well known by Mr Trask, and a Physician, that the occupation of shomaker did not suit me—and my health was much impared in conequence—said Physician Amos Putnam, advised my Master to change my employment, who thereupon proposed to me to give me my time, which proposal was acepted by me, and a Certificate to that effect was given me—The purport of which was that he the said Trask gave me my freedom with full liberty for me to transact any, or all business of every kind untill I should arive at the age of 21 years, and fully relinquished all claim upon me whatever—I was thence afterwards engaged in various ocupations some times as a Farmer at others as a Truckman in Salem—and untill I was Nineteen years of age—and had all the avails of my labour—and at the age of Nineteen I Enlisted as a Soldier in the War of the Revolution and served Nineteen Months and an half as a soldier by Three seiveral Enlistments. (Viz) first under Capt Joseph Butler Colonel Nixon, Thirteen and one half months—and Three months in the Campaign against Genl Burgoyn in Capt Flints Company of Colonel Johnsons Regiment of Militia—and Three months in a Campaign on Rhode Island under Capt Woodbury of Cape Ann. And also Twenty two months as Steward to General Timothy Pickering I remember that when General Pickering was about to hire me as his Steward I exhibited to him my Certificate of freedom, which I had received from Mr Trask, as before stated—and as I was to go to the Southward with said Pickering, I thought It adviseable to have my said Certificate of freedom well established by the authorities of this state, and accordingly I presented it to Governor [John] Hancock, who attached his Certificate unde the official seal of this Commonwealth, to my said Certificate. I had my Pocket book stolen at Dumfries in Virginia and with it I lost said Certificate and likewise Three Discharges from the Army, and have not seen either of them to this day. I am by ocupation a Soap Boiler & have acquired a small property in this City and elsewhere by my industry.

Reuben Baldwin sent the following letter on June 14, 1836, to James L. Edwards,

> I am instructed by said Primus to say that he never was literally considered a slave; especially after he was given to said Trask and that said Trask always repelled that appellation, when applied so said Primus, with imagination—but considered him merely as an apprentice to the shoemaking business and in no respect different from a white person under like cirusmstances.

The following is the reply from James L. Edwards,

> War Department/Pension Office/July 9th 1836 Sir [Reuben Baldwin] The supplemental statement of Primus Hall, alias Trask, respecting his emancipation, would have been more satisfactory if accompanied by the instrument which he avers he received from his former master. Under all the circumstances of the case, the Department is constrained to decide that the testimony is not sufficient to shew he was an enlisted soldier in the ranks subject to, and actually performing military duty agreeably to the discipline of the Army. He no doubt was with the Army, for one of the terms alleged, yet may have been a waiter, or in some other civil capacity. I am respectfully, J. L. Edwards

It should be noted that the words slave, servant, waiters, and apprentice were sometimes interchangeable. A servant could mean that the person was free or a slave. An apprentice could also be either a free person or a slave. There were young boys and men in the army that served as waiters to an officer. These waiters might be slaves, especially in the south, or they might be free boys or men. Some waiters that were slaves were never in the army, but they were brought from home to serve their master, who was usually an officer. Other waiters, usually in the north were considered soldiers. In addition to waiting on an officer they, at times fought, did guard duty, or performed other soldier duties. The following letter was sent by Reuben Baldwin to James L. Edwards on July 14, 1836,

> Mr [Primus] Hall is fully impressed with the belief that any further testimony he may be able to adduce, as proof of his service as a soldier in the War of the Revolution, will also be considered unsatisfactory, especially when it appears by your last communication that the department are more ready to give credence to the belief that he might have been in the Army as a *"Waiter"* and not a *"Soldier"* Altho all the testimony hitherto adduced in this case, is decidedly in favour of the latter and not of the former. Said Hall is not well pleased at the reiterated and often repeated enquiries as to the maner how, and in what manner he became free; since he has been so over 64 years—and Inded the fact of his being given (not sold) to Mr Ezra Trask was the act by which said Primus was liberated from all Bonds of every kind name or nature appertaining to slavery. Those of Paternity and Minority, superceeding the same. This assertion will be better explained by understanding that said

Primus was an adopted son of Ezra Trask; who to the day of his death never had any Issue, and further was at that early period what we should now call an Abolitionist, who altho a poor mechanic (shoemaker) undertook to bring up this coloured boy as his own Child— and perhaps never was Philanthropy more properly bestowed or better repaid, in after years when Mr. Trask became infirm and Indigent said Primus altho married and setled in business in this City, was nevertheless induced to hire a Farm in Danvers and from his own bounty paid the annual rent on the same for several years &c and otherwise contributed to the aid and assistance of his former much esteemed but Indigent Patron, or nominal Master. Said Primus is a man of good repute and well known in this City and adjacent Country—whose Character for Truth and Veracity is second to none either here or elsewhere (see Judge Thatchers Certificate attached to the Declaration) The probability is that said Primus will refrain from further Importuning the department in his behalf for a Pension—which he justly considers his lawful due, and refer his claim to the National Legislature at their next session—which he would have done before now—but relying on the justice of his cause and the magnanimity and liberality of his Country, hitherto bestowed on the relicts of the Revolution, without distinction of Colour, He was averse to apply for especial Legislation in his behalf when to himself and all others his case appeared so clear. He therefore considers his claim as put to rest for the present, as it is not intimated, that any further testimony is wanted. Very Respectfully sir I am/Your Ob't. Servant/Reuben Baldwin

The following letter was from John Brown and written on August 12, 1836, to James L. Edwards. Brown had served with Primus at the Battle of Freeman's Farm on September 19, 1777. Primus stated in his application that he was in the Saratoga battle fought in October. That was the Battle of Bemis Heights fought on October 7, 1777. Both men wrote of the death of Captain Flint. Captain Flint was killed at Stillwater during the Battle of Saratoga on October 7, 1777.

When the British Army under General Burgoyne was making fearful progress down into the States the Militia of Essex County were called into service—and amongst the rest, Captain Flint's Company from Danvers, for a tour of three months.—I belonged to said Company, and many of my neighbours. Amongst the number a free Coloured Man, by the name of Primus Trask. We marched to the State of Newyork, to reenforce the American Army under General Gates, then acting against Burgoyne, and arrived in camp after the first battle and soon thereafter had another, in which Captain Flint's Company were engaged. We had a hard fight [the words "hard fight" were written in large letters to give them emphasis], and took the British Artillery, but lost our Captain (Flint) and Lieut. Herrick—both were killed in the course of the engagement. I know that Primus was in said battle, for I was near him when Captain Flint was shot through the body, who immediately expired—Our Lieutenant Herrick, we found dead the morning after the battle, a short distance from where Captain Flint was killed. After the Surrender of Burgoyne's Army, we marched down the Hudson River, and were discharged on the Shore of Long Island Sound, in the State of New York—the term of our enlistment, three months, having expired. Said Primus was discharged at the same time with myself, and I know he served faithfully as a soldier the above tour of three months, and was much esteemed by the Officers & men, as a brave & faithful Soldier in the service of his Country.

On January 4, 1838, a bill was presented to Congress that Primus Hall, a free colored man be placed on the roll of revolutionary pensioners. The bill was passed and Primus was granted a pension of $60 a year retroactive to March 4, 1831. The bill further stated, "He is justly entitled to a pension for a faithful service of eighteen months as a revolutionary soldier, not merely in camp duty, or the ordinary performance of military obligations, but in the field of battle, where his bravery and good conduct are proved to have been such as would have done honor to any man."

In 1781 Primus became a steward to Quartermaster Colonel Thomas Pickering. Primus told the Colonel that he accepted being his steward because he knew that Pickering was a New England man and he knew the Colonel's character. Pickering was happy for Primus to accept the job and he told his wife that the new servant was "so intelligent as to be capable of learning anything."

One anecdotal story about Primus and George Washington appeared in several publications in the 1800s. When Washington visited the camp of Colonel Pickering he sometimes felt the need for exercise. Primus got a rope and fastened one end to a stake about breast high, and he would hold the other end taut at his chest several feet away. Washington then would run and jump over the rope again and again until he tired. Whenever Washington visited the camp he would say, "Come, Primus, I am in need of exercise."

Another story occurred late one night when Washington was at the camp of Colonel Pickering. Primus found some straw and a blanket and made Washington a bed. After the General had fallen asleep Primus sat on a box or stool and leaned his head into his hands to sleep. Primus had given the General the last of the straw and the last blanket for his bedding.

Washington awoke during the night and saw Primus asleep sitting on the stool and he realized that he had been given the last of the bedding. He woke Primus up and insisted that Primus join him in his bed since there was enough room for two people. It was not uncommon during that period for travelers to share the same bed at inns when space was limited or share on the ground during cold weather.

In 1798 Primus opened in his home the first separate school for African-American children in Boston. The school later moved to the basement of the African Baptist Church which Primus helped to found. Later he established a college for the education of blacks. Primus was active in his support of movements against the slave trade and slavery.

In 1842 one obituary stated he, "was well known, particularly to the younger portion of our citizens, to whom he was in the habit of recounting scenes of the Revolutionary War."

Sources: 1. *Report of the Committee Appointed to Revise the Soldier's Record*, page 153. **2.** Cunningham, *This is New Jersey*, page 46. **3.** Pension Application W751. **4.** Jones-

Wilson, *Encyclopedia of African-American Education*, page 200. **5.** Minardi, *Making Slavery History: Abolitionism and the Politics of Memory in Massachusetts*, pages 63–9. **6.** Flexner, *Washington: The Indispensable Man*, page 120.

Prince Hall (father of Primus Hall)

Prince Hall was born c. 1735, and the location of his birth has not been proven. The first documentation of his existence comes from a list of slaves in the 1740s owned by William Hall, a leather craftsman in Boston. The mother of his son Primus was a servant named Delia who worked in a nearby household. In 1762, at the age of twenty-seven, Hall joined the Congregational Church, and soon after married an enslaved woman named Sarah Ritchie. Eight years later, after Sarah's death, he married Flora Gibbs of Gloucester.

His master William Hall taught Prince to read and write. After the Boston Massacre on March 5, 1770, he was given his freedom by William Hall with a statement that read, "no longer a Reckoned a slave, but always accounted as a free man." Prince made his living as a peddler and leather craftsman.

Prince encouraged enslaved and free blacks to serve in the American army. He believed that if they served in founding a new nation, it would help them to achieve their freedom. He said that Britain's rule of the colonies was similar to the enslavement of the blacks. It is believed that Prince was one of the six "Prince Halls" from Massachusetts to serve in the American army. He may even be one that fought at Bunker Hill.

In 1775 Hall and other free blacks joined a British army lodge of Masons. When the British left Boston the group formed African Lodge No. 1. It was the world's first lodge of black Freemasonry, and Hall became the lodge's first Grand Master. After protesting the lack of schools for black children, he formed one in his own home.

He was one of four signers of a 1777 petition demanding the abolition of slavery in Massachusetts. Slavery in Massachusetts would not be abolished until 1783. Prince was involved in the Back-to-Africa movement and tried to get the Massachusetts legislature to grant funds for voluntary immigration to Africa. Hall died in 1807 and is buried in Boston.

Sources: 1. Sidbury, *Becoming African in America: Race and Nation in the Early Black Atlantic*, pages 73–5. **2.** Marable & Mullings, *Let Nobody Turn Us Around: An African American Anthology*, pages 17–18. **3.** Muraskin, *Middle-Class Blacks in a White Society: Prince Hall Freemasonry in America*, pages 32–5. **4.** Johnson, *Profiles in Hue*, pages 95–7.

Edward Harman

Edward Harman enlisted under Captain Kirkwood in the First Company of the Delaware Regiment in 1777 and remained until the conclusion of the war. In 1778 or 1779 Edward, served under Lieutenant Colonel Mitchell Kershaw who was the commanding officer of the Ninth Delaware Regiment.

Hezekiah Lacey wrote a letter to the Pension Bureau in support of Edward and he stated in the letter, "I saw him with others of the Delaware Regiment, with uniforms and equipment just as they returned home from the army—at the same time he heard people say to Harman he was a fool to spend so much time in the army without pay—that Harman replied he was willing to go again and that he hoped he should get pay at some time."

When Edward applied for his pension he listed his total worth at $13.56, and he was given a monthly pension of $8 for his service.

Source: 1. National Archives Pension Application S36000.

Jeffrey Hartwell

Jeffery Hartwell was born c. 1751 in Massachusetts, and he died there on July 22, 1816. He married a former slave by the name of Maria and they had six children. The following is the bill-of-sale that transferred Jeffrey from his owner Joseph Fitch to the new owner Joseph Hartwell,

> Know all men by these presents that I, Joseph Fitch of Bedford in the County of Middlesex, in the Province of Massachusetts Bay, in New England, gentleman for and in consideration of the sum of dL24 lawful money of New England, done, in hand paid at and before the sealing and delivery of these presents, by Joseph Hartwell of Bedford, above said yeoman, the receipt I do hereby acknowledge, have bargained and sold and by these presents do bargain and sell unto the said Joseph Hartwell a negro boy about 5 years old, called Jeffru, now living at the said Joseph Hartwells, to have and to hold the said negro boy by these presents bargained and sold unto the said Joseph Hartwell, his executors, administrators and assigns forever, and I the said Joseph Fitch for myself etc do warrant the above said Negro boy unto the said Joseph Hartwell, his heirs etc against me the said Joseph Fitch my heirs etc, all and every other person and persons whatsoever, shall and will warrant and defend by these presents of which negro boy I, the said Joseph Fitch have put the said Joseph Hartwell in full possession by delivering said negro at the sealing hereof unto the said Joseph Hartwell.

Jeffery joined the militia for three months in place of his master and was at the Battle of Bunker Hill. When Jeffery returned home his master took the pay he was given and kept all of it. After that Jeffrey left and enlisted on September 29, 1777, in Captain Edward Framer's Company, in Colonel Jonathan Reed's 6th Massachusetts Regiment. He was discharged on November 8, 1777.

On June 16, 1778, Jeffrey enlisted in Colonel Thomas Poor's Regiment, and they marched to White Plains to fortify the passes of the Hudson River. In the spring of 1779 Jeffrey was discharged and set free.

Sources: 1. Quintal, *Patriots of Color*, pages 124–5. **2.** *History of Dracut, Massachusetts* by Silas Coburn, pages 332–3.

Edward "Ned" Hector

Edward Hector was born c. 1744, and he died on January 3, 1834, in Pennsylvania. He was probably a free man since he owned four horses and a wagon. He served as a wagon driver and a bombardier [part of an artillery crew] in Proctor's Third Pennsylvania Artillery Militia. According to the muster roll he served from February 1777 until December 1780.

At the Battle of Brandywine he was in charge of an ammunition wagon. During the battle Colonel Procter commanded four cannons and caused many casualties until the British stormed their position. When the order to retreat was given and to abandon the wagons, Edward refused. He said, "The enemy shall not have my team; I will save my horses and myself."

As the British were advancing he gathered up a few weapons that had been left by the retreating Americans. He placed them in his wagon and safely retreated with his wagon and horses. Edward continued to use his wagon to deliver supplies for the army until 1780.

After the war he tried to receive a pension, but he was turned down. The Pennsylvania Legislature gave him a onetime gift of $40 for his service. When he died his wife of fifty years suddenly died about an hour after she returned from his grave.

Sources: **1.** Grundset, *Forgotten Patriots, National Society of the D.A.R.,* page 413. **2.** Summers, *Obituary Notices of Pennsylvania Soldiers,* pages 443–4.

Jeffrey Hememway

Jeffrey Hememway was born c. 1737, and he died on August 15, 1819, in Worcester County, Massachusetts. His first wife, Susanna Wright, and daughter died from smallpox. His second wife, Hepsibah, he married on November 3, 1792. She applied for and received a yearly widow's pension of $80.

Jeffrey served in the closing years of the French and Indian War in Captain John Nixon's Company. In the Revolution Jeffrey marched at the Lexington alarm on April 19, 1775, and served for four days. On April 24, 1775, he enlisted for eight months in Colonel John Nixon's Regiment. He probably fought at Bunker Hill in June of 1775.

In September of 1776 he again served under Colonel Nixon in the New York Campaign and the Battle of White Plains. On April 1, 1778, he enlisted in Colonel Nathaniel Wade's Regiment and later fought at the Battle of Rhode Island. Jeffrey served several short tours of duty, and he received his final discharge on November 28, 1781, after serving a total of 2½ years.

Sources: **1.** National Archives Pension Application W19757. **2.** *Massachusetts & Vital Records 1620–1988.* **3.** Tombstone

Lewis Hinton

Lewis Hinton was born in August 1758 in Lancaster County, Virginia. He served in the Virginia Navy as a substitute for his master William Hinton. He stated in his pension application,

> William Hinton who was at that time the master of the said Lewis, enlisted in or about the year 1777, for the term of five years to serve in the navy of Virginia, and entered service on board the ship Dragon—and after serving near one year, his health became so bad, that he was permitted to leave the service, provided he would furnish a substitute. That he the said Lewis Hinton took the place of the said William Hinton, and entered service on board the ship Dragon in the spring of 1778 as well as he recollects. The said ship was lying at that time at Frazier's Ferry on Mattapony river, and was commanded by Capt Callender. That some time, near two years as well as he can recollect, after he entered the service, Capt Callender left the command of the Dragon & she was then commanded by Lt Hamilton, & about that time Lt Joshua Singleton entered service on board sd ship. That whilst he was in service the Dragon cruised briefly at sea. that they had a fight with the British schooner Lord Howe, which schooner out sailed us & got away. That the said ship Dragon and several other vessels were besieged by the fleet of the enemy in James river, where after laying for some time, & finding no chance to escape, we left the said ship and we returned home. This was to the best of my recollection in the year 1781. The said Hinton states that he was in active service on board the said Dragon between three & four years.

Sources: 1. National Archives Pension Application S10831. **2.** *The Journal of Negro History*, Vol. XXVII—July 1942, pages 254–5.

Prince Hull

Prince Hull was born c. 1750 and on May 15, 1775, he enlisted for eight months in Captain Oliver Parker's Company in Colonel William Prescott's Regiment. Prince was part of the 1,200 men under the command of Colonel Prescott at the Battle of Bunker Hill.

On the night of June 16, 1775, Prescott's Regiment began to erect defenses on Breed's Hill. The next day, with little sleep and limited ammunition, they defended their position against the main British attack. Some historians believe that Prescott is the man that ordered his troops, "Do not fire until you see the whites of their eyes." It is debated who actually gave this order. The regiment repelled two British attacks, and because they were running out of ammunition they were forced to retreat during the third attack.

On January 1, 1776, Prince reenlisted and served in Captain Perry's Company, in Colonel Paul Dudley Sargent's Regiment for three months. It was reported that he deserted on April 19, 1776, and was dropped from the rolls. This would have occurred after his three months enlistment was up. It was not uncommon for militiamen to leave and go home during their tour if no fighting was going on.

Prince enlisted on August 26, 1777, in Colonel Thaddeus Cook's Militia Regiment, and at the Battle of Saratoga they were on the left wing under the command of General Gates. Prince was wounded in this battle, and he was discharged on November 9, 1777.

On March 28, 1818, Prince filed for a pension and stated in his application,

> He first enlisted in April 1775 for eight months in Capt. Parker's company & Col. Prescott's Reg. of Mass troops & served through that campaign, was engaged in the Battle of Bunker Hill & at the expiration of his eight months in December 1775 he enlisted for one year at Cambridge in the Cont. line in Capt. Hill's company & Col. Webb's Regt & at the expiration thereof he was enlisted again at Fishkill N. York for three years by Lieut. Smith but on account of sickness he did not join any Regt. & does not now recollect to what one he belonged—in consequence of his sickness he was about six months afterwards discharged. In August 1777 he again enlisted into Capt Wadsworth's company & Col Cook's Regt. for three months & was wounded at the battle of Saratoga.

On August 26, 1820, he had to reapply for his yearly pension of $96 in order to prove he was in need of the money. He listed his personal property and its value which amounted to $8.57.

Sources: 1. National Archives Pension Application S36596. **2.** *Massachusetts Soldiers and Sailors in the Revolutionary War*, page 481.

James Huzzey

James Huzzey was born c. 1747 in Massachusetts, and he died on March 11, 1822, in Townshend, Vermont. He was a slave when he married Susannah Tobey, also a slave, on January 20, 1776. James received a yearly pension of $96 for his service. He wrote in his pension application on March 18, 1818,

> He entered the service in the spring of 1775 and sometime in the course of the summer of that year after Gen. Washington arrived in Boston & engaged during the War and served through till the Peace in 1783.

James first enlisted in Captain Moses Harvey's Company and Colonel Jonathan Brewer's 13th Massachusetts Regiment on June 8, 1775. The regiment was made up of eight companies with a total of 390 men. On June 17th he and his company fought at the Battle of Bunker Hill. During the battle James and his regiment took a position to the left of a redoubt on the hill. They held their position all day until they were ordered to retreat. Seven men in the regiment were killed, and eleven were wounded including Colonel Brewer. After the battle, the regiment was stationed at Prospect Hill for the rest of the summer and part of the fall.

James enlisted on March 30, 1781, for three years in Captain Jeremiah Miller's Company in Colonel Joseph Vose's 1st Massachusetts Regiment. They were stationed around the West Point area in the Highlands Department until the end of the war.

After the death of James, Susannah applied for a widow's pension. She stated that they were married soon after the Battle of Bunker Hill and for the next several years James was not often home due to his service in the war. Susannah received a widow's pension of $80 a year. She stated in her application filed on May 28, 1859,

> He [James] lived on Cape Cod in the State of Massachusetts, that he served two terms of service as a substitute for the sons of his master or masters, he living at that time a slave, that afterwards in order to obtain his freedom, he enlisted as she believes for the term of during the war & served until the close of the ____?____ that he was in the battle of Bunkere Hill & many other battles.
>
> **Sources: 1.** National Archives Pension Application W18091. **2.** Culter, *Historic Homes and Places and Genealogical and Personal Memoirs Vol. 4*, page 1740. **3.** Hurd, *History of Middlesex County, Massachusetts Vol. 3*, pages 25–6. **4.** *Massachusetts Soldiers and Sailors of the Revolutionary War, Vol. 8*, page 595.

Peter Jennings

Peter Jennings was born c. 1752 in Pequarock, Connecticut, and he received $100 a year for his service. He stated in his pension application of 1828,

> I served in Col Brewster's Ridgement (mostly black man) Major Tamage, Captain Edgar's Company as above named. There was in the same Ridgement Lieutenant Pike, Lieutenant Ray—Hanly & Thos Jackson—with Capts. Richardson & Brooks, and several other Capts and Lieutenants that I cannot a this period mention. I served about four years before the taking of Lord Cornwallis and about ten months afterwards, before the close of the War and the issue of my discharge from Maj Tamage & others. I was discharged at the Town of Fairfield in the State of Connecticut, a few weeks after the taking of Forte Slongo on Long Island's and on our way to said Forte Col Brewster was wounded in the Belly by the Traitor Capt Haile & Company who no doubt supposed that we were after them—but the wound did not prove mortal. I will here mentions some of the persons who were in the part of the Company with me and whose names may be inscribed on the list of Revolutionary Soldiers. James James, Philip James, Brothers; & Ned Bradley. Three Black men, also Pomp Nichols from Purke Quanock Ned Sherman and [an] Indian, Corporal Eatonton, white man. David Harrisson and James Griffin white privates. I would also mention that General recognized me when in Nashville and that I could get evidence of that fact by taking great paines, but hope that foregoing evidence will be sattisfactory.

The Battle of Fort Slongo was fought on October 3, 1781, in New York at a fort overlooking Long Island Sound. Peter said he was at this battle and at the Siege of Yorktown [see pension statement below] several days before it ended on October 19, 1781. Peter would have had to walk about 400 miles between Fort Slongo and Yorktown.

The following pension statement was made August 23, 1832,

That he enlisted in the army of the United States, according to the best of his recollection in the year 1776 with Corporal Edenton and when he entered the service, he belonged to the 5th Regiment of Artillery of Blacks, in the Continental line, under the following named officers. He belonged to Capt'n. Vener Angel's company. The Regiment was commanded by Col. Edward Oney.

He thinks his Regiment joined General Washington's army at West Point; and after remaining there a few days, marched to Saratoga, where they remained a considerable length of time. At the same time they were encamped at Saratoga, thinks that Gen. Dickson, or Dickenson was encamped there with a division of Virginia Militia, and he thinks he remembers Colonels Campbell & Ferguson were there in the Virginia Militia. After remaining at Saratoga several weeks, he thinks his regiment was divided, and a part of it attached to the troops under the command of Gen. Green [sa part of it to the troops under the command of Gen. Gates; a part of it probably to the troops under Gen. Cadwallade; and a part of it Gen. Washington retained with the troops under his immediate command. He remained with troops under Gen. Washington's immediate command; and he thinks the Regiment to which he was attached, was commanded by Col. Clifford.

Shortly after this division was made of the black regiment, he thinks the battle of Trenton took place, and he well remembers he was in that engagement. He has a distinct recollection that on the night of the 25th of December after he first entered the service as a regular soldier, which would be December 1776 if it was in that year he enlisted, and he thinks it was, Gen. Washington crossed his Troops over the Delaware about nine miles above Trenton and marched upon the enemy and attacked them by surprise. A part of the American forces he thinks were commanded by Generals Ewing & Cadwallader, the former of whom belonged to the Virginia troops.The forces under their command he thinks were to cross the Delaware, higher up than the point at which declarant crossed with Gen. Washington, and were to attack the left wing of the enemy; but he well remembers the did not cross over, which he thinks was owing to the ice; for it was with extreme difficulty that Gen. Washington got his troops over, on account of the ice and the extreme cold weather. On account of Generals Ewing and Cadwallader failing to cross the river as had been previously arranged, we were compelled to make the attack with such forces alone as crossed over with Gen. Washington. The enemy so little expecting an attack from us, were thrown into great confusion, and we obtained a complete victory over them, killing many of them, and taking several hundred prisoners, who were principally Hessians. We also took a large amount of military stores, a number of pieces of Cannon, and a great many small arms. He thinks the greater portion of the enemy's forces were killed & taken prisoners. He thinks there was a Colonel, commanding the Hessian troops killed, but does not remember his name. There were but few on the side of the Americans killed and not many wounded; amongst the wounded, he thinks there was a Captain Washington [which he remembers from his being of the same name of his General—Washington.

The American plan of attack on Trenton consisted of three coordinated attacks from three directions. General Cadwalader would attack south of Trenton at Bordentown to prevent reinforcements from the south. General Ewing would capture the bridge over the Assunpink Creek and prevent the enemy from escaping. The main group under Washington would attack the town of Trenton.

Terrible weather conditions delayed Washington's crossing of the Delaware, and Generals Cadwalader and Ewing were forced to abandon the attack. Washington reached Trenton by morning and caught the enemy by surprise. The Hessians had twenty-two men killed, including their commander Johann Rall, and 896 captured. The Americans had two killed, however, many later died from exhaustion and exposure to the harsh weather. Future president James Monroe was severely wounded in the battle. William Washington, second cousin of George Washington, was also wounded.

> After this engagement he states he marched back across the Delaware with the prisoners and captured stores; and the prisoners, he thinks were conducted to Philidelphia. In a few days however, he returned with Gen. Washington to Trenton. They had not been long in possession of Trenton, when the British forces collected and marched towards Trenton for the purpose of giving battle, as was supposed; in fact they had actually commenced firing on the American troops in the evening and considerable cannonading took place between the two armies. The firing from our artillery, somewhat checked their advance upon us, and night coming on, they halted on the opposite side of a creek from us, and ceased firing. It was then supposed that they intended making a general attack upon us the next morning. We were ordered to light fires along our lines in our front, for the purpose, as declarant afterwards discovered, of deceiving the enemy; for instead of remaining at the fires we were marched off with all possible expedition towards Princeton where some regiments of the British troops were quartered. We reached there very early the next morning and made a vigorous attack upon them. Declarant has a perfect recollection of an occurrence which took place during this engagement, which will never be effaced from his memory. A part of our troops were driven back by the British and were threwn into much confusion. Gen. Washington perceiving it, seized a standard and rushed in front of our troops, and dashed sevral paces ahead towards the enemy, exclaiming "come on boys," or some such expression. His example had the desired effect of rallying our troops, and they followed the Commander with renewed ardour. While Gen. Washington was between the two armies at least one round was fired on each side, and he remained untouched. Soon after this occurrence, the British troops gave way and retreated into some public building, where we pursued them and kept up such a play of artillery upon them, that all those who had taken refuge, were compelled to surrender to us. In this engagement, the Brittish were completely routed & defeated. Many of them were killed & wounded and a great number taken prisoners. The loss on the American side he thinks was inconsiderable. He remembers that General [Hugh] Mercer, who he believes belonged to the Virginia troops was severely wounded in this engagement, and thinks he shortly died of his wounds.

On the night of January 2, 1777, Washington called his officers together to discuss whether they should fight the British who were camped nearby, or should they retreat. It was decided that they should launch a surprise attack on the enemy. By two in the morning the American army was silently moving toward the enemy camp. Along the way rumors began to spread that they were surrounded and walking into a trap. These false rumors caused some men to flee to Philadelphia for safety. The Americans again caught the enemy by surprise and was again victorious.

The British view the Americans victories at Trenton and Princeton as a minor thing. But these victories gave the American hope and a belief that they could win the war. Peter Continues in his pension application,

> After the battle at Princeton we marched to Morristown and took up winter quarters, and remained there until some time in the spring. From Morristown, he marched to Middlebrook; from thence to Peek's-hill [Peekskill, New York] where some fortifications were erected. From this point he marched towards the Delaware river; and the army was occupied for several weeks in advancing & receding, marching & countermarching, sometimes toward Philidelphia, and then towards the Delaware, for several weeks, until the battle finally ensued at Brandywine]. This engagement commenced early in the morning, and the attack was brought on by the British who were under the command of Lord Cornwallis. They crossed the creek about a mile above our forces, and made an attack upon our rear. We were about the same time attacked in front by a British General whose name is now not remembered. The American troops were compelled to retreat with great loss. He thinks he retreated towards Chester and was pursued a considerable distance by the enemy. He well remembers seeing Gen. Lafayette in this engagement, and saw him receive a wound, which he thinks was in his right leg. He also remembers that there was another American General wounded, but he has forgotten his name. He thinks Gen. Lincoln was in this battle [General Lincoln was not present at this battle].
>
> Two or three weeks after the battle of Brandywine, Gen. Washington having received a considerable reinforcement from Virginia, marched us to Germantown and made an attack upon the British stationed there. The attack was made early in the morning, and from its sudden & unexpected character, the British forces were thrown into great disorder; but it being a cloudy, foggy morning it was difficult for our troops to keep in regular order, which caused considerable confusion amongst us; and the enemy rallying from the confusion into which they had at first been threwn, drove back our troops, and we were at length compelled to retreat with great loss. In this engagment an American General Nash was killed.

The Battle of Germantown was fought on October 4, 1777, and was a near victory for the Americans. One of the main factors that prevented an American victory was the thick fog, and battlefield smoke which hampered the coordination of American forces. Brigadier General Francis Nash was struck by a cannon ball which glanced from a post or a tree. The cannon ball killed his horse and wounded the General in the thigh. He was taken to a house on the road side and attended by Dr. Clark the chief surgeon. He lingered in great agony and died several days later.

> After recovering from this defeat, we marched to a place called Whitemarsh, where we remained some time in expectation of an attack from the British, who had taken a position not far distant from us; they however, withdrew without making an attack, and we were marched to Valley Forge where we took up winter quarters. Declarant was at the battle of York town. When we reached there, Lafayette had been engaged in some severe fighting with the enemy. The princapal fighting however after he reached the place, was with the artillery, with an almost constant cannonading was kept up. He well remembers the position of the french fleet on this occasion, which had taken a stand in the Patomac river to prevent

Cornwallis from being reinforced by the British troops under the command of Sir Henry Clinton. He remembers that about two days before the surrender fourteen of the British soldiers deserted and came into the American encampment and surrendered themselves; and that from them we received a good information about affairs in the enemys camp. The Surrender he thinks was on the 18th October 1781. He has a most perfect recollection of the circumstances which occured when Cornwallis surrendered up his sword, for he was present and saw this transaction. Cornwallis offered his sword to Gen. Washington, who steped back and declined taking it, when Gen. Lincoln, who it had been he thinks previously agreed should receive it, steped forward and accepted it from him. Declarant remained at York town several weeks after the surrender; he thinks however he marched to Winchester Virginia with the British prisoners, and that Cornwallis was in company. After he returned to York from Winchester, he remained there five or six days, at the end of which time he was discharged from the service. He lost his discharge a few years after the war was over he thinks, on the eastern part of the Bahama Islands, where he was shipwrecked, being on a voyage in a merchantman bound from New York to Teneriff on a trading expedition.

According to legend, when the British surrendered the British drummers and fifers played the tune "The World Turn'd Upside Down." The participants on both sides made no mention of this song being played, and it would not have been appropriate under the circumstances. The British were embarrassed that they had to surrender to what they considered to be an inferior army. Many of the British soldiers threw down their muskets in disgust of the surrender. Some of them cried and appeared to be drunk at the surrender.

British General Cornwallis refused to meet formally with Washington and did not attend the surrender claiming he was ill. Cornwallis had his adjutant, General O'Hara, represent him at the surrender. O'Hara first presented the sword of Cornwallis to French General Comte de Rochambeau, who declined and deferred to General Washington. Washington declined the sword and deferred to General Lincoln, who took the sword and then returned it back to the British General. For several days after the surrender, the American and British officers dined together at night.

Sources: 1. Johnston, *The Yorktown Campaign and the Surrender of Cornwallis, 1781*, pages 151–58. **2.** Heyl, *The Battle of Germantown*, page 54. **3.** National Archives Pension Application S4436.

Prince Johonnot

Prince Johonnot was born on July 6, 1749, in Boston, Massachusetts, and he died on May 27, 1838. He married Mehitabel Emerson in 1773, and after the war they moved to New Hampshire. He was given a yearly pension of $26.26 for his service.

> He enlisted as a minute man in the service of his country in December 1774 in the company commanded by Capt. John Davis. Said company was kept organized and drilled two half

days in each week when the weather would permit. On the day of Lexington Battle [April 19th 1775] when news of that event being received at Methuen we marched with the aforesaid company to Cambridge & entered the service of the United States for eight months and was stationed in the Centre College Building was attached to the Massachusetts Regiment commanded by Col. Joseph or James Frys of Andover Mass. Brecket Lieut. Col. And Ebenezer Youngman was adjutant who was killed at the Battle of Bunker Hill.

On the night of the 16th of June 1775 we marched to Bunker Hill where a breast work & fort was thrown up during that night and the next day was in the Battle on that hill. Knew Colonel Prescott who commanded a company which was also stationed at Cambridge & belonged to the same Regiment.

After the Battle of Bunker Hill returned to Cambridge saw General Washington when he came into that place, and continued in the service till some of the last days of December 1777 when he was dismissed.

Prince said he was stationed at Centre College Building before the Battle of Bunker Hill. On May 1, 1775, the students at Harvard were dismissed for an early summer vacation. They were told that when classes resumed on the 2nd of October they would be held at Concord 20 miles away. The colonial army was quartered in the school buildings.

When the soldiers left in the spring of 1776 they left damaged buildings. They tore off the roof of Harvard Hall and took 1,000 pounds of metal to melt it into bullets. They also stripped brass doorknobs and box locks from the building to melt into bullets. They also removed some interior woodwork to use as firewood. In 1778 Harvard petitioned the Massachusetts government to pay for the damages, and they were awarded the sum of 417 pounds.

George Washington was voted commander-in-chief of the Continental Army by Congress on June 15, 1775. Prince saw Washington when he arrived in Cambridge to take charge on June 15, 1775. Washington was now commander of an untrained and undisciplined mob of shopkeepers and farmers.

Sources: **1.** National Archives Pension Application S18057. **2.** *Harvard's Year of Exile*, Harvard Gazette, 13 October 2011. **3.** Sons of the American Revolution Application.

Tim Jones

Tim Jones was a slave of Rolling Jones in Virginia. Tim received a yearly pension of $80 for his service. He stated in his pension application,

That he enlisted in the army of the United States in the year [left blank] with Captain Edward Digges and served in the third Virginia Regiment in the Virginia State line under the following officers for the space of four years and four months; that he went into service as a substitute for his master Rolling Jones under Captain Edward Digges; was then put under Captain Ewall and then under Capt'n Dudley and lastly under Captain Woodson who gave him a discharge which has been destroyed in consequence of the burning of his house. That he was at the battle of Camden Court house and also at the battle of York Town in Virginia in which last battle he lost his leg by a musket ball. That at Camden Courthouse (North Carolina) he was taken prisoner but was exchanged and again joined the army at Point of Forks in Virginia. That he went as the substitute of his master Rolling Jones and was given his freedom by the Country for the faithful discharge of his duty as a soldier.

Tim was probably at the Battle of Guilford Court House fought on March 5, 1781. There was no Camden Court House battle. Also, the Battle of Camden was in South Carolina and Guilford Court House was in North Carolina, where he said he was taken prisoner. During this time Tim was probably in a militia regiment, because most of the 3rd Virginia Regiment had been captured at Charleston in May of 1780.

Two fellow soldiers wrote interesting letters in support of Tim's pension,

> I Alexander W. Green aged 74 years last January do hereby certify that I was intimately acquainted with Rolling Jones the person named in the application of Tim Jones and I know that the said Rolling Jones in a drunken frolick enlisted in the revolutionary war and when he got sober he put Tim Jones the applicant in, as his substitute and the said Tim Jones was set free, for the faithful manner he discharged his duty while acting as a soldier.
>
> I Ansolem Bailey now in my seventy sixth year of age do hereby certify that I was well acquainted with Tim Jones a man of colour. That the said Tim Jones is a resident of the County of York. That the said Tim Jones was a soldier in the revolutionary war and I believe went into service under Captain Edward Digges in the third regiment of the Virginia State line in the year 1776 or 1777. That said Tim Jones was in service at the battle of York Town in Virginia where he received a wound in his leg, in that battle and was obliged to have his leg amputated I know that the said Jones is a very respectable man of Colour, and that he rendered much service in the revolutionary war.

Sources: **1.** National Archives Pension Application S18063. **2.** Grundset, *Forgotten Patriots, National Society of the D.A.R.,* page 520.

Moses Knight

Moses Knight was born c. 1756, and he died on April 2, 1848, in Indiana. He was African by birth and raised by General Alexander McIntosh of South Carolina. Moses married Marian Hopewell on December 25, 1795, or 96. He was a free man at the time of his enlistment and received a yearly pension of $100.

> That he enlisted in the Army of the United States in the year 1779, with Colonel Jack McIntosh and served in the [Blank] Regiment of the South Carolina line under the following named officers: Colonel Jack McIntosh other field Officers not recollected. Captain James Fontleroy Lieutenant [Blank] Maryweathers; that at the time of his enlistment he resided at General Alexander McIntosh's on big Pedee River, about three miles below the long bluff and four miles below Culp's Ferry in [Blank] County, South Carolina; that Colonel McIntosh was the commandant of Troop of Light horse, and was called a Regular Officer, and that at the time he (the said Moses Knight) enlisted, 2 other individuals by the name of John O'Neal and James O'Neal, brothers and one other by the name of [Blank] McClary enlisted,

under said McIntosh: that they were marched to Camden where they were placed under Captain Fontleroy and Lieutenant Maryweathers, and there they joined the Army. That he continued to serve in said troop of horse and the officers aforesaid until the year 1782, when he was discharged from the service at Windsor in South Carolina. That during his service, he was marched into North Carolina; was at the Shallow Ford on Yadkin River: was guarding horses in hearing of the guns at the time of the battle of Guilford Courthouse that he was at Princess Ann Court-house Virginia, and that he was near Savannah in Georgia. That his service was principally against the Tories; and that he was engaged against the Tories and rode by the side of one George Storms, at the time the Tories killed Colonel Culp and burned his house, at Culp's Ferry on Pedee. That sometime in the year 1782, he was appointed and commissioned a press-master to take a boat load of corn from Culp's Ferry to Windsor; and that he did press hands, and take 800 bushels of corn, from said Ferry to Windsor, for the support of General Green's Light Horse, where he received his discharge.

Sources: 1. National Archives Pension Application W10182. **2.** Grundset, *Forgotten Patriots, National Society of the D.A.R.,* page 584.

Pompey Lamb

The Americans employed many spies during the war, and one of them preformed a very spectacular deed. Pompey was an African slave that volunteered to spy for the American Army. The Americans had just lost Stony Point, New York, in May of 1779. As a result, Fort Fayette had fallen, West Point was in danger, and all communication to the north was threatened.

Pompey went to the fort at Stony Point with a basket of strawberries, and he asked the sentry for permission to enter the fort and sell his fruit. The sentry saw no harm in letting in the laughing and harmless Pompey into the fort. The British officers, who were eager for fresh fruit quickly bought all that Pompey had. They insisted that he return with more, so for the next three days he sold his strawberries to the officers.

The third day he told the officers that he could not come back because he had to work. The officers were unhappy about this, so Pompey agreed to come after dark with the strawberries. To do this he said he needed to know the password, and the unsuspecting officers were happy to share it with him. Each night there was a new password, and for the next nine nights Pompey showed up with his strawberries.

On the 10th night around midnight Pompey gave the password, and the gates were opened. Only this time Pompey had hiding near him three soldiers with blackened faces. When the gates opened, they jumped out of hiding and knocked out the sentry. Other American troops were hiding, and they rushed inside the gates as other American troops scaled the back walls of the fort.

The British were taken completely by surprise, and Stony Point was recaptured by the Americans. Pompey for his role in the victory was given a horse and excused from all work for the rest of his life.

Source: **1.** Kaplan & Kaplan, *The Black Presence in the Era of the American Revolution*, pages 58–9.

Plato Lambert

Plato Lambert was born on December 1, 1737, and was taken when an infant by Mrs. Martha Nichols of Framingham, Massachusetts. He later became the slave of Joseph Taylor, and was later given his freedom. He was described as a man of a very large size.

On May 1, 1775, he enlisted for eight months in the company commanded by Captain James Mellen in the 1st Massachusetts Regiment under Colonel Jonathan Ward. His regiment was probably deployed outside of the Massachusetts Colony. In June of 1775 Plato probably participated in the Battle of Bunker Hill.

After the revolution he was often seen roaming around the country with a large dog at his side. In time Plato and the dog disappeared. In 1810 workers were constructing a road near Lake Cochituate and the skeleton of a very large man and the remains of a dog were found. Plato and his dog were probably murdered and buried there.

Sources: **1.** Drake, *History of Middlesex County, Massachusetts*, 1880, pages 192–3. **2.** Barry, *A History of Framingham, Massachusetts*, 1847, page 64. **3.** Grundset, *Forgotten Patriots*, National Society of the D.A.R., page 119.

David Lamson (Lampsom)

David Lampson was born c. 1740 and he served in the French and Indian War. He answered the Lexington alarm in 1775.

On April 19, 1775, about 700 British troops, under the command of Lieutenant Colonel Francis Smith, were sent to Lexington and Concord to capture and destroy rebel supplies that had been stored by the militia. British General Gage believed that reinforcements might be required to assist Colonel Smith. He ordered several regiments, under the command of Earl Percy, to leave Boston and march toward Colonel Smith. After several delays the reinforcements left Boston about 8:45 in the morning of April 19th. As the 1,000 British troops marched out of Boston they marched to the tune of "Yankee Doodle" to taunt the colonist along the route.

During the march Percy encountered an absent minded tutor from Harvard College. Not sure which road to take, Percy asked the Harvard man. The man, oblivious to what was going on, pointed Percy in the right direction. Later the poor man had to leave the area, because he was accused of aiding the enemy.

Samuel Abbot Smith described what happened next, "Lord Percy's reinforcements had been delayed a little time at Brighton Bridge, the planks of which had been taken up by the direction of the Committee of safety. But, unfortunately, they were simple piled up on the Cambridge side, and it was the work of but a few moments to replace them sufficiently to allow the troops to pass."

Following in the rear of Percy's troops was a group of supply wagons that were having trouble crossing the Brighton Bridge. Further ahead at Cooper's Tavern Word reached the rebels about the supply wagons, and the rebels began making plans to capture them.

David Lampson, a free black man, told the following story to Colonel Thomas Russell, who told it to Samuel Abbot Smith who wrote about it in his book,

> Meanwhile an express was sent post-haste from Old Cambridge to Menotomy, bearing the information that these supplies were on the way. Several of our men met at once in Cooper's tavern, which stood on the present site of Whittemore's hotel, to form some plan for capturing them. They were of the exempts, or alarm list as it was called, all old men, for every young man was that day nearer the post of danger. There were Jason Belknap and Joe Belknap, James Budge, Israel Mead and Ammi Cutter, **David Lampson**, and others, in all twelve. Some of them had been soldiers in the French war, and age had not impaired their courage. They chose for their leader **David Lampson**, a mulatto, who had served in the war, a man of undoubted bravery and determination.

The twelve men took a position behind a wall of earth and stones, and they waited for the groups of wagons.

> The convoy soon made its appearance. As it came between them and the meeting house of the First Parish, Lampson ordered his men to rise and aim directly at the horses, and called out to them to surrender. No reply was made, but the drivers whipped up their teams. Lampson's men then fired, killing several of the horses, and, according to some accounts, killing two of the men and wounding others.

Once the firing began, the drivers jumped from their wagons and ran to the bank of Spy Pond. They threw their guns into the pond and then continued to run along the banks of the pond. They followed along the bank and met an old woman named Mother Batherick.

> They surrendered themselves to mother Batherick who was digging dandelions. She led them to the house of Capt. Ephraim Frost, where there was a party of our men, saying to her prisoners, as she gave them up. 'If you ever live to get back, you tell King George that an old woman took six of his grenadiers prisoner.'

Once the wagons had been captured, David Lampson had his men pull the wagons off the road and let the men take whatever they wanted. The following made the rounds in some of the British newspapers. "If one old Yankee woman can take six grenadiers, How many will be required to conquer America?" West Cambridge had the honor of making the first capture of provisions and prisoners of the American Revolution.

Source: **1.** Smith, *West Cambridge 1775*, 1804, pages 26–31. **2.** Sanders, *America's Black Founders: Revolutionary Heroes & Early Leaders*, page 38. **3.** Kaplan & Kaplan, *The Black Presence in the Era of the American Revolution* pages 19–20.

Benjamin Lattimore

Benjamin Lattimore was born free in Weathersfield, Connecticut, in January of 1762, and he died on April 28, 1838, in Albany, New York. After he was born his family moved to New Marbury, New York, where his family ran a ferry. He enlisted in the army at the age of fifteen and received a yearly pension of $80 for his service.

> That in the year 1776 and in the month of September he enlisted at New Malbury as a private in Captain Amos Hutchin's Company of the 5th New York Regiment then under the command of Colonel Lewis Dubois. That a few days after his enlistment he went with the Regiment by water from New Malbury to New York. On their arrival the American Army commanded by Genl. Washington & which had been fighting with the enemy was retreating from Long Island. Some day afterwards the American Army retired from New York—and a large part of it was stationed at King's Bridge. A very few days afterwards a skirmish was had between a part of our troops and the Enemy in which we had the advantage and the next day we sent a flag to the enemy and a truce was declared for the purpose of burying the dead. Some days after this skirmish our troops marched back to King's Bridge and after remaining there a considerable time they left and went to the White Plains. The enemy perused them thither there was several skirmishes or engagements between them and a part of our forces. In one of the engagements Gen Heath from the East—had the command of the left wing. One of the churches was burnt at this place and several skirmishes were had with the enemy afterwards. Here they remained until it was time to go into winter quarters when they passed through a place called Crumpson and Peekskill at this latter place they halted a number of days where they left and went by water to New Windsor. Here the declarant was taken sick & had permission to go home which the declarant did. The army at New York & White Plains was composed of Regular troops and militia. Some of our officers were killed at the battle at or near Kingsshire.
>
> In the month of April 1777 he left New Malbury where he had been living during the winter and went by water to Fort Montgomery at the High Lands. Genl Clinton had command of the Fort and they remained there without being disturbed or having any engagements with the enemy until in October following.

The Battle of Fort Clinton is sometimes referred to as the Battle of the Clintons. George Clinton was the Governor of New York, and he was also the General in command of Fort Montgomery. General George Clinton shared command of Fort Montgomery with his brother General James Clinton. General James Clinton was also in command of Fort Clinton, which was a smaller fort less than a half mile from Fort Montgomery. General Henry Clinton was the British General in command of the troops attacking Fort Montgomery.

> In the early part of that month some vessels belonging to the enemy came in sight and when within five miles of the Fort the wind having slackened they disembarked at a place

called Dunderberg on Thunder Hill and marched from thence to the Fort. Before they arrived at the Fort Geo. Clinton sent out different detachments of men to meet them and fire was kept up between them and the enemy until our men returned to the Fort.

On October 6 British General Henry Clinton landed 2,100 men near Fort Montgomery and encountered a scouting party sent out from the fort. After a small skirmish the British General divided his force into two groups to attack the fort. One group of about 900 men were under the command of Lieutenant Colonel Mungo Campbell.

> Shortly after orders were given by Gen Clinton to stop firing as the enemy had sent a flag by Col. Campbell. The Col approached near to one of the gates of the Fort near to me of the gates of the Forts and was met on the outside of the Fort by Gen Clinton & Dr. Cook after the usual salutations had passed between them and Col Campbell the Col. Was asked by Gen. Clinton the nature of his business who replied that he came to demand a surrender of the Fort which of done within one hour and our troops presented their arms they would be permitted to go as it was not wished to take them prisoners because they (the enemy) had more men with them than could be accommodated in the fort. Gen. Clinton replied that the Fort would not be surrendered as long as he had a man able to fire a gun. Col. Campbell then said he would eat his supper or would sleep & which it is not collected in the fort that night or in hell. They then parted. An attack was made in the fort by the enemy and was defended until ten or eleven o clock when it was taken. Gov. Clinton, Gen James Clinton, Col. Dubois, De Cook made their escape Col Bryan or Brown, Stephen Lush aid to Clinton and others and this declarant were made prisoners.

The major officers and aids escaped by going down the embankment to the river, where gunboats took them to safety across the river. The defenders of the fort were taken to prisons in New York City. A list of prisoners was sent to the various communities in the area to inform their families. The families were expected to send provisions to the prisoners, because otherwise they might starve in prison. Benjamin stated in his application,

> In taking the fort Col. Campbell was killed. He was stabbed on the walls of the fort by Capt. Ronorane of Fishkill. The Enemy and the prisoners of whom this declarant was one remained until the latter part of October when the Fort was destroyed by the Enemy and they all went by water to New York.
> Here the declarant remained until the middle of the following winter when he was taken to King's Bridge where he remained until sometime in March and was compelled to wait on the British officers as a servant. From this latter place he went in his capacity of a servant with Captain ___?___ a Lieutenant who had about thirty men with him on an cursion in the vicinity of Tarrytown where they were all taken by the Americans.
> The declarant after being taken was carried to Genl Putnam who on discovering he was an American and belonged to Col. Dubois' Regiment ordered him to join this Regiment which was then lying at New Windsor on the west side of the Hudson River and the prisoners were sent to Hartford. Col. Dubois had the command of the Regiment when the declarant rejoined it and Capt. Hutchmen was then under the arrest and was cashier for

being absent from Fort Montgomery without permission. They remained until the roads were good when they crossed over the river and marched to the White Plains and remained there until the next fall

On arriving at the White Plains they found a large force concentrated there Cols. Van Schaick, Livingston and Courtland were there and Genl James Clinton had the command. The object of the concentration of so large a force at this place was as the declarant understood to aid Genl Washington in an attack on New York and the declarant while here saw General Washington, Arnold, Stirling.

From the White Plains Col. Dubois' Regiment marched to Fishkill where it was embarked on board vessels for Albany and proceeded up the river as far as Claverack at which place owing to the ice in the river they left the vessels and marched on the East side of the river to Albany and stopped there ten or twelve days when they left for Schoharie passing on their route through Schenectady and arriving at Schoharie were stationed at the lower fort and remained there until April following without being required to act against the enemy except on one occasion when a band of Tories & Indians came to a place called Beaver Dam some miles from the fort and carried off some of our committee men who were pursued & almost over taken.

In the month of April Col. Dubois with his Regiment left Schoharie and went to Johnstown shortly after their arrival at their place a detachment of 40 or 50 men of whom the declarant was one was sent by Col. Dubois under the command of Capt. Henry and stationed as one outside guard at a block house near the fishing area of Sir William Johnson about eight miles from Johnstown.

Sir William Johnson founded Johnstown and named it after his son John. It was originally called John's Town. Sir William, who was a former British General, died in 1774.

They continued here for two months and were not during this time engaged in any skirmishes or affairs with the foe. From Johnstown they then returned to Schenectady and were there a few days and left there some in boats on the Mohawk and some on foot for Canajoharie where they found Col. Livingston's Regiment. Col. Livingston's Regiment was there forming a circle around a gallows on which was hung a Canada spy.

These two Regiments after the lapse of a few days left Canajoharie for Otsego Lake where they found Cols Verplanck's & Courtland's Regiments, while here they advanced up one end of the lake so as to raise it and enable them to carry their stores and baggage by water to the Susquehanna River on damming up the lake and the waters being raised they proceeded as far as Tioga Point where they found Genl Sullivan and stayed a short time.

In 1779 General James Clinton and his troops made the upper part of the Susquehanna navigable by damming the source of the river at Otsego Lake. It allowed the lake's level to rise, and when the dam was destroyed the flood of water carried the boats downstream. This event is described by James Fennimore Cooper in the introduction of his book *The Pioneers*.

The whole country was then a wilderness, and it was necessary to transport the baggage of the troops by means of the rivers—a devious but practicable route. One brigade ascended the Mohawk until it reached the point nearest to the sources of the Susquehanna, whence it cut a lane through the forest to the head of the Otsego. The boats and baggage were carried over this "portage." And the troops proceeded to the other extremity of the lake, where they disembarked and encamped. The Susquehanna, a narrow though rapid stream at its source, was much filled with "flood wood," or fallen trees; and the troops adopted a novel expedient to facilitate their passage. The outlet, or the Susquehanna, flows through a gorge in the low banks just mentioned, which may have a width of two hundred feet. This gorge was dammed and the waters of the lake collected: the Susquehanna was converted into a rill. When all was ready the troops embarked, the damn was knocked away, the Otsego poured out its torrent, and the boats went merrily down with the current."— From the introduction of *The Pioneers.*

Benjamin Lattimore's Regiment, under the command of General Clinton, was part of the Sullivan Expedition during the summer of 1779. This was a campaign against the Tories and Indians in the heartland of New York. Clinton was ordered by General Sullivan to march down the Susquehanna to meet him at Tioga and to destroy all Indian villages along his route.

While at Tioga they recounted the news of the capture of Stoney Point by Genl. Wayne [16 July, 1779] and the Regiment had a general rejoicing. From this place they proceeded through the woods to Niagara and halted within hearing of the Enemy's guns. On their way they passed through and destroyed a number of Indian Settlements friendly to the Enemy but had no battle with them except at a place called Newtown about two days march from Tioga Point. Here the enemy made a stand and threw up a breast work and after __?__ about an hour they fade way and fled.

The Battle of Newtown was fought on August 29, 1779, and it was the last major battle of the Sullivan Expedition. The British and Indians had built camouflaged earthworks on a hill. The Americans attacked the enemy, and when the British mounted a counterattack the regiment Benjamin belonged to was one of the regiments that repelled the counterattack and secured an American victory.

At Niagara they remained a short time possibly a fortnight when they all left and returned nearly by the same route they had gone until they reached Tioga Point which was in October. Here the declarant received his discharged.

In the 1790s Benjamin moved to Albany, New York, and had a license to haul cargo and trash. In 1809 he married Dina the servant maid for Dr. Wilhelmus Mancius and the couple had at least three children. Although Benjamin was born free in 1830, he was summoned to court to defend himself against charges that he was an escaped slave. Many people in the community testified on his behalf, and Judge Estes Howe declared Benjamin to be a free man. He was the founder of Albany's School for People of Color and a founding member of the Albany African Temperance Society.

Sources: 1. *New York History: Quarterly Journal of the New York State Historical Association,* Vol. 77; Vol. 95, pages 385–388. **2.** National Archives Pension Application S13683. **3.** Grundset, *Forgotten Patriots, National Society of the D.A.R.,* page 316.

Richard Leet

Richard Leet was born in Africa c. 1750, and he received a monthly pension of $8. A statement from a shipmate of Richard said that he received $5 a month while in the navy.

> That he the said Richard is a native of Guinea that he was brought to the United States when he was about five years old as a slave. That being desirous to obtain his freedom, he left his master and went to New London; according to best recollection in the month of February 1782 he shipped as mariner on board the Frigate *Alliance* then lying in the harbor of New London a vessel of war in the service of the United States and commanded by John Barry Esq. That soon after his enlistment the frigate sailed on a cruise against the enemy. That they captured a number of vessels during said cruise. Then he continued on board said vessel until her arrival in April 1783 having served one year.

The *Alliance* was a 36 gun sailing frigate. Richard stated he boarded the ship in February of 1782 which is the wrong date. The ship sailed on December 24, 1781, and was at sea in February.

Sources: 1. National Archives Pension Application S38908. **2.** Grundset, *Forgotten Patriots*, *National Society of the D.A.R.*, page 282.

Barzillai Lew

Barzillai Lew was born on November 5, 1743, in Groton, Massachusetts, and he died on January 19, 1822, in Dracult, Massachusetts. In the mid–1760s he sold the family farm, and he moved to Clemsford, Massachusetts, and set up shop as a cooper making barrels. He married Dinah Bowman, who he had purchased in 1767 for $400 from Major Abraham Blood. This was a large sum of money for a young black shop keeper. In today's money it would be nearly $30,000. Lew had the reputation as big, 6 feet tall, and a strong man with a remarkable talent for music.

When the Revolutionary War began Lew enlisted on May 6, 1775. His military service is listed in his pension application,

> Descriptive list dated June 15, 1775; Capt. John Ford's co., Col. Bridge's regt.; age, 30 yrs.; stature, 6 ft.; occupation, cooper; residence, Chelmsford; enlisted May 6, 1775; reported a negro; also, Fifer (also given Drummer), Capt. Ford's co., Col. Ebenezer Bridge's (27th) regt.; muster roll dated Aug. 1, 1775; enlisted May 6, 1775; service, 3 mos. 3 days; also, company return dated Sept. 25, 1775; also, company receipt dated Chelmsford, April 19, 1776, for wages for service from Feb. 5, 1776, to April 1, 1776, in Capt. John Ford's co., Col. Roberson's (Robinson's) regt.; also, company receipt for mileage [soldiers were paid for every 20 miles from home they traveled after their discharge], given to Capt. John Ford, dated Ticonderoga, Aug. 28, 1776; also, company receipt for wages to Oct. 1, 1776, given to Capt. John Ford, dated Ticonderoga; company marched from Chelmsford, July 25, 1776, and was discharged at Albany, Jan. 1, 1777.

Lew served a total of eight months and three days. He was one of the three dozen or so African Americans who fought at the Battle of Bunker Hill. It was said that during the battle, Lew kept American morale high with his fife version of "Yankee Doodle Dandy." On April 19, 1775, as the British regulars under General Percy marched out of Boston toward Lexington and Concord, they played "Yankee Doodle Dandy" as a taunt to the Americans along the way. When the defeated British troops marched backed to Boston, they were taunted by the song "Yankee Doodle Dandy." According to the May 20, 1775, "Massachusetts Spy" upon their return to Boston one asked his brother officer how he liked the tune now—"Damn them!" he replied, "they made us dance it till we were tired."

In September of 1777 Lew was a member of Captain Joseph Varnum's Company of Massachusetts volunteers who marched to Fort Ticonderoga to reinforce the Northern Army. Lew served there until the American fleet was defeated at Lake Champlain on October 11, 1776. With winter coming the threat of the British was over, and Lew was discharged on January 1, 1777.

Lew returned home and years later purchased a farm. In addition to farming he continued to work as a cooper. Lew, his wife Dinah, and several of his children sang and played various instruments all over the area. They formed a complete band and played at several large cities such as Boston and Portland. Dinah may have been the first African American woman pianist in the United States. After Lew's death his wife received a widow's pension of $29.70 a year for his service. In 1943 musician Duke Ellington wrote a piano piece in honor of Barzillai Lew.

Sources: 1. Mayo, *Profiles in Courage: African-Americans in Lowell*, page 4. **2.** *Pennsylvania Journal; and the Weekly Advertiser. May 24, 1775*, The New York Public Library Digital Collections. **3.** Putney, *Blacks in the United States Army: Portraits through History*, page 121. **4.** Guthrie, *Camp-fires of the Afro-American; Or, the Colored Man as a Patriot*, page 93. **5.** National Archives Pension Application W2046.

Ambrose Lewis

Ambrose Lewis was born c. 1758, probably in Virginia, and he died on August 26, 1833. He received a monthly pension of $8 for his service. He stated in his pension application dated December 2, 1812,

> On the August 1780 he was badly wounded by receiving a ball through his thigh and five thrusts of a bayonet through different parts of his body and limbs which wounds have so disabled your petitions that he is more obliged to go on crutches.

Ambrose stated in his pension application of January 24, 1821,

> That on the 15 April 1776 he entered into the naval service of virginia, on board the galley Sage, commanded by Capt. Markham; in which service he continued untill 30 March 1778. when he entered as a seaman into the naval service of the United States, on board the

United States Ship Dragon commanded by Capt. Callender: in which service he continued until the 15 April 1779; when having compleated three years of service in the navy of the State & of the United States, he quitted that service & enlisted as a Common Soldier in Capt. Halliday's Company in the 2 Virginia Regiment, commanded by Col. George Stubblefield: served in that regiment untill and August 1780, when he was severely wounded & taken prisoner at the battle of Cambden & was detained as a prisoner till the end of the war, at Charleston S. C. where he was confined a part of the time in barracks and the residue of the time on board the prisonship.

I have no occupation, except occasionally that of a barber; and am not able to pursue any regular occupation for a livelihood, in consequence of my age & infirmity; & more especially of the anguish & disability of the wound in my leg received at the battle of Cambden which wound, the greater part of my time, breaks out into an open ulcer, & is always in a condition to render me a cripple in that leg.

Benjamin Alsop wrote a letter supporting the service claim of Ambrose. He also mentioned Charles, the brother of Ambrose.

I do hereby Curtify that Charles Lewis was a Solder in Capt. John Holliday's Company of Militia from Spotsylvania County & that he was in Genl. Gates's Defeat at Camden in South Carolina, on the 16 day of August 1780 and that he was a Brother to Ambrose Lewis.

In 1787 William Foushes, a surgeon, described the wounds Ambrose received at the Battle of Camden on August 16, 1780, "I find a ball has passed through the right thigh. Two stabs of the bayonet appear to have passed through the left arm."

Ambrose first served on board the Virginia ship *Page,* and on March 30, 1778, he was transferred to the *Dragon.* This ship carried sixteen to twenty cannons on board. Ambrose is found on the ship's rolls from 1778 until he was discharged on April 15, 1779. His brother Charles served on the *Dragon* from April 13, 1776, to January 20, 1779. Afterwards, both boys enlisted and served in the same army regiment.

After the war Ambrose married a woman named Susanna, and they had three children. In 1782 he was living in Richmond, Virginia, and after the death of his wife he married Fanny Williams. Fanny and her brother Francis were slaves, and their freedom was purchased by Charles, the brother of Ambrose. Charles lived in Richmond and died there in 1833.

Ambrose, his wife Fanny, and their children lived in a Fredericksburg neighborhood made up of whites and free persons of color. Ambrose owned no property during his life but rented a home from John Benson. After the death of Ambrose his wife applied for and received 100 acres of land for his service.

Sources: 1. National Archives Pension Application S36041. **2.** Willis, *Notes and Documents of Free Persons of Color Four Hundred Years of an American Family's History*, pages 68–70. **3.** *The History of Virginia's Navy of the Revolution, Roster Rolls*, pages 214–215. **4.** American Revolution Virginia Navy datasheet 1775–1782.

Pomp Magus

Pomp Magus was born c. 1748, and he died November 22, 1832. He received a monthly pension of $8. He enlisted in the early part of the Revolutionary War in Massachusetts and stated in his pension application in April of 1818,

> I preformed the service as a private soldier in the year A.D. 1775. I served eight months in a company of Infantry commanded by Capt. Samuel Sprague's in Col. Baldwin's Regiment and also at the latter part of 1775 or fore part of 1776 I entered the service in Capt. Agerey's company of Infantry in Col. Bond's Regiment.

Pomp first served under Colonel Loammi Baldwin's 25th Massachusetts Regiment and later the 15th Regiment commanded by Colonel William Bond. Both regiments were present at the Siege of Boston.

> I continued in said Regiment & proceed with it to the State of New York and that being a man of color myself and some others were left on fatigue [work detail] there, & then I continued until regularly discharged.
> In the year 1777 I enlisted in a company commanded by Capt. William Stoner in Colonel Jackson's Regiment & that I continued in said Regiment until the close of the term of service. I was at the taking of Burgoyne in October 1777.

Pomp served in the 8th Massachusetts Regiment commanded by Colonel Michael Jackson. The Colonel had the distinction of being one of the few men that served in the Continental Army from the beginning of its inception in June of 1775 until it was disbanded in November 1783.

Pomp's regiment was at the Battle of Bemis Heights on October 7, 1777, when British General Burgoyne was taken. His regiment was in the center of the American Army and Benedict Arnold led them in an attack on a redoubt. Arnold was wounded in the leg during this attack.

Pomp added another statement to his application on May 1, 1819. This statement included his capture toward the end of his service. When he first applied he was probably unaware that being in a prison camp was considered as time in the service.

> I enlisted for the term of nine months in the Regiment under the command of Col. Michael Jackson. A few days before the expiration of said term of service I was taken prisoner and carried to New York and was in confinement for ten or eleven months. I afterwards obtained a regular discharge.

On April 19, 1819, Asa Hart wrote a letter to the pension bureau testifying that Pomp was taken prisoner while in the service,

> I enlisted in the 8th Regiment commanded by Col. Michael Jackson sometime in the month of February I believe in the year A.D. 1780. I was taken prisoner by the enemy and carried to New York and there remained about eleven months. Pomp Magus was in the service and was taken at the same time and carried a prisoner with me to New York and remained

with me the whole time of my confinement which was more than ten months. Said Pomp Mangus afforded me much assistance during the term of our confinement.

Years after the war Pomp was poor and unable to take care of himself. Pomp Mangus died in the Malden Almshouse.

Sources: **1.** U.S. Pension Rolls of 1835. **2.** Pension Application S33059. **3.** Grundset, *Forgotten Patriots, National Society of the D.A.R.,* page 120. **4.** Meltsner, *The Poorhouses of Massachusetts: A Cultural and Architectural History,* page 66.

John (Keto) Martin

The first African American to fight in a Marine role was John Martin, also known as Keto. He was the slave of a Delaware man and he was recruited in 1776 without his owner's permission. He served with the Marine platoon on the *Reprisal* for a year and a half and was involved with hard ship-to-ship fighting. He was lost at sea with the rest of his unit when the brig sank in October 1777.

Sources: **1.** Shaw & Donnelly, *Blacks in the Marine Corps.* **2.** Lanning, *The African-American Soldier: from Crispus Attucks to Colin Powell,* page 15.

Thomas Mason

Thomas Mason moved to Louisa County, Virginia, and in April of 1791 he married Elizabeth. They were married in the Protestant Episcopal Church by the Reverend Douglass. Thomas had enlisted three times and served one year in the North Carolina Militia. He was in several battles during his enlistment. He was preparing his application for a pension with the aid of Major James B. Risque, when Thomas died in October 1832. This application gives a look at the problems faced by people of color, when they tried to receive what was due them.

On May 1, 1854, Elizabeth Mason filed for a widow's petition, because she was very old and needed the money. Because she had no written proof of her husband's service she enlisted the aid of Charles W. Statham, a Virginia lawyer. Her statement of May 1st,

> That she is the widow of Thomas Mason deceased, who was a Free man of Color, and a Private in Captains [William] Wilson, Moore, or Lee's Company, and she believes the Colonel or Commanding Officer of the Regiment was Moore, the name or number of the Regiment she does not recollect; that he entered the service as aforesaid in 1777, in Caswell County North Carolina, and was in the Battle of "White Marsh" near Valley Forge Pennsylvania, she thinks this was in 1777; in this tour he served six months in a Horse Company to the best of her recollection. He then volunteered again under Captain Wilson and Colonel Moore, and was in "Gate's Defeat" Aug 16, in 1870 in this tour he served three months. Again volunteered in 1781, under Captain Wilson and Colonel Moore, and was in the battle

of "Guilford Court House" March 15, 1781, and served in this tour, three months, and was honorably discharged at the termination of each tour. That she is now very old and infirm and scarcely able to walk, and has frequently heard her deceased husband narrate scenes and circumstances which occurred during his service in the Revolutionary War, and has frequently seen his "Discharged," and that they were given to Major James B. Risque to prosecute a claim for her husband under the Act of 1832, and that her husband died in October 1832, while they were preparing his claim.

Mr. Statham had several people write letters that supported the service of Thomas and his marriage to Elizabeth. An example of a letter is by Samuel George dated May 1, 1854,

> That he [Samuel George] was well acquainted with Thomas Mason deceased, in his life time—that this knowledge of him extended back for fifty years—and that he frequently heard the said Thomas Mason relate his services in the war of the Revolution; that it was always currently reported and believed that he served in the said war by his neighbors, and never heard it questioned by anyone.
> That the said Thomas Mason and Elizabeth lived together as man and wife from the time he first knew them fifty years ago.

The North Carolina Comptroller sent a letter showing that Thomas was paid for military service in the war,

> State of North Carolina/ Comptroller's Office I, William J. Clarke, Comptroller of Public Accounts in and for the State aforesaid, do hereby certify that it appears of record in my office, among the payments made by said State to sundry persons for Military services in the Revolution War as follows, to wit: Thomas Mason Vol. C entry 4516, £12—specie Book No. 14 page 113, £9—specie Book No. 26 page 44, £6 specie.

The claim filed by Elizabeth was rejected in a letter dated on May 19th by the Commissioner of Pensions, Loren P. Waldo. Mr. Waldo gave several reasons for the rejection. He said that the declaration Elizabeth gave should have been made before a court of record and not before a Justice of the Peace. He also stated that the certificate provided by the Comptroller of North Carolina did not show that the soldier referred to in the certificate was a man of color. Waldo also said that the marriage between Thomas and Elizabeth had not been properly established. His last objection was the declaration claimed service in the line of the Army, while the payments show militia service only.

This author has reviewed hundreds of pension applications, and many contain less proof of service and marriage than the application of Thomas Mason. If the application had been filed in a northern state, it probably would have been approved. Likewise, if Thomas was not a "man of color," it probably would have been approved.

Attorney Statham quickly replied to the letter of rejection from Mr. Waldo on June 5, 1854, and sent the following reply,

As one of the Attorneys for Elizabeth Mason, widow of Thomas Mason, deceased, a soldier of the Revolution, and whose claim I had filed some month since, for her pension, I ask a reconsideration of her claim, and write to clear up some of the objections, in your letter of suspension of the 19th May last. First– "That the Declaration should have been taken before a Court of Record, and not before a Justice of the Peace as such." You are doubly aware that Justices compose our Court of Record, having a Presiding Justice, which Court has as high jurisdiction and its members separately as the Judges in many of the states. In fact, I believe most of them have not as high power as our Justices. We have no county Judge at all in Virginia, though we have what is called a District or Circuit Judge, embracing a large number of counties in his Circuit. In this case, Elizabeth Mason is wholly unable to attend in open Court, and if that is required, it is impossible for me to get her there, and I shall be under the necessity to abandon the case. Mr. Jno. P. Knight, the Justice before whom she made the Declaration, had just left the bench, where he was presiding as one who constituted a Court of Record, and went with me from the Courthouse to visit this old woman, and take her Declaration. He certifies to her inability to attend in open Court, on account of old age and infirmity, which is literally true, and it would be impossible for me to get her to the Courthouse. She is 90 years old and very infirm, and is physically unable to move about. If it is regarded as essential by the Department, I will get the Presiding Justice to visit her, and certify as to her inability to attend in open Court, for I have to get them to go to see her. Heretofore I have had but little difficulty in getting this admitted by the Department, and I hope in this case they will not be more rigid than in others I have had. I should like to know your decision on this, as it would be unnecessary to proceed to comply with the other objections until this is removed. 2nd—"The certificate of the Comptroller of North Carolina does not show, that the soldier referred to in his certificate was a man of color." In answer to this, I will say, no such distinction was made on the muster rolls or in any certificate given to free negroes from North Carolina or Virginia. Both black and white, if free persons, stood on the same footing at militiamen, no distinction being made as to color, which I hope will remove that objection. But if the Department thinks proof necessary as to that fact, I will procure the letter or certificate of the Comptroller, that these certificates never specify the color. It is proper for me to say, that Benjamin Farmer and William Lee Fair, two of the witnesses, are white gentlemen of the highest respectability in the country. The other two witnesses are free persons of color (Samuel George and Thomas Mason) and whose testimony are entitled to the most ample credit, as they are thrifty and prosperous and educated—one of them, quite so. I refer you to the Hon. Thomas L. Bocock, if necessary, whom I suppose knows one them, Thomas Mason, who is a butcher, in regular attendance in the Lynchburg market. But if you think it best or necessary, I will get the Presiding Justice, who knows Mason well, and I believe he knows George, to certify as to their respectability and truthfulness. Of course, in speaking of respectability, I mean as colored men for as citizens our laws do not recognize their political equality with white persons, though their testimony, is lawful and valid in all cases, in which their own color is involved, as in the case of Elizabeth Mason, and that was the reason I annexed the testimony of two of each. 3d– "That the marriage has not been properly established." Please let me know what will be proper for me to do to prove the marriage, when no records can be found. Recollect that the marriage of free persons of color are not kept with that attention, which is paid to whites, and it is a rare case that one is ever returned by the Minister to the Clerk's office, as no law to fine him in that case exists, as is the case, when he makes a failure to return the marriage of whites. Their marriage, is therefore, seldom to be obtained from the records, though they generally get a minister to marry them, but he can do it without even the usual Clerk's certificate or license as is essential in the case of whites. Another objection urged is, that the Declaration embraces service "in the Line of the Army," while the payments shew "Militia service only." I am rather surprised that it is so in the Declaration, for the old widow informed me from the beginning, that the whole of her husband's service was in the militia, and that he volunteered the first time together with his whole company from Caswell Col, N.C. and went to Pennsylvania. In looking over the original draft, I discover it so stated, but not knowing what law to claim under, I sent the Declaration and paper as written by myself, to my assistants in Washington, Jno S. Pollard & Co., and asked them to look over and write the Declaration anew, if the one I sent did not answer, or was too voluminous, which the wrote, and I did not discover by that Declaration, at least I did not understand that he was made anything but a volunteer of militia in any case. He certainly was never any but a militia company which volunteered as a whole. If I can be allowed to do so, and the Department think it necessary, I beg leave to amend and correct the Declaration in that particular, for Thomas Mason always served as a volunteer of North Carolina Militia, and in no other capacity—his company as a whole volunteering and entering the service. This claim has been suffered to stand unattended to for a great while, because free persons of color are but little noticed or cared for. Such claims are overlooked, and the testimony is more obscure, as they never have any acquaintances but those that live adjoining or near them. I hope on this account, that the Department will be as lenient as it can be with due regard to its interest and rules. Please answer this, and remit all the objections you can, and inform me what is necessary to perfect the claim.

The Secretary of the Interior of the United States, Robert McClelland, wrote to Mr. Waldo about marriage between free colored people in Virginia,

In reply to the question submitted to this Department in your communication of the 16th Inst. arising in the case of Elizabeth Mason, a claimant for a Pension under the Act of July 7 1838, viz: "Can the relation of husband and wife exist between free colored people in the State of Virginia—the ceremony of Marriage taking place in said State, so as to constitute the wife upon the death of the husband, his 'widow' within the meaning of the laws of Congress granting pensions to widows of deceased revolutionary soldiers"? I have to say: That from the examination which the library of this Department affords, nothing has been discovered in the Statutes or Code of Virginia prohibiting marriage between free negroes or to deprive those who have entered into that relation, of any of the legal rights incident thereto—on the contrary, the rite of marriage is expressly recognized, and consequently legalized between servants [slaves] and between a free person and a servant [slave] (6 Henning, page 83-4) Such being the case, I would recommend a consultation, upon the question submitted with some of the Virginia delegation, and be guided by their opinion. In cases of this kind, the Department would not be disposed to be too technical and rigid. It may not be amiss to call your attention to the Act of Assembly of Virginia, entitled "An Act for regulating ad disciplining the militia," of May 1777" (9 Henning page 267 &c)* "that all free male persons, hired servants apprentices" &c were directed to be enrolled the kind of service in which free mulattoes" were to be employed designated and provision made against the enrolment of slaves, by requiring "any negro or mulatto" to exhibit a certificate of freedom to the recruiting officer before enlistment. It appears also by the same act, that no distinction was made in the pay and bounty offered to such recruits.

Elizabeth died before the pension matter was resolved. It remained closed until 1884 when Elizabeth Merchant, granddaughter of Thomas Mason, filed to receive the pension, back pay, and bounty land due her grandfather. The request was rejected by the pension commissioner William Dudley. He said since Thomas or his wife had not been approved to receive benefits, then the heirs could not receive any.

Years after the death of Elizabeth Mason, her lawyer Charles Statham wrote that it was an injustice to deny Elizabeth's claim for a widow's pension. He believed the rejection was due to the political feelings regarding race and slavery in the 1850s.

Sources: 1. National Archives Pension Application R6993. **2.** *The Rejection of Elizabeth Mason*, Prologue Magazine, Summer 2011, Vol. 43, No. 2.

Saul Matthews

Saul Matthews was born in Virginia and was a slave of Thomas Matthews a General in the Virginia Militia. Saul served as a soldier and a spy for the Continental Army during the Revolutionary War.

As a spy Saul was able to get very valuable information for the Americans. In 1781 the British were in the vicinity of Portsmouth, and Saul was sent by Colonel Parker to the British garrison to gather information. The same night he returned to Colonel Parker and served as a guide to take the Americans to the enemy's garrison.

On one occasion when many people fled to North Carolina Saul was sent to Norfolk to gather important information on the British. Many of the top American officers including Lafayette and Greene said that Saul deserved the applause of his country.

After the war he returned home as a slave to Thomas Matthews. In 1792 Saul petitioned the Virginia legislature for his freedom in consideration for his service during the war. The legislature granted his request and wrote, "In consideration of many very essential services rendered to this Commonwealth during the late war ... full liberty and freedom ... as if he was born free."

Sources: 1. Kaplan & Kaplan, *The Black Presence in the Era of the American Revolution*, page 59. **2.** Davis, *Black Heroes of the American Revolution*, page 57. **3.** Hine & Jenkins, *Manhood: A Reader in U.S. Black Men's History and Masculinity*, Vol. 1. **4.** *The Journal of Negro History*, Vol. XXVII, July 1942, No. 3, pages 271–2.

Prince McLellan

Prince McLellan was born c. 1729 in Guinea, Africa, and he died on July 19, 1829, in Maine. He was brought to Maine as a slave when he was about twelve years old. When his master, William McLellan joined the army during the Revolution, Prince ran off and went to sea.

Prince filed for a pension and he stated in his application dated March 15, 1821,

> The said Prince McLellan served as a seaman on board the Frigate Deane on a cruise to the West Indies under Capt. Nick son, on which cruise we captured several prizes and then returned home to Boston.

The *Deane* was built in Nantes, France under the direction of Benjamin Franklin. The ship was brought to the United States in May 1778. She was named *Hague* in 1782, and taken out of commission in 1783. The *Deane* cruised in the West Indies with the ship *Confederacy* in 1782 and captured four prizes. In April 1782 she captured the cutter HMS *Jackal*.

> Said Frigate was then called The Hague Frigate and I served on board her on another cruise under commodore Manley of 124 or 15 months. We was at Martinique when we first heard of the Peace. We then returned to Boston in the fall of 1783 where I was honorably discharged.

On March 16, 1821, Peter Smith wrote a letter to support the service of Prince when he applied for a pension. Peter stated,

> I served on board the Frigate Deane on a cruise to Barbados on that latitude and about Bermuda under Command of Capt. Nickel son or Nick son, we took a prize called the Regulator of 20 guns and several other prizes and then returned home to Boston. I also testify and say that Prince McLellan served on board said Frigate, said Frigate was then called the Hague Frigate.

A letter in the pension file of Prince is from Hugh McLellan and dated March 22, 1858, or 68. This is many years after the death of Prince. Hugh states that he wrote to the pension bureau hopping that their file would contain the cause of death of Prince. Hugh was collecting facts about his family history. In his letter he wrote,

> He was a slave to a Great Uncle of mine. He was owned by the family from twelve years of age till he was free, and from that time till he died, lived on a small farm given him by said uncle. When he died he was over 100 years of age. While his master was in the army Prince ran off to Portland shipped in Capt. Manley's Colonial Privateered and went on a cruise on his.

After the war Prince was still a slave and returned to the farm of William McLellan. He married a woman named Dinah who died in 1800. He then married Chloe who died in 1827.

When the slaves in Massachusetts were emancipated, his master gave Prince a horse and cart and told him to take what he wanted. Prince and his wife filled the wagon with items they considered most useful and left for the town of Wells. They later left Wells and returned to the farm of Mr. McLellan. His old master gave the couple twelve acres of land, a house, and ten acres of pasture land. Prince and his wife lived out their lives in that house. Prince received a monthly pension of $8 for his service.

Sources: **1.** National Archives Pension Application S37228. **2.** Grundset, *Forgotten Patriots*, National Society of the D.A.R., page 23. **3.** *Celebration of the One Hundred and Fiftieth Anniversary of Gorman, Maine May 26, 1886*, pages 80–2. **4.** Lock, *African American Historic Burial Grounds and Gravesites of New England*, page 91.

Oliver Mitchel

Oliver Mitchel was born in September of 1762 in New York County, New York, and he died on March 10, 1840. He died when he fell out of his boat on the Connecticut River, while returning home after drawing his pension at Hartford. He received a yearly pension of $46.66. He married Anna Wright in 1796 or 97. He stated in his pension application of April 27, 1833,

> He enlisted in the Continental guard stationed at Windsor for the protection and defense of the hospital and army stores there gathered in very large quantities.
> As no building in Windsor was sufficiently large to contain said stores they were distributed into various buildings and continually under the guard of a military formed force Capt. James Hooker of said Windsor had the general charge of said stores.

Sources: **1.** National Archives Pension Application W1632. **2.** Grundset, *Forgotten Patriots*, National Society of the D.A.R., page 284. **3.** *The Connecticut Magazine*, Vol. 15, 1899, page 324.

Ambrose Month

Ambrose Month was born on March 4, 1764, or 65 in Hawsfield, Virginia, and he died on June 8, 1842, in Tennessee. He married Daphne on November 12, 1833. Ambrose received a yearly pension of $80. He stated in his pension application,

> That at the time he was 16 or 17 years of age he was drafted in the said County and was enrolled as a private in the army of the United States into a company commanded by Captain Crane, and Lieutenant Robot. Spill Coleman, that this company was attached to a Regiment commanded by Col. Buckner. Under these officers applicant marched from New Market, the place of rendezvous, to Hobbs hole where they were stationed several months to repel an attack which it was thought the British meditated in Virginia. after remaining here several months applicant marched he thinks under his same captain Crane, though of this he is not certain, to some place in North Carolina he thinks Hillsboro where there were many of the continental troops collected after Gates defeat; here applicant was induced by a call from the officers of the Continental army to join their ranks—and he with several others was enrolled into a company under the command of Captain James Wilson which company he thinks belonged to the 39th Regiment [there was no 39th Regiment, he was probably in the militia since most of the Virginia troops at this battle were in the militia], but of this he is not certain. Applicant does not know whether his name was entered on the rolls of the enlistment or not. He knows however that he voluntarily entered the regular army, was put under the command of the said Captain, was invested with a musket, knapsack, and canteen and done military service as a volunteer soldier. He states that he continued

in the regular army under Gem's. Greene. Marched to Charlotte N. C. and to the various other places, not now recollected which were occupied by that officer, until at the battle of Guilford where he was engaged by the enemy and was wounded in the belly by a bayoneted. after his said wound he was taken from the field of battle and carried to Halifax Va. where he remained a few weeks until his wound got well, when he joined the army again at Mecklenburg courthouse Va. and from there marched to York Va. where he remained doing duty until after the surrender of Cornwallis—shortly after this time he was discharged at Portsmouth Va. and returned home. Applicant states that he is of mixed blood, having part Shawnee and part Negro that he was born free.

The following is an undated letter in the pension file of Ambrose concerning his wife Daphne. The question was raised if she was free or a slave after the death of her husband. If she was a slave then she would not be entitled to a pension. It must have been established that she was free, because she received a pension until her death.

> Pension Agency/ Knoxville Ten. Sir, I have on my pension list Roll, since 23d Decry. 1853, a pensioner, whose name is Daphne Month, widow of Ambrose, private, $80—pr. annum, who has been regularly paid to the 4th Sept. 1856. She is a free Negro, living in this county, & perhaps in the suburbs of this city. And on yesterday, the attorney general for this district, called on me to know whether it was a fact that I was paying a pension by order of the Department to a free Negro; and I answered in the affirmative. The question with the attorney is, whether she, the pensioner, could, under any act of Congress, be entitled to a pension, being a slave until sometime after the death of her said husband Ambrose. Her case was brought to his notice by taking a deposition of some gentleman in relation to the estate of the former Mistress and owner of said pensioner. At the close of our conversation on the subject I promised the attorney that I would state the case to you and get your opinion on the legality of the pension. Neither the attorney nor I knows anything of the evidence by which the pensioner's claim was established, nor whether she was represented to the Department as indeed and truth she is, a free Negro of full blood. Your early attention to this subject will be an obligement to the attorney gen. and information to myself which will be thankfully received. Isaac Lewis Pension Agent

Daphne's last pension payment was on September 4, 1860. When the Civil War began on April 12, 1861, pension payments were suspended to those receiving a pension living in insurrectionary states. After the war to have the pension reinstated, the pensioner had to swear an oath of allegiance and swear that they did not participate or show sympathy to the south during the war. Daphney died on July 22, 1864.

Sources: 1. National Archives Pension Application W7477. **2.** Grundset, *Forgotten Patriots, National Society of the D.A.R.,* page 523.

Abraham Moore

Abraham Moore was born in October of 1738 in Maryland. He may have been a slave owned by Augustine Moore, or he may have worked for him. Abraham served a total of eight months and twenty-eight days in the militia, and he received a yearly pension of $29.76. He stated in his pension application,

> In the year 1751 he was living with one Augustine Moore in Fayette County Pennsylvania. The said Augustine Moore was drafted in the militia to go on an expedition to the west against the Indians. That this declarant went out as the *substitute* of said Augustine Moore, in the company of militia commanded by Captain George (or William) Fox in the Regiment commanded by Colonel Thomas Giddes in the Brigade of General Broadhead.
>
> That he marched with said company from the town of Uniontown and marched acrossed the Ohio River at the Mingo Bottom where there was then a Black house from thence he marched through the wilderness to wapatamika in said state of Ohio where they arrived in the month of June in said year 1781. Here the American troops attacked the Indians, and defeated them. Several Indians were killed and several taken prisoner in this expedition. The declarant was wounded by a ball passing through his arm. Captain Fox was wounded in the breast.
>
> Shortly after this engagement the company returned to Uniontown. Their return was in the year 1781. Declarant was absent on this expedition *two weeks* was discharged at Uniontown.
>
> In the fall of the same year (1781) the Indians again became troublesome on the frontier settlements and then said Augustine Moore was again drafted in the Pennsylvania Militia in an expedition against the Indians, and this declarant again entered the service as a substitute for said Moore. He was under the command of Capt. Edward Stewart in this expedition, the aforesaid Col. Giddes still commanding the regiment. He was marched from Uniontown to what is now called Holliday's __?__ on the Ohio River and crossing the Ohio at that place, the troops proceeded through the wilderness to the Muskingum river, where they met and engaged with a body of Indians, defeated them, and returned to Uniontown. Declarant was absent on the expedition *six weeks*.
>
> The following spring (1782) the Indians committed some murders and another draft was made from the Pennsylvania Militia to go out against the Indians, and this declarant again entered the service as a substitute for Augustine Moore in the company of Pennsylvania Militia commanded by Capt. Sharpe. We marched from Uniontown, crossed the Ohio River, at the mouth of short creek, and proceeded on to Stillwater and had an engagement with a body of Indians who were defeated and routed and the company returned to Uniontown.
>
> In the spring of 1783 Augustine Moore was again drafted and this declarant was his substitute. The company acted in the capacity of scouts and was stationed at a Black house, at what is now called Beach Bottom in Brock County, Virginia.

Sources: **1.** National Archives Pension Application S2855. **2.** Grundset, *Forgotten Patriots, National Society of the D.A.R.*, page 413.

Mark Murray

Mark Murray was born c. 1755 in North Carolina. He had two sons at the Battle of New Orleans during the War of 1812. He stated in his pension application why it took him so long to apply. Mark had placed the information in the hands of Colonel Dew, who gave the papers to his brother-in-law William

Sypert, a lawyer. William made all the necessary proofs for the application, but for some reason he did not send the papers to Washington for eight or ten years.

When Mark obtained the original papers he gave them to another lawyer named Jordan Stokes. Stokes made the papers out new, and he sent them to the court but failed to date them. They were sent to Washington not completed and were later sent back. This is the statement Mark made on April 21, 1849, when he again filed for his pension based on six months and fifteen days service,

> That he entered the Service of the United States on the last Saturday being the 29th day of April 1780 in the following manner to wit he volunteered as a private soldier under Captain Nathan Mayo in Martin County North Carolina he lived in Halifax but was invoted to go to a Muster over the line by his neighbors Thomas Weathersby, William O'Cain and Jonathan Drake they agreed all for to mess together and volunteer to join General Gates who was then stationed in South Carolina. There Colonel's name was Benjamin Sowel and William Brukle was there ___?___ Colonel's name their Ensign's name was James Cooper and their ___?___ name was Benjamin Whitley they were mustered into service at a place called hogstown on Roanoke but afterwards altered to Williamstown Colonel Long was Sometime furnishing arms which he finally did he Colonel lived close to Enfield (Halifax Court house) to which place they had marched leaving Scotland Neck race ground and reached Colonel Long's on the 9th May following under orders which was given eight days previous they were three Companies one from Halifax one from Martin and one from Bertie Counties they were then marched to Chatham Courthouse where they met General Sumner with the troops of North Carolina. They stayed there but a few days before they were marched in the direction of South Carolina to meet with the General Gates who was stationed near Camden crossed Deep River at Ramsey's Mills next to Coles bridge on drowning Creek thence to Pee Dee] to the long bluff. They would have Joined Gates but the battle took place and they could not reach in time and orders was then to march back this was the battle called Gates defeat and orders were then given to join General Sumter But before they could join Sumter orders were received to join General Green and Sumter having been used up in a battle they were in neither of these engagements they were then Stationed at the Shallow ford on the Yadkin and waited with expectation the British Army finding they would not cross there they marched to Salisbury where they were Stationed Some time. At the last place General Sumner went home and the troops were then placed under General Butler when the three months of the first service was out they were on Pedee and they volunteered again for six three months on account there was no relief as they were called at that time which was there was no new soldiers come to fill up their place and they could not be spared Captain Mayo and Lieutenant Whitley took sick were sent for by carriages and went home. Their places were filled by Captain Richard Cooper was still the efficient officer. They were again marched from Salisbury to Charlotte but finding they could not stand before the Main Army of the British they retreated on the other side of the Yadkin about this time the Virginia troops had a battle with the Tories near the Moravian town they got there time enough to see the last of it they were then placed under General Green about some time in October of the same year and were finally discharged at Salisbury on the 15th day of November 1780 by General Butler he returned home and gave his discharge to his father who kept it and Declarant does not know what has become of it he

thus served 6 months and 15 days in two three-months tours rather continued in service and 15 days over on account that they were held in service until new soldiers had arrived.

Mark's first pension statement was made on May 5, 1845. It contained a briefer version of the statement above and was dated April 21, 1849. The first statement did have some unusual information in it about an incident just before the regiment received news of Gates' Defeat. Mark described a "show battle" that was left out of other pension statements,

> The Company drew the arms and were then marched to Chatham Courthouse then head quarters in that part of the State, at which place General Sumner had the command, and from this point they were marched with the view of joining the Army under the command of General Gates; intending to cross the Big Pedee at the Long Bluff—the Army arrived at the Big Pedee on Saturday evening the day of the month not recollected, and there encamped for the night, intending to cross the next morning, that the urgent request of some gentlemen in the neighborhood, the General agreed to entertain them on the next day Sunday, with a show-battle. So in the next day a large crowd came in composed of ladies and gentlemen, and the show-battle was regularly fought—no damage done except a fine horse, ridden by Major Knight, was killed. On Sunday night the news of General Gates defeat came to General Sumner by some Gates's *flying soldiers*. General Sumner then retreated to Cole's Bridge on Drowning Creek—at this place orders were received for General Sumner to march and join General Sumter but at the end of two or three days march, they heard that Sumter was defeated. They then retreated to Ramsey's Mills upon Deep River, from that point they marched to Salisbury, from Salisbury to Charlotte, from Charlotte to a point on the Catawba River below where the British Army was stationed—here the British stole a march on us and we forced to retreat—the pursuit continued for 3 days and nights—we crossed the Yadkin River at the Shallow Ford in boats, and that night there fell a very heavy rain by which the march of the British Army was stoped. Each Army lay several days in this position, when a reinforcement came to the assistance of the Americans, and Genl Green then took the command, if the applicant recollects correctly,—the British retreated and were pursued by the American Army a day and a half, or two days, where each Army stationed, and at this point this applicant was regularly discharged.

On September 18, 1851, Mark amended his previous pension statement, which contained information about his family and why he enlisted,

> That his Great Grandmother came from Ireland and had to be Sold for her passage and his parents always told him a gentleman by the name of Colonel Walk [could by Walk] bought her She was free and fair Skinned and after serving out her passage Mancy married a man a had children by a Negro which accounts for his being mixed blooded. When the British took Charlestown His father came to him where he was mauling rails in the new ground and told him Mark I have bad news to tell you the British has taken Charlestown you must go and fight for your country. You are a free man and you Serve your country and never do you return unless you get an honorable discharge and bring it to me. It was in the spring of the year say about March.

Later, in the same letter he described the problems that faced the poor and ignorant troops that were cheated by land speculators. After the war many of the soldiers were given a bounty paper that was good for sixty or more acres of land. Greedy speculators took advantage of many soldiers, both black and white, and bought for just a few dollars their bounty papers or papers promising to pay for time served.

> When the war of the Revolution was over a great many speculators were through the Country who told Declarant and others "boys I am sorry for you, you will never get nothing," they bought up the claims of the Soldiers. There was one James Alsbrook who bought affiant's claims to wages or pay for his services in one or 2 of his tours for one dollar. There was one other the Sherief who agreed to pay his taxes for one year or two years for another tour of service and so affiant got nothing for he got his living by hard labor could only read his Bible but could not write.

When Mark first applied for his pension it was rejected for lack of proof of service. He had numerous comrades and neighbors write on his behalf about his service. One letter was sent by Elizabeth Pope who was a friend of Mark,

> I knew Mark Murry he lived in Halifax County North Carolina. The family lived about three miles from me in time of the Revolution. They lived across deep Creek a very marshy Creek and was difficult to get over. Mark and his wife used to cross to go to meetings on fishing Creek. They were very respectable for coloured people the old lady Mark's mother was a great midwife was sent for a great deal among the most Respectable people I know he was out in the Service in the war of the Revolution. I am certain he served nine months but I cannot say whether him three months tours or nine months but he was absent in the Service from early in the spring to the winter following.

Another interesting letter was sent by Jesse Grimes who said he had known Mark for thirty years. The letter is dated July 27, 1853,

> Jesse Grimes of Wilson County, Tenn., aged 64, who testifies that he was born in NC; has lived in Wilson County some 30 years; has known Mark Murray ever since he (Grimes) was born near Murray in NC; has frequently heard Murray talk with his fellow soldiers in the Revolution, Jethro Harrell, James Harrell, Joel Harrell, Henry Kent, Jesse Rawls and William Rawls, all of whom were in the same company as Murray. "...Have been with them all when I was a boy at log-rollings & house raisings & have heard them joke one another about their campaign exploits. Henry Kent was a small man, & they were accustomed to run a joke upon, saying that he wished to get behind Mark, if they should get into a battle, & Mark declared that he would be breastworks for no man. Mark Murray is now somewhere in the neighborhood of 100 years of age, according to witness's understanding of these years. He has been a man of irreproachable character, a man whose veracity & honesty I have never heard anyone impugn. I live near him now. He is unable to work. His family assists in taking care of him, are all poor. He does not travel about much now. He is well thought of by his neighbors.

The pension bureau first rejected the pension claim, because there was lack of proof of service. After many people wrote testifying to his service, the bureau gave a new reason for the rejection. On May 15, 1854, a new rejection letter was sent to Mark. It stated that Mark's first statement in September 1851 said he entered the service at the insistence of his father after the British had taken Charlestown. The letter went on to say that Charlestown was taken on May 12, 1780, and Mark said that he enlisted on May 9th or right after the taking of Charlestown. So the news could not have reached Mark for several weeks. This would mean that he served less than six months and could not receive a pension.

The bureau ignored the letters from others stating that Mark had served over six months. Also, Mark was pushing 100 years old, and his memory of dates could have been somewhat vague. Did the fact that Mark was a black man play a part in the bureau's decision? At this time tensions were building toward a civil war which could have affected fairness.

Sources: 1. National Archives Pension Application R7523. **2.** Grundset, *Forgotten Patriots, National Society of the D.A.R.,* page 523.

Peter Nash

Peter Nash died on January 8, 1825. When he and Lydia were married on September 10, 1785, by Congregational minister Hezekial Ripley, they were both slaves. Lydia was a slave owned by Doctor Jesub, and Peter was owned by Captain Thomas Nash. Lydia applied for a widow's pension on September 18, 1851, and stated,

> That in the early part of the Revolutionary War said Peter, being a slave of Captain Thomas Nash who commanded a company of Coast Guard, went out with and attended Capt. Nash as a waiter. That said Peter served as a force and in all a little more than three years. That said company had a cannon or field piece & when that was in use that said Peter was attached to that & when not carried a musket. That said Peter was in the skirmish with the enemy at Compo in Said Fairfield where one Wakeman when he was shot in the head by a bullet—that Peter stood by the side of Wakeman when he was killed & that said Wakeman's cap was given to Peter & he afterward wore it.

Lydia's application was rejected, because Peter was a slave while he served as a waiter and was not entitled to a pension. There is no record indicating if or when Peter was freed.

Sources: 1. National Archives Pension Application R7558. **2.** Grundset, *Forgotten Patriots, National Society of the D.A.R.,* page 285.

Isaac Perkins

Isaac Perkins was born free in 1761 in Craven County, North Carolina, and he died there on May 23, 1830. He received a yearly pension of $96 for his service. He stated in his application on June 9, 1818,

> That he enlisted as a private soldier in the tenth North Carolina Regiment in the Continental line in the year One thousand seven hundred and seventy seven, in the Company

commanded by Captain Silas Sears Stevenson, was marched to Valley Forge in Pennsylvania, where the tenth Regiment was distributed & deponent passed into the Second Regiment and into the Company commanded by Captain Clement Hall. he served in that Regiment in its northern Campaign, marched with it to South Carolina and was taken prisoner at Charleston. he escaped from the enemy, returned to North Carolina & served until peace in the militia of the State. His whole service in the Continental line of the State of North Carolina against the Common Enemy exceeded three years.

When Isaac enlisted in the 10th North Carolina Regiment he was marched to Valley Forge. The regiment had been in Battles at Germantown and Brandywine and was depleted of manpower. The men that were left in the 10th Regiment were placed in the 2nd Regiment. This regiment fought at the Battle of Monmouth in June 1778, and it was then transferred to the Southern Department. In May 1780 the regiment was captured by the British at Charlestown.

Several of Isaac's neighbors wrote a letter in his support for a pension. They said in the letter, "though a man of Colour we do believe him to be too honest in principal to practice anything like a frawd." In addition to his pension, Isaac also received a 274 acre bounty land warrant. He is listed in the 1790 census for Craven County as a "free Negro" with a family of two.

Sources: 1. 1820 Federal Census. **2.** National Archives Pension Application S41953. **3.** Salter, *Combat Multipliers: African-American Soldiers in Four Wars*, page 15.

Nimrod Perkins

Nimrod Perkins was born c. 1760 as a freeman in Virginia, and he received a yearly pension of $80 for his service. He stated in his pension application on July 31, 1832,

> He enlisted as Drummer on board the Diligence Gally, in the service of Virginia in the Revolutionary war in 1777 & continued on board until she was laid up 1781 & that he was in board & in the service more than three years, that when he entered Johannas Watson [sic: Johannes Watson] was Captain, Richard Parker [pension application R81] was 1st Lieutenant & Jesse Cannon [R19] 2nd Lieutenant, that he was born in the County of Accomack, was a resident in that county when he was enlisted & when discharged & never has been a Resident of any other County, that he has received a Virginia Military Land warrant for one Hundred acres, & scrip for the same, for the said service.

Nimrod received a Virginia Military Land Warrant for 100 acres, and in 1830 he was granted 666 acres and in 1832 a pension. Elcanah Andrews stated that he and Perkins sailed together in the Chesapeake Bay and Atlantic Ocean on the vessels *Diligence* and *Accomack*. Andrews also said that they were laid up in the cold winter of 1779–80 when Chesapeake Bay was frozen.

Sources: 1. National Archives Pension Application S5904. **2.** *The Journal of Negro History Vol. XXVII*, July 1942, No. 3, page 279.

Jesse Peters

Jesse Peters was born c. 1764 in Virginia. Jesse's pension was rejected, because it needed further proof. He stated in his pension application of May 25, 1835,

> That he enlisted in the Service of the United States in the year 1780 under Captain John Lucas in the aforesaid County of Surry and remained in the said County about Seven Weeks, when he marched to a place Called Mackies Mills and was stationed there about the same length of time from thence he Marched to Brunswick Courthouse where he was also stationed a short time, from there he marched to South Carolina and was put under the command of Captain Morgan, Colo. Campbell and Gen'l. Nath'l Green at the battle at Guildford Courthouse was in the battle at Campden, when the british attacked Gen. Green and cause him to retreat, he was also in the battle near the Eutaw Spring and well recollects that Colo. Campbell was killed in said engagement. he was after the Battle stationed at the high hills of the Santee, where they rec'd information of York Town having been taken by the Americans, that from the high hills of Santee he went with Captain Morgan (who was wounded in the hip) to Cumberland Courthouse at which place the said Morgan gave him a discharge.

At the Battle of Eutaw Springs on September 8, 1781, Jesse was part of 350 Virginia Continentals led by Lt. Colonel Richard Campbell. The day of the battle was very hot, and Jesse and his comrades were short of rations and had little rest. The Virginia troops took the right flank, and when they took the British by surprise the British left their uneaten breakfast as they ran for the woods. When the hungry American troops entered the camp, they stopped to eat the abandoned breakfast rather than chase after the British.

The British regrouped and attacked the American troops. For four hours the two sides fought in the heat and sometimes fighting hand-to-hand. One witness described the battle by saying, "Blood ran ankle deep in some places." Finally, both armies decided they had enough and they broke off the fight. During the battle Colonel Campbell was shot in the chest and was carried from the battlefield.

After the battle American Major Pendleton visited the wounded Colonel Campbell. The Colonel asked Pendleton, "Who had gained the battle?" Pendleton replied, "We have completely defeated the enemy." Colonel Campbell replied, "Then I die content." The Colonel died shortly after that.

Sources: **1.** National Archives Pension Application R 8146. **2.** Tomes, *Battles of America by Sea and Land Vol. 1*, pages 886 & 889. **3.** *The Southern Review*, Vol. 1, 1828, page 106.

Salem Poor

Salem Poor was born a slave c. 1747 in Salem, Massachusetts. It is believed that he was purchased as an infant as part of a dowry. According to legend one of the grandmothers of the bride or groom brought the baby from Salem to

Andover on horseback. Salem purchased his freedom in 1769 from John Poor for twenty-seven pounds, which is about $5,600 in today's money. This was about a year's salary for the average man, so Salem must have saved for many years.

In August of 1771 Salem married Nancy Parker, who was a servant for Captain James Parker. They had a boy named Jonas who was baptized on September 29, 1776, in the church. In 1780 he married his second wife, a window by the name of Mary Twing, who was described as a "free negro." Salem and Mary moved to Providence, and according to city records they were asked to leave because they could not support themselves.

The marriage ended in 1785, and Salem placed an ad in the Boston Gazette to disavow the debts of his wife. The ad said, "forewarn all Persons from trusting Mary." Salem married a third time to Sarah Stevens in 1787. He married a fourth time in 1801 and died the next year on February 5, 1802.

In 1775 Salem enlisted in Captain Samuel Johnsons' 5th Regiment under Colonel James Frye. On June 16, 1775, the Regiment marched from Cambridge to Charlestown. At Charlestown Salem and the rest of the Americans built fortifications on Breed's Hill and awaited the British. After the third British assault the Americans began to retreat from their fortifications. During the retreat British Lieutenant Colonel James Abercrombie, who commanded an elite group of grenadiers, "mount a redoubt and wave his arms in triumph." At that moment Salem shot the British officer. The officer was carried from the battlefield and taken to a hospital, where he died a week later.

Salem's gallantry at the Battle of Bunker Hill was noted by fourteen officers, which included Colonel Prescott. Salem was cited for heroism, and the General Court of Massachusetts made the following statement,

> The Reward due to so great and Distinguished a Character. The Subscribers beg leave to Report to your Honorable. House (Which We do in justice to the Character of so Brave a man) that under Our Own observation, we declare that A Negro Man Called Salem Poor of Col. Fryes Regiment, Capt. Ames. Company in the late Battle of Charleston, behaved like an Experienced Officer, as Well as an Excellent Soldier, to Set forth Particulars of his Conduct would be Tedious, We Would Only beg leave to say in the Person of this Negro Centers a Brave & gallant Soldier.

Salem continued to serve in the army. In 1776 he served in upstate New York under General Arnold. He enlisted for three years in the continental Army in 1777 and was at Saratoga. In the winter of 1777–78 he was at Valley Forge, and he fought in the Battle of White Plains. In 1779 he was stationed at Providence, Rhode Island, and he was discharged in 1780.

Sources: 1. Smith, *Notable Black Men, Book II.* **2.** Finkleman, *Encyclopedia of African American History, 1619–1895*, page 526. **3.** Bailey, *Historical Sketches of Andover*, pages

323–4. **4.** Pulsifer & Burgoyne, *Battle of Bunker Hill, Comp. from Authentic Sources,* 1872, page 58.

Jabez Pottage

Jabez Pottage was born c. 1745 in Connecticut. He received a yearly pension of $96, and he stated in his pension application,

> He enlisted into the Revolutionary War in the year 1775 and in Col. Ethan Allen's Regiment assisted in taking Skenesboro, Ticonderoga and Crown Point & served against the common enemy more than nine months & was then dismissed.

In late April 1775 Ethan Allen received a request from the Connecticut militia for assistance in capturing Fort Ticonderoga. In May Jabez and other militiamen from Connecticut joined with Ethan Allen's men who left on an expedition to capture the fort. On the 10th of May Allen's men and some troops led by Benedict Arnold captured Fort Ticonderoga. Included in the supplies they captured were 111 canons, of which twenty-nine were sent to Boston. The next day they captured a small British garrison at Crown Point and some small boats at Skenesboro.

> In the Spring of 1776 he enlisted into a Company commanded by Capt. Sharp in Connecticut and again served at the north under the command of Genl Arnold about nine months, and was then dismissed & soon after enlisted for a short time and went to providence in Rhode Island under the command of General Spencer and at Providence aforesaid in the spring of 1777 he again enlisted a private soldier for three years into the Continental Army in a company commanded by Capt. Vine ___?___ in Col. Herman Swifts Regiment in the Connecticut Line of the American Army.

Jabez enlisted in the 7th Connecticut Regiment commanded by Colonel Swift from January 1, 1777, to January 1, 1781. Jabez may have fought at the Battles of Brandywine and Germantown in 1777. After spending the winter at Valley Forge he fought at the Battle of Monmouth in June of 1778. In this battle Jabez's Regiment was on the right wing of the American Army under the command of General Nathanael Greene.

> During the said three years he was in several skirmishes & in the battle of Monmouth, and afterwards while in a scouting party near Kings bridge he was taken prisoner by the enemy & carried into New York and there kept in the sugar house [prison] four months & two days and was then exchanged and again joined said company & served out the whole term of three years.
>
> He also declares that in the Spring of 1781 he again enlisted at Pomfect in the company commanded by Capt. Benjamin Hoglen in Col. Sheldens Regiment of light horses. Benjamin Tallmadge Esq, being a Major in the Regiment and he enlisted into the last mentioned company & regiment for another term of three years. He served until 14 June, 1783.

Jabez enlisted in the 2nd Continental Light Dragoons under Colonel Elisha Sheldon. They were sometimes called "Washington's Eyes" because of their spy work. Major Tallmadge was the chief intelligence officer for Washington. Tallmadge organized the famous Culper Spy Ring.

Sources: 1. National Archives Pension Application S36241. **2.** Grundset, *Forgotten Patriots, National Society of the D.A.R.*, page 287.

Caesar Prutt

Caesar Prutt was born in June of 1727 in Hadley, Massachusetts. His mother, father, and six brothers and sisters were slaves owned by Parson Isaac Chauncey of Hadley. The Parson gave a slave to each of his married daughters and two sons. Caesar was given to Josiah Chauncey.

The Chauncey brothers were strong supporters of the Tories. Caesar and his master left to fight in the French and Indian Wars in 1758. Caesar was sent to enlist in Captain Elisha Pomeroy's Company in Colonel Israel Williams' Regiment.

When the Revolutionary War began, Caesar must have run off to join the American cause. Since his master was a Tory supporter, Caesar would not have been allowed to join the American Army. Caesar enlisted on May 8, 1775, for eight months in the company of Captain Reuben Dickinson in Colonel Benjamin Woodbridge's 25th Regiment.

Woodbridge's Regiment arrived at Bunker Hill just before the battle began. Caesar and the Massachusetts men were stationed on the right flank of the American defenders. It was reported that they fought well and covered the retreat of the Continental Army when the hill was taken by the British. Caesar enlisted in Colonel Paul Dudley Sargent's Regiment in December of 1775, and in 1777 he enlisted in the same regiment for three years.

In April of 1801 it was noted in the Amherst annual town meeting that Caesar, now the town pauper, was auctioned off to Asa Smith for $1.00 a week. Each year Caesar is brought before the town meeting and auctioned off. The last time he was auctioned off was in the year 1807 for $65 for that year. The person that won the bid in the auction was responsible for feeding and clothing Caesar. In return Caesar would do small chores.

Sources: 1. Walker, *Historic Hadley, A Story of the Making of a Famous Massachusetts Town*, pages 49–51. **2.** *Massachusetts Soldiers and Sailors of the Revolutionary War*. **3.** Carpenter, *The History of the Town of Amherst, Massachusetts*. **4.** *History of the Connecticut Valley in Massachusetts*, page 239.

Kenaz Ralls

Kenaz Ralls was a slave born c. 1763 in Stafford County, Virginia. He was probably one of the few slaves in Virginia that could read and write. He received a yearly pension of $20 for his service. He stated in his pension application on March 29, 1833,

> About the first of March 1781 two companies of militia were called out from Prince William County under Captains Brent and Warren, he was hired by Benjamin Harrison of Prince William County to take place of his overseer Walter Stallard who belonged to Captain Warren's Company—that Mr. Harrison let him a horse and he overtook the Companies low Fredericksburg Captain Warren received him as a substitute for Stallard, and Stallard returned home with Mr. Harrison's horse, when he overtook the troops, there were 4 or 5 Companies of Militia, and Captain Coleman (longing as he believes to the Continental Army) with two pieces of brass cannon. In Warren's Company, Charles Ewell was Lieutenant and Charles Atwell Ensign. He does not remember any Officer higher than Captain. They marched through New Kent and King William to Williamsburg and quartered in the Governor's Palace. While in Williamsburg, he saw Colonel Churchill of Fauquier, who had command over Militia. After having been in Williamsburg about a week, intelligence arrived that the British were in James River, in the militia were marched to the halfway house between Hampton and Williamsburg, and remained a few days—thence they returned to Williamsburg, and quartered in the barracks at the lower end of the Town. They remained there a few days, until they were driven out by the British Army. The 1st night the militia retreated six miles, and the next day took up the line of march for Richmond. When they arrived at Richmond, they quartered at the rope walks, at the lower end of the Town. They remained there for about two weeks. The British appearing in the River the Baggage Wagons under charge of Sergeant White with a group of whom I was one retired to the high grounds above Richmond. From this position, this affiant saw the British march into Manchester and burn the warehouses. A short time after this he returned home with Sergeant White & two others having been out more than three months. He does not remember to have received any discharge.

On January 5, 1781, British troops under the command of the traitor Benedict Arnold marched into Manchester, which was a part of Richmond, Virginia. Arnold wrote to Governor Jefferson that if he was allowed to move the city's supplies of tobacco and military equipment, he would leave Richmond unharmed. Jefferson was angry and refused to cooperate with the traitor.

The reply from Jefferson then angered Arnold, and he ordered his men to burn Richmond. The British troops burned buildings and homes, and then they ransacked the city.

> 2nd Tour. In the latter part of July 1781, he marched from Falmouth in a company of militia from Stafford County, commanded by Captain William Harding, Joseph Combs Lieutenant (the Ensign forgotten) several other companies assembled at, and marched for the same place William Philips and James Gerrard were the Colonels, Gregg was Major and William Ballard the adjutant. The whole proceeded to the lower part of the State, and when the siege of York commence, the company of Captain Harding was marched and posted on a rising ground before the Town. Captain Harding returned home, and the company was commanded by William Ballard the adjutant. He worked in the entrenchments about two reliefs—were appointed sergeant, and with twenty men and a Lieutenant or Ensign was sent on a relief party. We marched to an Oak growth, and procured fascincs and __?__ for

the use of the besieging Army. He was taken sick in days before the surrender of Cornwallis. Before he recovered the Army marched off. He was not mustered afterwards. His term of service expired before his recovery.

    He did not get a discharge, and does not believe that an officer was left to do that duty. He was absent from home in the second tour considerably more than three months. He remembers Major Southall of the regular Army and General Lincoln. After returning from York—town he thinks in the month of December 1781—he met the third division of the British Prisoners near Falmouth in Stafford County, Virginia, on their way to Winchester Barracks. They numbered about one hundred guarded by a Lieutenant and about thirty men. He then took the place of Thomas Weston of the guard, and assisted in conducting those prisoners through Fauquier County to the barracks near Winchester, and was absent from home in that service from 18 to 19 days.

A letter supporting the service of Kenaz was made by Henry McInteer on February 16, 1833,

> That he is well acquainted with Kenaz Ralls of the County of Fauquier, who is about to apply to the War Department of the United States for a pension, that he has known the said Ralls upwards of fifty years, and believes him to be about seventy years of age, that the said Rawls went with him the said McInteer to the siege of York, during the Revolutionary War. We went from Stafford County under command of Captain William Harding, Regiment being under the command of Colonel William Phillips, when we arrived at York, we were ordered to stack our arms and sit down. In a little _____?_____ enemy commenced a fire of cannon at us, one ball struck a stack of arms to my right, and took off a man's thigh, stuck a bayonet through another about the groin, and a ramrod flew out and struck another across the forehead and wounded him. That it was understood and believed that the said Rawls had been in service before.

Sources: 1. National Archives Pension Application S18561. **2.** Grundset, *Forgotten Patriots, National Society of the D.A.R.,* page 525.

Jack Randall

    Jack Randall was born c. 1754, and he received a monthly pension of $8 for his service. He stated in his pension application dated April 17, 1819,

> Sometime in the Spring of the year 1778 I believe, volunteered in the state of Rhode Island, I was duly enlisted in the service of the United States for during the war and belonged to the Regiment of *Blacks* raised in the state of Rhode Island Commanded by Col. Green. I obtained my emancipation from slavery having been previously a slave belonging to Richard Lord of Lyme in the State of Connecticut.

    Jack belonged to the 1st Rhode Island Regiment under the command of Colonel Christopher Greene. Colonel Greene was given the command of the Regiment on January 1, 1777. If Jack had enlisted in the spring of 1778 and stayed until the end of the war, he would have taken part in the New York campaign, the Battle of Red Bank, Battle of Rhode Island, and the Siege at Yorktown.

In 1778 Rhode Island was having trouble recruiting enough soldiers to meet quotas set by Congress. On the 14th of February the Rhode Island Legislature voted to allow the enlistment of people of color. Slaves that were accepted would be given their freedom upon the end of their enlistment, and their masters would be compensated by the state government in an amount equal to the slave's fair market value.

Sources: **1.** National Archives Pension Application S35593. **2.** Grundset, *Forgotten Patriots, National Society of the D.A.R.,* page 227.

Robert Randall

Robert Randall was born c. 1758, and he died on May 24, 1823, in Hanover, New Hampshire. His pension claim lists several officers that are not found on any military rolls, which may suggest that the claim is fraudulent. His claim was accepted, and he received a monthly sum of $8 for his service. He stated in his claim dated May 2, 1818,

> That he the said Robert Randall enlisted in the Revolutionary Army in the Virginia line, in the State of Virginia in the company commanded by Lemuel Rogers of the continental establishment; that he continued to serve in the said corps, or in the service of the United States for more than four years, when he was discharged from service and received a written evidence thereof but lost the same when afterwards a prisoner to the Indians and that he is in reduced circumstances, and stands in need of the assistance of his country for support; and that he has no other evidence now in his power of his said services.
>
> I Robert Randall of Hanover in the County of Grafton & State of New Hampshire a free black man of the age of sixty years testify & declare that I served as a soldier in the revolutionary war betwixt the United States of America & Great Britain for more than four years in the whole, on the Continental establishment. I enlisted in Fairfax County in Virginia under Lim'l. Rogers who brought me to Rhode Island where I joined the Regiment under Col. Patterson under the command of Gen'l. Gandlebuss [& remained under his command for the term of two years, in which time I march'd to Fort Stanwix by order of Gen'l. Clinton, & was confined six months in the Hospital at Albany, by reason of a wound I received in my arm from a musket shot—after which (having served out my time) I had a discharge from Col. Patterson at Albany & went home to Virginia. Afterwards, I enlisted under one Capt. Richardson & with a great number of other Soldiers was put on board of a 70 Gun Frigate commanded by Capt. __?__ at Williamsburgh in Virginia, & we were the next day taken by the British, & taken to the Isle of Wight & there detained six months. We were then brought by the British to York Town & came to the forks of James River, where I ran away from them, intending to go home; but met Capt. Sharpe & inlisted under him & went again into the service & remained about two months when we were dismiss'd by Col. Lines. The money I received for my wages would not bring hardly anything & I about lost the whole of it. Afterwards I went to the westward to get the land granted to me as a Soldier, when I was taken by the Indians between Limestone & Fort Wheeling on the Ohio & kept as a prisoner eighteen months. I then run away from them & by way of Detroit went to Montreal & from there to the State of New hampshire about twenty five years since, & whilst with the Indians I lost my discharge.

Sources: **1.** National Archives Pension Application S45165. **2.** Grundset, *Forgotten Patriots*, National Society of the D.A.R., page 526.

Joseph Ranger

Joseph Ranger was born c. 1760 and served for nine years, which was longer than any other black seaman in the war. He received a yearly pension of $96 from the government, and the state of Virginia gave him 100 acres of land for his service. He stated in his pension application dated October 25, 1832,

> That he the said Ranger entered the service of the State of Virginia in the Revolutionary war to wit as a private or seaman in the navy of said State, that he said Ranger resided at the time of his entering said service in the county of Northumberland in the State aforesaid, that he said Ranger entered the service aforesaid early in the war of the Revolution, the ___?___ time he cannot recollect, though he thinks in early part of the year in which Independence was declared that he said Ranger entered first on board the Hero Gallery [Galley] commanded by Capt. John Thomas on board of which he continued but a short time, to the best of his recollection about three months, when the said Ranger was transfered to the ship Dragon of the Virginia Navy aforesaid an armed vessel of the same, that he said Ranger continued on board said ship about four years, that said ship was commanded while said Ranger was on board, first by Capt. Eliazer Callender and then by Capt. Edward Travis of Williamsburg, that Thomas Chandler was Lieutenant of said ship. that Edward Eskridge was a midshipman of the same. that he recollects also William Booth, who was a pilot. That a Joseph or Josiah Saunders was also a lieutenant of the same. That said Ranger was transferred from said ship Dragon to the Brig Jefferson of fifteen guns. The Dragon having been converted into a fire ship. That Lt Chandler was also turned over from the Dragon to the command of the Jefferson, that the said Ranger served on board of said Brig Jefferson about 12 months, when she was blown up by the enemy at a place called Osborne's on James River that the said Ranger was lastly turned over to the Boat Patriot about 5 or 6 months before the siege of York. That in an engagement near Newport news on James River the crew of the Patriot was taken prisoners and confined until after the siege of York, when he said Ranger with other prisoners was discharged.

Sources: **1.** National Archives Pension Application S7352. **2.** *The Crisis*, Feb. 1976, page 69.

Thomas Ray

Thomas Ray was born a free man on October 11, 1752, and he died on March 21, 1807, in Rhode Island. He married Sarah on the Sunday after Christmas in 1776. They were married at her uncle's house by Joseph Clark the Justice of the Peace. When she applied for a widow's pension she had people send letters to the bureau testifying to the fact that they were married. She must have been a beautiful bride, because Barney Lisson stated in his letter dated January 6, 1840,

He well remembers when said Thomas brought his bride home to his, said Thomas' Mother's house, that there was much talk in the neighborhood about the Bride, and how handsomely the Bride was dressed as she lived in Col. Bennets family and dressed in a style better than was used in the country at that time; and despondent further says that he and many others went to see the said Thomas, and his Bride when they came to said Thomas' house, that they remained there that night, & the next day the wedding party went to Mr. Joseph Babcock's and spent the day.

Thomas received a yearly pension of $50, and he stated in his pension application,

He first enlisted in Providence in the month of March 1777 as a private in the Artillery Company commanded by Capt. Ebenezer Adam Regiment commanded by Col. Elliot— first quartered about two weeks in the college at Providence, employed in making cartiages. Afterwards removed to Darwick Neck and was then stationed with our field pieces in the Battery, and continued through the spring and summer—he was then ordered in said company in September to go to Rhode Island in Spencer's Expedition. First marched to Tiverton and then quartered a short time to wait further orders, thence marched to Sakannet in Little Comptom and afterwards returned to Tiverton and stationed in Fort Barton, and then served until March 1778, when his time expired making one year.

Fort Barton was a defensive post that overlooked the main ferry crossing between Tiverton and Aquidneck Island. It was the crossing point for American troops during the Battle of Rhode Island in 1778.

Spencer's Expedition was a secret one against the British in Rhode Island, and it was led by Major General Joseph Spencer. It was a planned invasion by 8,000 troops on Aquidneck Island. Weeks before the invasion Tories warned the British of the assembling American troops. The British assumed that they were forming to join General Gate's army in upstate New York. The troops had been preparing for the attack for several weeks. However, they encountered delay after delay. Bad weather and lack of coordination hampered the expedition.

The long delay was not popular with the American militiamen. One morning General Spencer coming out of his tent saw the following verses written in large letters,

> Israel wanted bread,
> The lord sent them manna;
> Rhode Island wants a head,
> And Congress sends a granny!

General Spencer would now forever be known as "Granny Spencer." Finally, the word was given for the troops to gather to cross over from Tiverton to Aquidneck Island. Before they crossed, heavy gales of winds came and made the crossing impossible. The element of surprise had been lost, and the attack was abandoned. Many of the militiamen were tired of the delays and went home. By the time news of the surrender of British General Burgoyne reached the Americans the expedition was officially over. Thomas returned home to Sarah, who he had spent very little time with after they were married.

Sources: 1. Lossing, *Lossing's Field Book of the Revolution Vol. 1.* **2.** National Archives Pension Application W13843. **3.** Hamilton, *History of Bristol County, Massachusetts, Part 2*, page 542.

William Redman

William Redman was born c. 1750 and probably in South Carolina. After the war he was a keeper of a mill owned by Samuel Bell. His pension application was rejected, because in his first statement he reported that he joined in 1794. His next statement dated October 7, 1820, gave a different date,

> That he the said William Redman enlisted for the term of 15 months sometime in the month of May in the year 1775, in the State of South Carolina in the company commanded by Captain Francis Prince in the Regiment commanded by Colonel Huger in the line of the State of South Carolina Continental establishment; That he continued to serve in said corps about 6 months, when he was placed under Captain Benjamin Tutt in the Regiment commanded by Colonel Hammonds in said establishment in which corps he continued until sometime in the month of August 1776 when he was discharged from said service in the Cherokee Nation at a Fort called Seneca That he was at Charleston South Carolina at the time of the first Battle of Sullivan's Island and was then sent to guard the frontiers against the Tories and Indians, and was in the Battle at Seneca, then in a Battle at the Grassy Valley where he was wounded in the left shoulder, supposed to be by a rifle ball, also in a battle at Brass Town, in a battle on Tennessee River.

William first enlisted in the 5th South Carolina Regiment under Colonel Isaac Huger. At the Battle of Seneca, William was under the command of Colonel Samuel Hammond. This battle occurred on August 1, 1776, when the South Carolina militia raided several Cherokee towns. The militia was ambushed by Tories and a group of Cherokee Indians, but the Americans were eventually victorious. A militiaman, Francis Salvador, became the first Jewish patriot killed during the Revolution. The Battle at Grassy Valley, where William was wounded, and the Brattle of Brass Town were also fought against Tories and Indians.

Sources: 1. National Archives Pension Application R8645. **2.** Grundset, *Forgotten Patriots, National Society of the D.A.R.*, page 565.

Richard Rhodes

Richard Rhodes was born in Africa and sold as a slave. He married Catherine Spencer in October of 1786. He was wounded in battle, which caused a stiff elbow joint. After the war he went to sea for several years. He received a yearly pension of $80 for his five years of service. He died on January 17, 1823. He stated in his pension application on September 4, 1818,

> In the year 1778 I enlisted in Capt. Arnolds company & Col. Greene's regiment. In which regiment I continued until June 1783 when I was discharged. I was in the battle of Monmouth I reveiced a serious wound in my arm from a musket ball. I was born in Africa and I entered the army for the purpose of obtaining my freedom.

Richard enlisted in the 1st Rhode Island Regiment which was under the command of Colonel Christopher Greene. A total of 88 slaves enlisted in the regiment at the time Richard joined. The regiment eventually had about 140 African Americans.

At the Battle of Monmouth Richard's regiment was a part of the advanced guard under the command of Major General Charles Lee. During the battle Lee ordered his men to retreat, and while retreating Lee encountered General Washington. Washington, was angry about the retreat, and he relieved Lee of his command and had him withdraw to the rear. Washington then rallied the troops to re-engage with the British. The two armies fought to a draw on a very hot day in June. Lee was later court martialed and relieved of command for one year.

Richard received a serious wound in the arm during the battle. The British used a seventy-five caliber ball, which did not cut into flesh like smaller bullets today. Instead, it smashed through the skin, muscle, and bone resulting in wide spread damage. The lead ball would flatten out when it hit a solid object like bone. Richard was lucky he did not have his arm amputated when he was treated.

Sources: 1. National Archives Pension Application W22060. **2.** Grundset, *Forgotten Patriots, National Society of the D.A.R.,* page 228.

Charles Riley

Charles Riley was born c. 1756 and probably in Virginia. He applied for a pension, which was rejected for unknown reasons on June 8, 1841,

> That he entered the service of the United States in the latter part of January 1800 [1780] under Captain Thomas Montague and he thinks Major George Bird and Col James Montague. he remembers distinctly that the last named gentlemen were field officers but at this late date he can not be positive as to their respective ranks That on one occasion he was sent express to the county of Caroline for a detachment of men under the command of Capt Thomas Dogward That is the spring of 1781 he assisted in the capture of a vessel belonging to one Richard Bird of Parrots creek which had been employed in furnishing the enemy with arms and provisions and that in August following he also assisted in the capture of another vessel employed on the Rappahannac in the enemys service belonging to one Capt Gutridge that in the latter expedition he was commanded by a Capt Walker. That he was employed about a month in keeping guard over Richard Birds vessel after her capture and in the effort to catch the said Bird. That he was a resident of the said county of Middlesex when he entered the service and performed the greater part of his duty in said county until a short time before the commencement of the siege at york town, at which

time he was marched to Gloucester town and continued in service there until after the surrender of Lord Cornwallace when he was discharged together with the other militia troops of Middlesex That he continued in service the whole time from January 1780 to about the 1st of November 1781 sometimes sent in express between the troops in Middlesex and Gloucester and sometimes ordered out upon foraging services.

Sources: **1.** National Archives Pension Application R8824. **2.** Grundset, *Forgotten Patriots, National Society of the D.A.R.,* page 525.

Reuben Roberts

Reuben Roberts was born c. 1761. He served in the 1st Rhode Island and he stated in his pension application on March 31, 1818,

> I enlisted as a private soldier in the month of February 1777 in Capt. Thomas Arnolds Company and Col. Christopher Greene's regiment in the Rhode Island line. I continued five years three months and ten days & was then discharged.

On November 30, 1820, a doctor wrote to the pension bureau stating the reason Reuben could not work and needed the pension, "Reuben Roberts is subject to a ___?___ of his left leg, arising from a fracture of the bone, which happen while in the service of his country as a soldier and that the leg occasionally becomes sore & disqualifies him for labor."

John Cole, a friend of Reuben, wrote to the bureau on November 21, 1818, "Reuben has been crippled by having his feet very badly frozen while he belonged to the army." Reuben received a monthly pension of $8 for his service.

Sources: **1.** National Archives Pension Application S39834. **2.** Grundset, *Forgotten Patriots, National Society of the D.A.R.,* page 228.

Prince and Mingo Rodman

Prince and Mingo served in the 1st Rhode Island Regiment. Prince was a slave that belonged to Robert Rodman, Jr. According to records Prince was born in South Kingston, Rhode Island, his trade was a cobbler, and at the age of sixteen he was a little over 5'4" tall. Mingo was a slave owned by William Rodman. The two slaves were from the same county, and both were valued at 120 pounds.

After the war the men that served received a land bounty for their service. Unfortunately, dishonest men would prey upon these individuals, many times African Americans, because they could not read. The men would cheat these soldiers out of their land bounty either by getting to them to sign it over to them for some reason, or they would buy the land bounty paying pennies on the dollar for them. The following is a letter dated July 12, 1837, and written to the War Department on the behalf of two black men in Rhode Island that were cheated out of their land bounty,

> There are several poor colored families in my neighbor who think they have a claim on the government for Revolutionary Bounty Land. The following is the information as nearly recollected which they give—that prince Rodman & Mingo Rodman served a term of regular service in the war. A few years ago a gentleman from Connecticut came here and bought one of these rights and they signed or made their marks on the papers conveying it. They cannot tell which of the rights they were imposed upon, as they were unable to read and papers were not read to them.
>
> If there are any papers in the Department which could give any information upon this subject without too much trouble, I would be very much obliged. Signed Elisha R. Potter

Mingo had died several years after the war, and his brother Aaron was entitled to receive the land bounty. On September 28, 1830, Aaron made his mark on a legal document that gave the rights to the land bounty to Gurdon Huntington, according to the document Aaron's true and lawful attorney. So, Aaron gave his right to his brother's land to Mr. Huntington for free.

Sources: 1. Bounty Land Warrant 7687-100. **2.** Grundset, *Forgotten Patriots, National Society of the D.A.R.*, page 228. **3.** *The Narragansett Historical Register*, Vol. 1, April 1883, No. 4—A List of Slaves Enlisted in to the Continental Army. **4.** Saffell, *Records of the Revolutionary War: Containing the Military and Financial Correspondence*, page 154.

Jack Rowland (Freeman)

Jack Rowland was born a slave on March 1, 1753, in Fairfield, Connecticut, and he probably died there on February 1, 1839. He received a yearly pension of $50 for his year of service. He stated in his pension application (which was very difficult to read) dated July 5, 1833,

> Born the slave of a one Burritt in Fairfield, at the age of seven he was purchased by Jonathan Booth of NewTown with whom he lived until he became the age of thirteen when he was purchased by Hezekiah Sanford.
>
> In the month of January 1777 and as early as the 10th of said month he enlisted for the term of during the war as a private soldier in the company commanded by Captain Ezekiah Sanford in the Regiment commanded by Colonel Philip B. Bradley in the continental line of the army.

Jack enlisted in the 5th Connecticut Regiment under the command of Colonel Philip Burr Bradley. Jack was at the Battle of Germantown fought on October 4, 1777. His regiment served on the left wing under the command of General Greene.

> That on the 1st day of April 1777 he joined the said regiment at __?__ Pond in the county of Putnam in the state of New York and from thence marched with said regiment to Peekskill on the Hudson River [this is about 15 miles] and there he continued to serve with the continental troops there.
>
> He was engaged in the battle of Germantown in the month of October of that year

and afterwards marched with said Regiment to Philadelphia from thence the said Regiment into winter quarters at Valley Forge. He was [several words cannot be read due to paper damage] and he __?__ the severe winter of 1777–8. He participated with the rest of the army in all the hardships endured by the soldiers during that miserable winter. On the opening of the spring the said Regiment was marched to Princeton there he was discharged under the following sickness.

When he was discharged Jack's master hired a substitute to serve out his enlistment. A letter written to the pension bureau in support of his one year service explained the reason for Jack's sickness. It was written by the son of Jack's master and is dated August 2, 1832,

> I William Sanford say that Jack a colored man (a slave to my father) enlisted under Captain Ezekiel Sanford [Ezekiel is William's uncle] & that he went off in the spring of 1777 & that he was gone one year. Said Capt. Came home in the course of the year & told how homesick Jack was & wanted his old master to hire a man in his room & he would come back and be a good slave, my father did hire a man, I understood took his place, Jack came home & served I think three years for his freedom, he enlisted for three years or during the war, I cannot tell, I have understood he went by the name of Jack Freeman.

Three years after Jack returned home he was given his freedom by his master.

Sources: **1.** National Archives Pension Application S17066. **2.** Grundset, *Forgotten Patriots, National Society of the D.A.R.,* page 229.

Silas Royal (Ryal Varnum)

Silas Royal was purchased as an infant in Boston, and he was brought to the household to be a servant for General J.B. Varnum of Dracut, Massachusetts. In January of 1776 he enlisted in the company of Captain Joshua Reed in the 9th Continental Infantry and he was under the command of Colonel James Mitchell Varnum and served as his servant. Colonel Varnum was the brother of General J.B. Varnum, the master of Silas. The Colonel was in favor of allowing African Americans to enlist in the army, which led to the 9th Continental being re-designated the 1st Rhode Island Regiment as an all-black unit.

After he was discharged from the army in April of 1776, Silas entered the navy as a privateer. Records show he served on the Privateer *Franklin*. The *Franklin* was commanded by Joseph Robinson. Silas drew thirty pounds as prize money after one voyage.

While Silas was a free man and home in 1778, he was taken prisoner to be sold as a slave in the South. The number of free African Americans gaining their freedom by serving in the war increased in the north. They became prey to unscrupulous men, who would kidnap them and sell them as slaves in the south. These men later hid behind the 1793 Fugitive Slave Act that allowed runaway slaves to be captured and returned to the south. The kidnappers would destroy any freedom papers the black person would have. The courts would not allow testimony from a black person to defend themselves, and due to racism most whites did not care to get involved.

The following account of the kidnapping of Silas is preserved in an old Varnum family diary,

> Jan 19 1778–This morning while at breakfast heard that Joshua Wyman had sold Ryal Varnum [Silas Royal], that ye News was brought from Westford by Jos. Varnum Jr. & that said Ryal was carried off in a covered waggon. Handcuffed—on hearing of which I immediately called for my horse, Galloped to Jos. Varnum's to Know ye Certainty. He confirmed it, Sent him to Capt. Jo's to come Immediately. Sent Jonas with my horse. Gave Jonas $20 to bare his expenses, with orders to pursue with all possible speed, overtake, Bring back and not suffer arbitrary voyalance to Escape with Impunity. They pursued, came to Woburn, found the News confirmed. That it was the Infamous Joner White, the Scurrilous Tinker of Haverhill, that Bought him (at ye same time knowing sd Ryal was a free man) sd White had Imprisoned him, Woburn people had liberated him. Sd White laid a false charge against him. Said he was an Inlisted soldier in ye Continental service: that he had received $20 Continental money & had Deserted, that he had stole from Sundry persons & was a thief & that if ye prison Could not hold him ye Guard should & profanely swore that he had bought him & would have him some way on that Complaint Altho he knew it to be false he put him under guard. There is ye Infamous White that hath worked himself by some means as some way to be a quartermaster for ye Army at or near Boston, a fine post to get money when Truth Nor Honor is not regarded.
>
> Jan 20. Capt. Joseph & Jonas Varnum went to Boston, Complained to General Heath against said White, had sd Ryal Liberated, and a promise from the Genl. that he would take Notice of said White. They gave sd White Just Character to ye General, he promised he would take Notice of it. They went to White, Informed him what they had done. He was extreamly angry. Curst & swore very profanely. They delt with him very sharply for his Conduct to Ryal. He said he did not know that Ryal was free. They told him that he Did know that his Crime aledged against Ryal, for which he was put under gaol was true, but that he knew ye contrary. He said that all such Neagrows ought to be slaves. They told him that Ryal was as Good a man & of as much Honor as he, at which he was extremely angry & profain. Laid his hand on his Hanger by his side. They told him they had seen Hangers & men before they had seen him or his, that they were Ready to answer him any way he pleased, that they on sd Ryal Behalf, should Bring an action of Damage for false Imprisonment, that such men stealers should not go unpunished. They came to Wymans same Day. Gave him ye like Trimming.

The jury came back with the verdict, "that the said Silas Royal recover against the said Joshua Wyman One Hundred Pounds lawful money." However, it did not end there. General James Varnum filed an action against Joshua Wyman. John White had purchased Silas from Wyman, and White published the following deposition in 1779,

> I, John White solemnly declare that I purchased a Negro named Royal of one Joshua Wyman of Woburn in the County of Middlesex, State of Massachusetts Bay, sometime the last of spring or beginning of summer 1778, for which I paid nine fifty six pounds lawful money,

> sd Wyman declaring to me on his word of honor that if I would sell the sd Royal to some other Southern Officer, so that he might never again return to New England, he would give me some consideration therefor (as he said on account of his infamous character as a thief &c) and that the said Wyman still retains the money from me that I gave him for said Negro, alledging that he is my slave for life and that it is my fault that I do not make him so. This I solemnly protest to be the truth. John White Newburyport Sept 28 1779.

It was written that Silas held respect from all. He was described as "dignified old darky with autocratic ways." He felt respect was due him as Gen. Varnum's servant. "If any young men failed to take off their hats to him when they met him on the road, he would cry out, 'Boys, where's your manners?' and failing recognition, would send his cane after them in double quick time."

When Silas was old and diseased, he was cared for by the family, and he had his own room in their mansion. Silas died on May 3, 1826, several years after General Varnum, and he requested to be buried alongside an Indian in one corner of the Varnum burial plot.

Sources: 1. *Massachusetts Soldiers and Sailors in the War of the Revolution*, page 637. **2.** Coburn, *History of Dracut Massachusetts*, pages 334–338.

Peleg Runnels

Peleg Runnels was born a slave c. 1752, and he died September 11, 1832. He married fifteen-year-old Martha in the spring of 1777. They were married in Salem, Massachusetts, by a Baptist minister. Peleg served for two years in the 1st Rhode Island Regiment and received a yearly pension of $80. In his pension application dated April 21, 1818, he stated,

> That he the said Peleg Runnels sometime in the spring of the year 1777 was placed in the company commanded by Captain Alexander Hopkins and regiment commanded by Col. Christopher Green this regiment was composed mostly of blacks he don't know whether they were considered as belonging to any particular line on Rhode Island the condition upon which he was placed in said corps by his master was that if he would serve two years in said service he should then have his liberty or Freedom. That he continued to serve in said corps by the United States in said war from the year 1777 until the year 1779 making the full term of two years and he returned to his master and received his freedom. He was in the battle of Rhode Island in 1778.

Sources: 1. National Archives Pension Application W15295. **2.** Grundset, *Forgotten Patriots, National Society of the D.A.R.*, page 229.

Peter Salem

Peter Salem was born a slave c. 1750 at Framingham, Massachusetts, and he died there on August 16, 1816. He was first owned by Captain Jeremiah Belknap, and later he was sold to Major Lawson Buckminster. Peter was granted his freedom when he marched on the Lexington Alarm on April 19, 1775, and he served as a minute man in Captain Simon Edgell's Company. On April 24, 1775, he enlisted for eight months in Captain Drury's Company in Colonel Nixon's 6th Massachusetts Regiment, which was raised on April 23, 1775.

Peter marched with his Regiment to fight at the Battle of Bunker Hill on June 17, 1775. The Regiment was placed near the redoubt on Breeds Hill. During the battle Salem and some other men were sent from Captain Drury's Company to support Colonel Prescott in the redoubt. When Salem reached the redoubt, Prescott's men had just run out of powder.

Judge Needham Maynard later wrote what happened next, "I saw a British officer come up with some pomp, and he cried out, 'Surrender, you damned rebels!' But Prescott made a little motion with his hand, and that was the last word the Briton spoke; he fell at once."

Peter Salem had shot Major John Pitcairn as he scaled the redoubt. The major fell into the arms of his son, who carried him from the battlefield. The major was taken to a house near Boston where he later died. Salem and the rest of the Americans, were out of powder and were forced to retreat. There are some historians that cast doubt that Salem was the soldier that fired the fatal shot.

After the eight months were up Salem returned home. He enlisted in September 1776 in Captain Micajah Gleason's Company in the Regiment of Lt. Colonel Nixon, and he served in the New York Campaign. He later was at the Battle of White Plains. Upon his return home Salem joined the militia commanded by his former master Major Buckminster. When British General Burgoyne's army began to threaten northern New York, Salem once again answered the call for volunteers. Salem enlisted for three years in the Continental Army under the command of Colonel Thomas Nixon.

Before he was discharged in 1783 Salem had spent the cold winter at Valley Forge, fought at Saratoga, Monmouth, and Stony Point. Salem had served his country for nearly eight years, and many of them were as a waiter to Colonel Nixon.

After the war in September of 1783 he married Katy Benson, which proved to be an unhappy marriage. The marriage was dissolved sometime before the 1790 census. He lived in several places in Leicester, Massachusetts, and he finally settled into a cabin which he built for himself. In the front of the cabin he planted a couple of poplar trees and cultivated a small garden. He earned a small amount of money mending baskets and putting new bottoms in chairs. Many times when people would pass him he would stand erect and give a sharp military salute.

A number of young children would gather around him when he was mending chairs. Salem would entertain them with stories about the war, when he was out with "Massa Nixon." He enjoyed entertaining and swapping stories with anyone that had been in the service.

As he became old and knew his time was short, Peter went around visiting his friends and gave them one last salute. On August 16, 1816, the old soldier joined his comrades that had gone before him.

Sources: 1. Alexander, *History of the Colored Race in America*, page 330. **2.** Federal Census of 1790. **3.** Barry, *The History of Framingham, Massachusetts: Including the Plantation, from 1640 to the Present Time*, pages 64, 160, & 181. **4.** Wilson, *The Black Phalanx African American Soldiers in the American Revolution*, page 22. **5.** Temple, *History of Framingham, Massachusetts, Early Known as Danforth's Farms, 1640–1880*, pages 324–6.

Caesar Shelton

Caesar applied for a pension on February 6, 1840, and he stated that he served with the company commanded by Captain Potter in a Regiment under Colonel Meigs. He told of places he marched to and spent time at. He said he was in the Battle of White Plains and was in a skirmish where he was wounded in the back. The problem is that his statement was not completely true.

His pension was rejected, because he did not serve in the Regiment of Colonel Meigs. He told his story to John Heath who wanted to aid him in getting a pension. John apparently served with Colonel Meigs and wrote that Caesar did also, but knowing it was a lie. John never told Caesar what he had written, and Caesar being around 80 years could not read or write, and his memory was not very clear.

The following are true facts about Caesar, and were found within his pension application. Caesar was born c. 1760 at sea when his mother was brought from Africa. He was a slave of John Shelton of Bridgeport, Connecticut. He served in the 4th Connecticut Regiment under Colonel John Durkee from May 14, 1777, to May 17, 1780. He enlisted so that he could obtain his freedom.

Several people that knew Caesar considered John Shelton to be very truthful and a man of good character. One man, Josiah Hulet, gives some insight to the attitude of many of the people in New England toward blacks. Josiah wrote on July 13, 1840, "…he is an Industrious & good citizen for a black man."

On April 2, 1844, Caesar filed a new and correct statement with the pension bureau about his service, "He served under the command of Col. Durkee for three years. He was at the Battles of Germantown, Red Bank, and in the Battle of Monmouth. He thinks the Monmouth battle was in the summer of 1778, it was very hot weather and he remembers the army was expected to fight again next day—but the enemy made off."

At the Battle of Red Bank fought on October 22, 1777, Caesar was one of

400 militiamen who successfully defended Fort Mercer against 1,200 Hessian troops.

Caesar was in the 4th Connecticut Regiment and part of the 2nd Massachusetts Brigade on the left wing of the American Army. The Battle of Monmouth was fought on June 28, 1778, on a day so hot that more men probably died from heat stroke than by musket fire. By six in the evening the smaller American force had fought the British to a draw. Washington wanted to resume the battle the next day, but during the night the British withdrew and returned to New York City.

> Before he enlisted he was out in the Militia in the place of his old Master's son, he was wounded at Horse Neck, and he was just relieved from guard and had laid down with his pack on & fell asleep when he was awakened by the order "Surrender." He jumped out of the window and escaped to the bushes and received one blow with a cutlass across his back. He was also struck by a ball on the shin at the same time & that was the only time during the service he was wounded.

Caesar was probably wounded at the raid on Horse Neck, New York, on May 23, 1780. Colonel James DeLancey raised a Tory unit known as "DeLancey's Cowboys" or "DeLancey's Refugees." The Tories rode to Horse Neck where Caesar and other militiamen were stationed. The attack was so sudden that the militiamen could not fire more than twice before they were routed. Their losses would have been greater, if it were not for the woods nearby where they took shelter.

Caesar Shelton was granted a yearly pension of $80 for his service.

Sources: 1. National Archives Pension Application 19764. **2.** Grundset, *Forgotten Patriots*, *National Society of the D.A.R.*, page 290. **3.** Horton & Horton, *In Hope of Liberty: Culture, Community and Protest among Northern Free Blacks*, page 65.

Jack (Prince) Sisson

Jack Sisson was born c. 1743, and he was a slave owned by Thomas Sisson. Jack was described as tall, stout, and muscular.

On the morning of December 13, 1776, American General Charles Lee, second in command of the American Armies, was captured at White's Tavern by the British. The General was still in his nightshirt when he was captured. It was common at the time to exchange officers of equal rank. Unfortunately, the Americans had no British officer equal to the rank of general for the exchange.

Lieutenant Colonel William Barton was given the task to raid the sleeping quarters of British General Richard Prescott and take him captive. Barton asked five regimental officers to volunteer for a secret and dangerous mission. To keep the mission a secret he waited until the last moment to ask for volunteers of the enlisted men.

Barton appealed to the 1st Rhode Island Regiment, "I am about to undertake an enterprise against the enemy. I wish to have about forty volunteers and those who dare risk their lives with me on this occasion will advance two paces to the front." It was reported that every many stepped forward.

Since the raiding party would have to travel by water, he picked experienced rowers and men familiar with the area. Jack Sisson was picked because he was experienced as a boat steerer. A Native American was selected to steer another boat.

After a setback due to bad weather, the boats carrying the raiding party landed on the beach of Aquidneck Island the morning of July 10, 1777. Intelligence had informed the Americans that the British General was sleeping in a farmhouse owned by Mr. Overing. A British deserter had given the Americans details about the security around the General.

Outside of the farmhouse the Americans encountered a guard who asked, "Who comes there?" The Americans replied they were looking for deserters, and when the guard asked for the countersign Sisson rushed the man and seized him before he could fire a shot. The guard was tied up and the raiders entered the darkened farmhouse. According to an account published later in the *Pennsylvania Evening Post*, "The colonel went foremost, with a stout, active negro close behind him. They slipped in through the entrance way and swiftly rounded up the occupants. Bounding the stairs, they found Prescott's door locked. The negro, with his head, at the second stroke forced a passage."

After Sisson had shattered the door open, the British general and his aid were captured and taken away wearing just their nightshirts and barefoot. The raid was a success without the loss of a man. Ballads were written and stories told about "the sturdy Negro (Jack Sisson) who broke through into the general's chamber, grabbed him, and hauled him out the door."

After the raid Jack served in the 1st Rhode Island Regiment at the Battle of Rhode Island and the Siege of Yorktown. He died around the age of seventy-eight in Plymouth, Massachusetts.

Sources: 1. Falkner, *Captor of the Barefoot General,* August 1960, American Heritage Magazine. **2.** Quarles, *The Negro in the American Revolution.* **3.** Burney, *Kidnapping the Enemy: The Special Operations to Capture Generals Charles Lee and Richard Prescott.*

Edward Sorrel

Edward Sorrel was born c. 1763 probably in Virginia, and he died July 7, 1857. He married a woman named Darcis on December 15, 1814. An 1810 federal census lists him as a "free mulatto."

> That he enlisted in the Army of the United States in the year 1779 with Capt Thomas Downing a militia officer and served in the 2nd Regt of the Virginia line, under the following

named Officers Genl Gates. Colo Porterfield, Capts Drew & McGill Lt. Mann & Ensign Vaughan. That he lived in the County of Northumberland & State of Virginia at the time he enlisted which was in the fall of the year 1779. He marched from the County to Williamsburg Virginia in February or March of the following year, with a recruiting officer by the name of Carvell, he there joined the Regt of Colo Porterfield, after a few days stay at Williamsburg he marched with the Regt. of Colo Porterfield for Charleston South Carolina.

The Regt marched through North Carolina by Sallsbury, Hillsborough & Guilford court house. the Regt. arrived in one or two days march of Charleston before it heard of its surrender. He was in frequent skirmishes with the british. He was at the battle of the Point of Forks where Genl Gates was defeated. he there received musket ball in his right shoulder. Colo. Porterfield was their wounded. Seargent Booth to others & my self were carrying Colo Porterfield off after he was wounded but were so closely persued by the enemy that they had to leave him he was taken prisoner. The defeat of Genl Gates was in August 1780: after the defeat of Genl. Gates he with others collected at Hillsborough & with Maj. Marzard marched to Richmond City Virginia, where he joined Capt Smith late in the fall & went with him to the western part of Virginia to obtain wagons & teams for the Army. they returned in the spring following, in a few days after their arrival at Richmond, he was ordered to Camden by Capt Smith for the purpose of attending Colo Porterfield to Virginia on parole. Colo Porterfield was confined a prisoner in Camden he went in company with Capt Singleton of the Maryland line to the neighbourhood of Camden he found Colo. Porterfield still a prisoner & being ill, he died in four or five days after he arrived in Camden. he immediately brought Colo. Porterfields baggage to Richmond City Virginia & delivered it to Capt Smith it was then in the fall of 1781. He then obtained for the first time his discharge from Capt. Smith (which has been lost) he served more that six months after his enlistment had expired (which was for 18 months) before he was discharged. Immediately after returning home he volunteerd in Northumberland County Virginia & went to York Town Virginia he was put under Colo Ennis command on Gloucester Point opposite York Town his whole service in the Militia was about six months.

Sources: 1. National Archives Pension Application W26493. **2.** Grundset, *Forgotten Patriots, National Society of the D.A.R.*, page 526.

Richard Stanhope

Richard Stanhope was born March 1, 1748, at Fredericksburg, Virginia, and he died September 20, 1862, in Champaign County, Ohio, at the age of 114. He and his family became servants of George Washington's family, as part of an inheritance of ten slaves Washington received after the death of his father. It is believed that Washington gave Richard his first name and influenced his last name. Dr. Jan Ebert regent of the D.A.R. wrote,

> Many of the maps and in the deeds refer to him as Stanup, or in one case Standup. The history of that reportedly is that when he was working for the Washington family as a slave he was told by his mother repeatedly that he should stand up in the presence of the Washingtons. And so, he evidently heard it enough times, Stanup! Stanup! That he thought it was his name.

During the Revolutionary War he was Washington's personal valet throughout the war. Richard applied for a pension and recorded his statement on January 17, 1859.

> He was a servant in the military family of General George Washington during the war of the revolution. That he was by permission of said general engaged in the Battle of Stony Point where he received a wound in the left had from a sword in the hands of a British soldier. That he was in the Battle of Long Island prior to the evacuation of New York by the American army. That he was then shot through the right leg just above the knee and that he continued in the service and family of General Washington until the termination of the War.

His pension application was rejected, because there was no proof of service and he was not on any military rolls. Since he was brought as a servant by Washington, he never enlisted in the army. By the time he applied for a pension, anyone that served with him was probably dead. In 1914 his heirs applied for his pension, and that too was rejected.

After the war Richard was still a slave and returned to Washington's home and his duties included supervision of the slaves at Mount Vernon. He was at the foot of Washington's bed when Washington died. Washington freed only one slave in his will, William Lee his personal body slave. Washington did request that the slaves he personally owned be freed at the death of his wife Martha. She freed her husband's 123 slaves on January 1, 1801.

Richard moved to Ohio in 1808 and soon bought eighty acres of land and built his home. In the War of 1812 Richard again answered the call of his country. Richard was past sixty years old when he drove a four horse wagon team to Detroit with the American troops commanded by General William Hull. The sneaky British had their Native American warriors make as much noise as they could around Fort Detroit held by the Americans. This convinced General Hull that he faced superior numbers, so he surrendered the fort on August 16, 1812. Hull was later court-martialed, convicted, and sentenced to death, but he received a pardon from President Madison. After the surrender Richard was ordered to drive his team for delivery to the British. He refused to do it, unhitched his saddle horse, and made his escape back home.

During his life Richard was noted for three things: well digging, preaching, and fatherhood. Being stout, hardy, heavy-set, and chunky he would travel around the county and dig wells for various people.

He also claimed to have twenty-seven children. Richard married three times and was still raising children into his nineties. He instilled the abolitionist cause in his children. Three of his sons took part in the Underground Railroad to move escaped slaves through the area.

He was a Baptist preacher, and even though he was illiterate he was considered one of the ablest preachers around. He ministered mostly to white people, and he served as pastor of the Kings Creek Baptist Church founded in 1805.

> Sources: **1.** *Proceedings of the 21st Continental Congress of the D.A.R.*, April 1912, Vol. 21, page 796. **2.** *The History of Champaign County, Ohio, 1881*, page 506. **3.** Writer's Program, *Urbana and Champaign County*, 1942, pages 26 & 143.

Jordan Stewart

Jordan Stewart was born c. 1750 in Dinwiddie County, Virginia, and according to the census he was alive in 1860. In the 1810 Federal Census it stated that he lived with Cresey, probably his wife, and they were both free. The 1860 Federal Census states his age as 112, and he was probably living with his son's family in Wake County, North Carolina. His pension application was rejected for lack of proper proof of service.

> That he joined the melitia on the 4 day of Feb 1780 and remained in said County of Macklenburg Va in Service Seven months, and upwards and that he was marched from Said County of Macklenburg Va to Taylors ferry on the roanoke River in N.C. not verry far from Halifax Town N. Carolina where there was about three hundred soldiers where declarent Staid about six weeks then was marched to the County of Granville N.C. then to the County of Wake where he remained some time thence to Randolph N.C. thence then on his way to Gilford Court House and got within twenty or thirty miles of Gilford Court house declarent met his farther a Soldier William Stewart Returning with a great many others in one body after the Battle at Gilford Court House in N. Carolina. declarent further states that all those with him amediately countermarched or returned and made for Peyton Skippers ferry on the Roanoke River N.C. where he was Stationed and knews came that Lord Corn Wallace was taken in Little york and the following december Thereafter & on the 22 or twenty third day of December 1781 Seventeen Hundred & Eighty One he rec'd an Honourable Discharge which has been lost a great many years since. Declarent states as a reason for his not making a former application that he did not know that the melitia soldiers was entitled to a pension and only those in the Regular Continan army altho his services was verry Faithfully rendered and run many narrow Risks of loosing his life while in actual Service yet he was not apprised that he was Entitled to a pension for the above reason until verry lately.

> Sources: **1.** Federal Census 1810 & 1860. **2.** National Archives Pension Application R10160. **3.** Grundset, *Forgotten Patriots, National Society of the D.A.R.*, page 527.

William Stewart

William Stewart was born free c. 1759 in Brunswick County, Virginia. According to records he enlisted in the 2nd North Carolina Regiment on June 22, 1777, for two years, and on March 12, 1779, he re-enlisted. His pension application stated that he deserted in January of 1780, which forfeited his pension and bounty. He stated in his pension that he was discharged in June of 1780,

He enlisted in the year 1777, under Major Hardy Murphy a Continental recruiting officer in the month of June, he was then marched to Halifax North Carolina, and from that to Alexandria in Virginia, where there were assembled fifteen hundred new recruits where those who had not the smallpox were inoculated, and in the last of September of the same year we were marched to a place called the White Marsh in New Jersey and there joined the headquarters of Genl Washington, where the detachment was placed in the company of Captain Robert Fenns in the Second Regiment North Carolina line our Colonels were Colonel John Patton & Colonel Harney. We there wintered and in the spring marched to West Point the Valley Forge on Schulkill [Schuylkill] River and from thence to West Point on North River and was there at the time the British took Stoney Point, Declarant was marched among other places to the White Plains, Pyramus, Hackensack & Long Island, Declarant was in the Battle of Monmouth, under the command of General Hogans we marched to various places in jersey and finally marched, through Baltimore, to North Carolina under the command of General Hogan, and was discharged in the month of June in the year 1780 in North Carolina, his discharge was signed by General Hogan, having served three years the full term of his enlistment. He preserved his discharge for many years until it was worn out, & lost.

Source: **1.** National Archives Pension Application R10173.

Samuel Sutphin

Samuel Sutphin was born a slave on January 1, 1747, at Bridgewater, New Jersey. Samuel was a black slave and also raised as a Dutchman. In the early part of his life he did not speak much English. He applied for a pension with this statement given August 15, 1832,

That he entered the service while a slave of Casper Bergen as his substitute on promise of receiving his freedom, and continued therein more than two years. That he enlisted in the company at Millstone under the command of Captain Coon Rod Ten Eyck, that he continued in said company one month, went with said company to Communipaw, That after one month entered the company of Captain Jacob Ten Eyck, went with the company to Elizabeth Town, Staid there one month and returned, After one month he entered Captain John Ten Eyck's company, went to Elizabeth Town and staid one month, saw the British soldiers. That he afterward served under Captain Philip Van Arsdalen one month and next under Captain Jacob Jennings one month, That Previously to the forgoing Services he entered the company of Captain Philip Von Arsdalen, remembers General Sterling was the superior Officer and that Frederick Frelinghuysen and Richard Meddagh were Colonels, That at the time of his entering the company it was warm weather. That he went with the company from Hunterdon to Elizabeth Town and thence to Communipaw, staid out one month, Shortly after he entered the company of Captain Westcott under Colonel Seely, remembers Lieutenant Davis was an officer in said company to Van Nestes Mill, That the British were on the opposite side of the Millstone river, the company could not cross the bridge, several Pieces of cannon being stationed thereon, by the British, That the company crossed the river about a mile below the bridge, approached the enemy, fired upon them killing one horse, pursued after but could not overtake them. Then the company went down toward Brunswick, saw a small detached part of the British lying in ambush near the road, fired upon them, and drove them away, seizing upon and taking five cannon which they left behind in their flight. That about a hundred of the British army stationed near by, took Doctor Lawrence Van Dorveer Prisoner, which he saw. That the company then retreated and returned to Van Nestes Mills, Deponent took one of the enemy prisoner, for which general Dickinson Presented him with a Gun which he still Possesses.

The Battle of Millstone, also called the Battle of Van Nest's Mill, occurred on January 20, 1777. A British foraging party of about 600 men and more that forty wagons was sent by General Cornwallis to capture the mill. A force of about 400 New Jersey militiamen, which included Samuel Sutphin, were dispatched to meet them. What happened next was reported in a letter printed in *The Pennsylvania Journal and Weekly Advertiser* at Philadelphia on January 29, 1777,

> Last Monday [January 20] a party of Jersey militia and Pennsylvania riflemen marched to attack a body of the enemy, consisting of about 600, who were posted at a bridge at Millstone River, near Abraham Van Nest's mill, which is two miles from Somerset Court House. In order more effectually to prevent our men from crossing, the enemy had placed three field-pieces on a hill, about fifty yards from the bridge. When our men found it impossible to cross there, they went down the river, broke through the ice, waded across the river up to their middles, flanked the enemy, routed them, and took forty-three baggage-wagons, 104 horses, 115 head of cattle and about sixty or seventy sheep. We lost four or five men. We took twelve prisoners, and from the best accounts the enemy had about twenty-four or twenty-five killed and wounded. A man who came from New Brunswick this afternoon says the enemy allow that they lost thirty-five or thirty-six men, but say the rebels lost 300. There were not more than 400 of our men crossed the river. The enemy report that they were attacked by 3,000 of General Washington's troops, and were absolutely certain they were not militia. They were sure that no militia would fight that way!

The British had no respect for the American militiamen. In most battles the militia would fire a shot or two and then run. The British did not believe, or want to believe, that a militia unit could defeat a larger British force. British General Cornwallis was very impressed with what the Jersey militiamen accomplished that day. Samuel continued with his pension statement,

> After this he entered the company of Captain Cornelius Lanes under Colonel Frederick Frelinghuysen, That it was at the time of Cutting Grass and near harvest, That the company went from Readington to meet Col. Frelinghuysen at Millstone, From Millstone they marched to Griggstown and thence to Princeton, Where they arrived at Princeton in the morning, That the *battle* commenced between nine and ten in the morning of the arriving and continued until three in the afternoon, That he fought in said battle. That at three in the afternoon of the same day orders came from General Washington that the army should retreat. That the company in which he served left Princeton at three in the afternoon, and encamped at night on the mountain near Rocky hills, and thence returned to Readington,

The Battle of Princeton occurred on January 3, 1773, which was seventeen days before the Battle of Millstone. Samuel had this battle out of order, which he corrected in a pension statement made two years later,

That after the battle of Princeton he was drafted in the company under the command of Captain Isaiah Younglove, in which company Robert Robinson was Lieutenant, Went with the company to Head Quarters at West Point marched thence to Utica in pursuit of the Indians, taking wit them two friendly Indians as guides, their names were Shawnee John and Indian Ben, Marched thence to Buffaloe, made an attack upon the Indians and killed three, it was late in the fall, They kept garrison until winter then returned to Head Quarters, was placed on picquet guard That a number of Hessians approached him while standing on guard, he shot at and killed one, saw him fall. at this time the main guard coming up attacked the Hessians, killing 16 and taking forty six prisoners, the number killed inclusive of the one was seventeen, Deponent wounded at this time in the leg, which disabled him from performing any duty two and a half months, That he then returned with the company to Hunterdon, That he served in said company nine months, Deponent commenced performing the duties of a soldier in the beginning of the revolution, and continued in readiness to serve, during the whole of said time, That at the commencement of the Revolution he lived at Readington in Hunterdon County, Was a slave of Casper Bergen, and is now free, That he has no documentary evidence of his services in the war, and that all who knew of his services in the War, are now deceased. That after the revolution he was sold to a second master of whom he purchased his freedom

Samuel's pension application was rejected for lack of proof of service, and because he was a slave and not required to serve. On May 26, 1834, he wrote another letter to the pension bureau with more details of his service and how he came to enlist. It also gave an interesting insight to the selling of Samuel Sutphin and the trust Samuel had with his master.

I am the same Sutphin, who heretofore made a declaration of my militia services in the war of the revolution, to obtain a pension under the act of Congress of June 7th, 1832, before the Court of Com. Pleas of Somerset Co. which declaration having been rejected, is now on file in the Pension office. the reason of the rejection as I understand them, form a letter of Oct. 30, 1833, signed by Commissioner Edwards, addressed to Lewis Condict and that being a slave originally, I was not bound to serve in the militia, the circumstances of each tour of actual service not having been stated, as was required, the claim is rejected. My story was a long one, whilst so many other cases were urged pressed on the attention of the Court, I caut hardly expect 10 minutes circummtanial a detail would be committed to writing, as was required. The writer of my story, was much hurried, I presume he did not state in writing, any thing more than a *general* outline of my services. Knowing however that I served *faithfully* many months encountered many hardships dangers, I will ask of the Secretary of War Commissioner Of Pensions, a patient hearing, I will endeavour, as far as old age will permit, to give an honest circumstantial account, as well of the motives inducements to engage in the service, as of the services themselves.

And 1st ... as to the inducement motives. In the beginng of the war, I was a slave to Guisbert Bogart of Somerset co. N. Jersey, living on the Raritan river. Casper Bergher a neighbor, of Readington in Hunterdon Co. but living within some two or 3 miles, proposed to buy me from my master Bogart, give me my freedom at the end of the war, if I would take his place in the Militia service, perform militia duty in his stead. To obtain my freedom, I agreed to the offer, master Bogart sold me to master Begher for 92 pounds, 10 shillings, hard money, which I believe was paid. Master Begher had served one month in the Militia, said he was tired of the service. I believed the white man's word hoping to be free when the fight was over. I took no paper to shew the bargain, but trusted to my Master.and now, I will try to tell my *services*, to the best of my knowledge. I went to live with Master Bergher in the spring when it was muddy cold. I do not know the year, only as the folks called it 76. when they talked about it. We served our flax just after I moved to Master Berghers, then he was called on to go out with the militia. He went out himself this time, left me at home, to plow the corn ground get ready for planting. Directly after I had planted 4 acres, another call was made for the Militia. Master Bergher belonged, as I understood, to Capt. Tire Lanes company. or Matthias Lane's as his name was called in English (we being all Dutch) the company was dessed as I was told, so I was put in Master's place. Captain Lane agreed to take in Master's stead, as a soldier, I was willing that I might be a *freeman* when the war was over. The whole company did not always go, in a body together sometimes half sometimes a quarter. When *part only* went, a part *only* of the *officers* went with them. In my first tour, I think I went out under Capt. Lane himself. I think colonel Taylor was Col. of the Rejemt at home, to which Capt. Lane belonged We marched from the Branch of Raritan where Master lived, through Bound Brook, Scotch plains, Newark so on to Bergen Communipaw. It was in warm weather. A great many militia were there along the shore of North river. We were in sight of N. York. I remember Col. Abm. Ten Eyck was there Col. Schamp Col. Hunt Major Linn. We helped build a small breast work. The ships of the enemy were expected. We mounted guard at night every night staid out our month, were discharged by word of mouth, went home.

We had not been home long (say a few weeks) before we come again called out to the same place. the same duty of mounting guard throwing up breastworks. It was in hay and harvest season when we left home, under command of Capt. Jacob Ten Eyck, as it now appears to my memory. I remember a ship called the Asia was laying in N. York harbor, which we were on this tour, the British fleet arrived. A large body of Militia was collected here, Col. Schamp, Col. Frelingheiysen [Colonel Frederick Frelinghuysen] I believe were both on the ground other officers not remembered. I best remember our *Dutch* Officers because I could talk but little English, knew our Dutch Officers. After staying out our month here, my impression is, that we went home, after being discharged but if we recruited home

Our tarry there was very short for all the Militia were soon called out to meet the enemy, who it was said, had landed on Long Island. Capt. Lane took command of our company, we were hastened to Long Island as soon as practicable. Our company was in the heat of the Long Island battle. Lord Stirling had command of the Jersey troops, I think he was made a prisoner. I believe it was Col. Frelingheiysen who commanded our Regiment. Our company was broken up dispersed in the battle, we lost our officers, or our officers lost the men. Two of our company were taken prisoners in this fight viz: Peter Low John Van Campen. Some months after, they were exchanged got home. Jacob Johnson, a man with one eye,Wm. Van Syckel myself (3 of us) all of Capt. Lane's company, got together, secreted ourselves as well as we could from the notice of the enemy, until we had a chance to make our way down to the narrows opposite Staten Island. I found a colored man with a skiff, who took us across to Staten Island. The black man piloted us through bye ways across Staten Island, we crossed the Sound over to Eliz. town point then through the town, by the Wheat sheaf Tavern Short Hills Quibbletown Bound Brook home.

The Battle of Long Island was fought on August 27, 1776. The outnumbered Americans under General Washington were forced to retreat. On the night of August 29, Washington took his entire army across the East River to Manhattan without a loss of supplies or life. Like other soldiers Samuel found his own way across the river. The army was later driven entirely out of New York.

> In the fall of the same year, after the nights had become frosty, we were again ordered out under Capt. Philip Van Arsdalen was stationed for a month guarding the lines in the neighborhood of Bergen along the Bay shore Capt. Van Arsdale lived at Pluckemin I believe he commanded me on this tour. My next tour was in cold winter weather, under Capt. Van Arsdale Col Schamp. It was about the Christmas holidays. We were marched from Raritan, up the Millstone river escorted Gen'l, then Col. Frelingheiysen, by Griggstown to Princeton. We heard the firing of guns before we reached Princeton, were marched directly into the battle.
>
> Soon after the battle I think Genl' Washington went into Winter quarters near Pluckemin. The morning after this battle, Cornelius Lane, one of our company, was accidentally shot through the hip by one Todd. Lane was lying against a sapling the ball passed in near the navel, came out near his back. Thomas Oliver I carried Lane home on a litter made with poles a bed between two horses. I was absent from home on this tour, according to the best of my memory, 10 days. I had been with my Master but a very few days, before we were summoned in haste to take a body of Tories refugees of 500 to 700 men, led on by one Christopher Vought, or Stosh Voke, as the Dutch called him. They were said to be from Lebanon in Hunterdon Co. + were making their way toward N. Brunswick, then headquarters of the enemy. They were discovered by Doctor Jennings in the night. Captain Lane Capt. Jacob Ten Eyck their companies the neighbors were immediately called. We fell in with them at the 2 bridges, where the 2 branches of the Raritan come together. We had a fight with them here, Wm. Van Arsdale of our company was shot in the heel they ran to a fording place near to Cornelius Van Derveers mill, where they crossed made their retreat. Most of them were mounted Capt. Ten Eyck took one prisoner, kept his horse. We pursued them, but they made their escape towards N. Brunswick, knowing the country well.

In this pension statement he mentions the Battle of Millstone as occurring after the Battle of Princeton.

> This was in cold weather, we mounted guard almost every night all winter along the Raritan to protect the people against the Tories and Refugees, who were very troublesome in this quarter. I was stationed with Lieutenant Davis a party of militia at the 2 bridges performing this guard duty for a month, toward the latter part of winter or perhaps in March, when an Express rider, on a black horse, was sent from Col. Frelingheiysen bringing news that the enemy was out in a large force from N. Brunswick coming out towards Van Ess's Mills in the Millstone river. I piloted Lieut. Davis with his company as many others as joined us, to a fording place across the South Branch well known to me, we hurried our march to the Mills. The enemy had plundered the Mills at Van Ess' of flour grain~had loaded about 10 wagons of 4 horses, started them. They had not yet got out of the lane heading fro the mill to the big road. We fell in with the teams first, before we discovered the enemy. Lieut. Davis ordered us to fire, we did. We shot some of the horses in the front team, which stooped the whole. the drivers left the teams fled, the guard escorting the teams also escaped. We took

the teams wagons, which were sent off under an escort to Morristown. A short time after, a company of Hessians opened a fire upon us from behind a hedge with some 3 or 4 field pieces retreated. Doctor Van Derveer who had rode very near them before they were discovered, was taken prisoner by them carried off to N. Brunswick. A large body of Militia was out, there was a sharp fight with the main bodies of the two armies. I understood Gen'l Dickinson commanded, that Col. Frelingheiysen was with him. Lieutenent. Davis who commanded our guard station was said to be from Cumberland below Philadelphia his Captain, who name was Westcott, was also said to be from Cumberland. He, Westcott, had been left very sick at my old masters, Guisbert Bogarts house, where he died was taken to Cumberland. On this excursion we were engaged not more than 2 or 3 days, before our company returned to its former station near the two bridges, mounting guard every night, which duty we performed faithfully, till the season of plowing came. From the time of the battle at Princeton, I was constantly on duty, either mounting guard along the Raritan, or engaged upon the excursion which I have endeavored to describe, until early in April. I performed at least, from three to four months of duty, in this inclement season hoping the time of my freedom was not far off.

About the time for early Corn planting, as near as I can remember, our company was called on to furnish men to go to the North against the Indians. Three men were taken from our company, as I understood, 3 form each company. Hendrick Johnson~James Ray, a free mulatto man, myself, were taken from Captain Lane's company and 3 from Capt. Ten Eycks company. Captain Isaiah Younglove, Lieutenant Robert Robertson, were along the Raritan the branch, enlisting or raising men for the services which was for a term of 9 months. My Master Bergher, ordered me to go, my name, as I suppose believe, was entered by *Capt.* Younglove for this service period. Colonel David Seely, who was said to be from Cumberland, commanded our regiment our company under Capt. Younglove joined Col. Seely the regiment at Cornelius Stacki tavern at Succasunny plains in Morris County. When we joined our Regiment at Stackis the farmers were just finishing their corn planting. From succasunny plains, we were Marched through Sussex, Goshen in Orange County, to West Point. Here I recollect there was a huge chain of Iron stitches across the north river, anchored into the rocks, to prevent vessels passing up down.

Samuel was called to join the Sullivan expedition during the summer of 1779. It was a campaign to eliminate the threat of Indians and Tories in upper New York. On the way Samuel encountered the Hudson River Chain. This was a massive chain that stretched across the Hudson River to block British ships from sailing up the river. It was constructed between 1776 and 1778, and when completed the chain contained huge iron links with each being two feet in length. The chain weighed sixty-five tons and went 600 yards across the river.

We marched through N. Windsor, Newburg, Esopus Utica at or near which place there was a fort, called Fort Stanwyk or fort Schulyer perhaps I am wrong in the name. We remained here a few days. The Indians had just left the place, having massacred some of the inhabitants. The bodies of three children were found here, that had been massacred by them. We marched through a place called Cherry valley, which the Indians had also visited destroyed, as well as fort Montgomery. I think the name of our General was Sullivan, he joined the expedition took the command somewhere over the North river, I believe at West Point. The Indians had destroyed most of the new settlements villages through which we passed, only a few days before. We found them deserted burnt. We pursued them through the wilderness Country to the Lake Country the Indians retreating as we advanced. We had some 4 or 5 small field pieces with us. When we arrived near the lake, it was about husking corn time in the fall, + we did not begin or march homeward, We a week after the new year began. We returned by the same route, or nearly the same. We halted at West Point. One cold night, when the snow was knee deep, as I was standing sentry, a party of Hessians or Highlanders, who had crossed the river on the Ice came upon us by surprise. I hailed the first I saw, he giving us answer, I fired by moon light saw him fall. i loaded my gun, as they they fired rushed upon me, I fired again, retreated to the main guard who were coming to my relief. They immediately fired killed wounded 16 of the enemy. Our light horse had rallied for our relief coming in their rear, they soon surrendered and we 70 prisoners. They were dressed in short wide plaid trousers wore broad swords. I rec'd a bullet upon the button of the gaiter of my right leg. both bullet button were driven into the leg just above the outer ancle bone. The wound was dressed by Doctor Parrott, the surgeon of our Regiment, who extracted both ball button from the leg, with the knife, the next morning. The fight was in the fore part of the night. In the same affair, I rec'd a wound just above the heel, as high as the ancle, which appeared to be a cut, almost dividing the legs cord behind the ancle, in the same leg. Both these wounds and scars, are yet plain to be seen felt, a lameness has remained from them to this day. I was confined 2 weeks 5 days by this wound at West Point. Doctor Parrott attending dressing the wounds daily. Capt. Younglove was wounded in the fleshy back part of the thigh, the same night, by a ball. the Regm't remained here about 3 weeks, as I believe, when we took up our homeward march, I hobbled along with them as well as I was able. We reached home late in the winter were discharged but a little before the spring season began, having served out the full time our engagement. (in all in active 16 months service.)

It was said by some that his last engagement or service for 9 months would excuse me or my master form Militia calls for some time to come. For this or some other cause, I performed no other service in the war. After the war ended I spoke to my Master for my freedom. I found not long after that I was sold to Peter Ten Eyck a slave for life, for £110. Col. Frelingheiysen some others, endeavored to obtain my freedom, by talking to my old master Bergher, Master Ten Eyck. but Master Ten Eyck sold me as a slave again to Domine Duyea for £ 92.10. 00 I lived with him 2½ years he sold me to Peter Sutphin for the same sum. I lived with him his son 2 years as a slave, after his death, with my Mistress for one year. She then agreed to let me have my freedom, provided I would pay her £ 92. 10. I paid her down, in cash £ 30. which I had laid up in small sums, by selling furs skins of rabbits, raccoons, muskrats for years the residue I paid her by the process of my labor, have been since, a free man. until within a short time, I have been able to feed clothe myself my aged wife from our labor, but now, in my 87th year, I find my working days are ended. If I can receive the pittance which I believe I have faithfully honestly earned by my Militia services in the war **fighting for the white mans freedom**, it would gladden my old head & my wife's. I have told the story of my service in the war, according to the best of my remembrance.

On May 2, 1834 Dr. Lewis Condict wrote to the pension bureau at the request of Samuel to describe the wounds he received while in the service,

> I hereby certify to the Sect's of War Commissioner of Pensions that at the request of Samuel Sutphin, the colored man within named who claims a pension, I examined his right leg &

foot, alleged by him to have been wounded in an engagement with the enemy in the night, upon the Hudson river. the following is the result of my examination. viz: A hard knotty scar, is seen & felt, in the large tendon, called by anatomists, "tendo Achilles," which is formed by the muscles making the calf of the leg, & is inserted into the heel bone. This scar or knot- is about an inch & a half above the heel, & it would Seem, as though the two on had been once divided, or nearly divided, by some rough or harsh instrument. It must have caused a tesious & painful lameness, under the best practicable treatment, & is, as I verily believe, the cause of a palpable & visible lameness, which yet afflicts Sutphin, at this day. On the outside of the same leg, about 3 inches above the ancle, is another scar, somewhat depressed, the size of a half dollar, I should think that the small bone of this leg. (the *fibula*) must have been shattered, as the cover-membrane (priostrum) has been destroyed~ the tendons & integements, being now all firmly fast to the bone- & the motions of the ancle joint are greatly impaired, when contrasted with the other limb.

Samuel also had several friends write to the pension bureau testifying to his character. Unfortunately, no one wrote a letter that served with him, and since he could not prove that he actually served other than his own statement, his pension application was again rejected. They also reasoned that since he served for someone else he should not receive a pension.

After the war Samuel and his wife Catherine moved around several times in New Jersey. After his pension was rejected a fifth and final time, the New Jersey Legislature did the right thing. On March 10, 1836, they passed an act "For the Relief of Samuel Sutphin of Somerset." This act gave the sum of $50 a year for Samuel's service to his country. Samuel died in 1841 a free man and respected for his service to his country.

Sources: 1. Hodges, *Root and Branch: African Americans in New York and East Jersey, 1613–1863*, pages 141–2. **2.** *Official Register of the Officers and Men of New Jersey in the Revolutionary War*, 1842. **3.** Harvey & Smith, *A History of Wilkes-Barre, Luzerne County, Pennsylvania*, Vol. 2, page 903. **4.** Messler, *History of Somerset County* [New Jersey], page 81. **5.** National Archives Pension Application R10321. **6.** *Harper's Encyclopedia of the United States*, Vol., IV, page 447, 1905, Hudson River Chain. **7.** *Acts of the Legislature of the State of New Jersey*, page 436.

William Taborn

William Taborn was born c. 1758 in Northampton County, North Carolina, and he died February 4, 1834. He married a woman named Nelly on January 2, 1778. William received a yearly pension of $34.44 for his service. No evidence was found to show if he was born or raised a slave. However he was described as free when he filed for his pension on August 10, 1834.

> That he entered into the Continental service of the United States when he was about the age of twenty or Twenty one years under James Saunders as Captain, his other Company officers he cannot recollect but he remembers that Col. William Taylor commanded the Regiment, the other field officers he cannot recollect. He entered the Service by Enlistment

for two years and a half. The destination of the detachment to which I belonged was for Wilmington, North Carolina and our place of rendezvous was in Williamsborough in this County. Here we were mustered for a short time, and as soon as preparation could be made the company marched off to Wilmington. There being great difficulty in procuring baggage Waggons for this company and I owning a pretty good one and Team and the departure of the company being delayed for want of a Waggon I was importuned again and again to let my Waggon go with them, but I felt great repugnance to this course, but Col. Taylor and Captain Saunders joining in entreaty to effect this object I at length consented and accepted their proposal to discharge me from any Term of Enlistment on condition of sending my Waggon to carry the Baggage. But I had some difficulty in getting a driver; by arrangement with said officers a man by the name of John Davis who also had a Waggon to accompany the soldiers agreed to and did take charge of my Waggon upon condition I would tend and cultivate his Crop for him in his absence. This contract was fully and honestly complied with on my part and Davis took my Waggon and Capt. Benjamin Hester drove his Waggon went with the detachment and brought my Waggon back and delivered it to me. I cannot state the day, month, or year in which these occurrences took place but it was at an early period of the Revolution. I never took any discharge or written evidence of this service.

    I next engaged by draft in a Southern tour of five months service under Richard Taylor as Captain, the other officers and field officers I am unable to recollect—We marched from Oxford Granville County by Cross creek now Fayetteville to Charleston S.C. or near to it, we thence marched to the river Savannah and joined the American army—I am unable to recollect who was the commander in chief but I rather think that Col. Lytle was the Colonel of the Regiment to which I belonged. This circumstance recurs to my memory from the fact that Col. Lytle had me put under guard for a whole day for getting drunk and cursing him. While in service in that country an engagement took place between the British and our men. They were too hard for us and we had to retreat, indeed we were routed & put to flight and I made the best of my way home. On my arrival at home I found my captain had returned before me. I rather think the battle in which the Americans were routed as before spoken of was that of Briar Creek.

William was a member of the 6th North Carolina Regiment under the command of Lt. Colonel Anthony Lytle at the Battle of Brier Creek on March 3, 1779. The American militia under the command of General John Ashe was caught by surprise by the British. The Americans ran from the camp leaving their cooking fires burning, and many of the men threw down their weapons without firing a shot. William's regiment tried to cover the retreat of the Americans, but soon Colonel Lytle told his men to retreat and avoid capture. Many of the men had to run through a deep swamp for two or three miles.

    American General Moultrie wrote, "General Ashe's affair at Brier Creek, was nothing less than a total rout; never were men more panic struck."

My next Tour of duty was again by Draft from Granville County under the command of James Fuller Captain, Thomas Bradford Lieutenant, and Blake Maulder Ensign Capt. Fuller had received a wound in his Instep and became unable to travel and Shadrack Parrish took the command of our company. We marched to Hillsborough, & were then put under the command of Col. Farmer Lieutenant Colonel Harrison & Major Sharpe. My memory is refreshed as to this last fact and that of Parrish taking the place of Fuller by talking with Thomas Jordan a soldier who served in the same company with me. From Hillsborough we marched through Salisbury to the Catawba about Beaties ford and Joined our army under Genl. Davidson. The enemy were on the opposite bank of the River. I was stationed at Cowan's ford when the attempt was made to cross the river at this place as well as at Beaties ford three miles above. I was stationed very near General Davidson who rode upon a Black horse, when he received the ball that put a period to the life of the ablest, kindest & best officer that ever commanded an army. As soon as he was struck by the ball he called out 'Help me down, Boys, I am a Dead man—give the news to the men at the Island and above' and expired. We were soon thrown into confusion by the death of our beloved General; the Enemy took advantage of it, crossed the river overpowered our men and put us to flight- we scampered for life and made our way as well as we could to the Widow Torrance's land where we were stopped & formed into order of Battle by our company & field officers. It was raining like a Torrent, Tarlton with his light Horse pursued and here overtook and charged upon us. Our guns were so wet we could not discharge them and we were all put to flight in the utmost confusion. I ran and escaped as well as I could. I fell in with an old Horse without Saddle or Bridle and was enabled to get hold of & mounted him. I traveled that day and night and near day stopped at a house to get something for my horse and myself to eat. I was then informed that I was only about twelve miles in a North West direction from the Widow Torrances' lane where we had been beaten & put to flight. I then bent my course so as to escape the enemy & coming near to, but north of, Salisbury learned that the enemy had just passed through that town. I directed my course up the river and crossed the Yadkin high up and passed along through Salem thence a winding and crooked course so as to avoid the enemy until I got entirely clear of them and then struck a direct course toward home.

William was at the Battle of Cowan's Ford fought on February 1, 1781. Less than 1,000 American troops were trying to slow an army of 5,000 British troops advancing across the river. There had been a heavy rain, and at daybreak the British began to cross the swollen stream. General Davidson began to rally the Americans to stop the British.

Soon after the General arrived he was shot in the left breast with a small rifle ball, and he never moved after he fell from his horse. Frederick Hager, a local Tory guide, was known to have a rifle of that description, and it is believed that he shot the General. After the war Hager moved to Tennessee, and when some of the Davidson family moved there, Hager left for Arkansas.

> Shortly after my return home I was attacked by sickness and was unable to Join the company under my captain who had crossed Dan River passed down the Roanoke, crossed over at Taylor's Ferry & had come on to Harrisburg. Being too unable to travel I remained at home when they marched to Hillsborough. In a short time I was so much improved in health and strength that I set out to Join the army and at Johnson's old store on Little River, I met the remnant or a part of our company returning home. I was informed by them that as the term of service was within a few days of expiring, and there was great demand for arms to supply the new recruits who had Joined the army without arms, we were discharged & I returned with them and in a few days afterwards we heard of the Battle of Guilford.

> In the Summer of 1781 I performed another tour of three months duty by Draft I was commanded by Wm Hargrove Searcey Captain, the other officers I cannot recollect. We were drafted and marched from Oxford in Granville County to Hillsborough thence to Cross creek, from which place Genl. Butler marched us to the Raft swamp in the neighbourhood of which the enemy consisting of British & Tories were collected in considerable force. After being in service some time Capt. Searcey obtained a furlow or discharge and left the Army and I took his rifle shortly after I was selected by General Butler as a Cook and continued in that character until I was discharged, which was upon the reception of news of the capture & surrender of the British Army under Cornwallis at York town.

In 1832 Thomas Jordon, who served with William, wrote a letter to the pension bureau in support of William's service. He provided an interesting story about William,

> The said Jordan that he entered the service of the United States in the Company commanded first by Jones Fuller & afterwards by Shadrach Parrish. He [Jordan] was but a little the rise of fifteen years of age at this time was small & slender and marched in company with said Taburn, who taking a liking to him the said Jordan, whenever we had to cross a deep Creek or other water course Taburn would stoop down and take him this affiant on his shoulders and carry him across the stream.

Sources: 1. Graham, *General Joseph Graham and His Papers on North Carolina Revolutionary*, pages 288–95. **2.** National Archives Pension Application W18115. **3.** Moultrie, *Memoirs of the American Revolution*, pages 321–6.

Drewy Tann

Drewy Tann was born a slave c. 1759 in Wake County, North Carolina. He received a yearly pension of $50 and his freedom for his fifteen months of service. He stated in his pension application on March 17, 1834,

> That he enlisted under Capt. Hadley in the County of Wake in the State of North Carolina, and states the manner he came in the service as follows, that being born free in the county of Wake he was stolen from his parents when a small boy by persons unknown to him, who were carrying him off to sell him into Slavery, and had gotten with him, and other stolen property, as far as the mountains on their way, that his parents made complaint to a Mr. Tanner Alford who was then a magistrate in the county of Wake state of N. Carolina to get me back from those who had stolen me, and he did pursue the Rogues & overtook them at the mountains and took me from them & my parents agreed that I should serve him (Tanner Alford) untill I was twenty one years old, when he had served Alford several years (six years) it came Alfords time to go in the army (or he told me so) and told me if I would go in the army he would set me free on which condition I readily listed under Capt. Hadley for eighteen months as he was told and marched to Charleston & thence to James's Island where he served out his tour of enlistment that he had a discharge and was about returning home when a Capt. Benjamin Coleman who told me he lived in Bladen County N. Carolina took his discharge from him and tried to compel him to remain in the service & be his waiting man. his name is to be found in the Records of the State of North Carolina as he is informed by Mr. Deverieux of the City of Raleigh N. Carolina & the time of his inlistment as well as the fact of his inlisting under Capt Hadley as stated above. he cant state at what

period of the war he entered the service. General Green was the commander in chief, Col Lightly & Capt Lightly adjutant Ivy.

Sources: 1. National Archives Pension Application S19484. **2.** Grundset, *Forgotten Patriots, National Society of the D.A.R.,* page 566.

Quom Tanner

Quom Tanner was born c. 1762, and he received a pension of $8 a month for his service. He served in the 1st Rhode Island Regiment and was a prisoner of war. He gave his pension statement on April 2, 1818,

> That the said Quom Tanner enlisted in the state of Rhode Island in the month of February or first of March [1777] for during the war in the company commanded by Captain Elijah Lewis in Colonel Christopher Green's Regiment Rhode Island line. Was stationed the 1st year in East Greenwich in said state the next year he was in the expedition under General Sullivan on said Island was in said battle and retreated from the Island to East Greenwich and remained there through the winter.

The Battle of Rhode Island took place on August 29, 1778. The Americans under the command of General John Sullivan had abandoned their Siege of Newport, and they were withdrawing when attacked by the British. The 1st Rhode Island Regiment which had a large number of African Americans, including Quom Tanner, took part for the first time. Side by side these newly freed slaves fought with their former masters.

The Regiment drilled by Colonel Christopher Green, Lt. Colonel Jeremiah Olney, and Major Samuel Ward was stationed in a grove in the valley on the right flank of the main army. The Regiment led by Major Samuel Ward was attacked by the Hessians, and three times the 1st Rhode Island Regiment repelled their attacks. The Hessian Colonel who had led the attacks applied for a change of command, because he was afraid that if he led his Regiment in another attack his men might shoot him for causing them so great a loss.

The battle was a draw, however, with the retreat of the Americans Aquidneck Island remained in the control of the British. The African Americans in the 1st Regiment had their first taste of battle, and they received praise for their actions under fire. They had three men killed, nine wounded, and eleven missing after the battle.

> In the following season was detached with twelve others as a guard on Quitnesick Neck and were surprised by a party of British and taken prisoner and carried on to Rhode Island put in prison and there remained until the British forces evacuated Rhode Island and was taken by them to New York and remained a prisoner until the close of the war when he obtained his liberty.

Sources: 1. Lippitt, *The Battle of Rhode Island,* pages 11–13. **2.** Murry, *General John Sullivan and the Battle of Rhode Island,* pages 21–23. **3.** National Archives Pension Application S42445.

Primus Tyng

Primus Tyng was born c. 1760 in Salem, Massachusetts. His father was Jack, and his mother was Priscilla Crowingshield and a native of Guinea, Africa. Primus applied for a pension on August 20, 1833.

He enlisted in May or June 1776 and Primus said he served three months as a private in Captain Flint's Company, Colonel Tarleton's Regiment [Captain Flint was in Colonel Johnson's 4th Essex County Militia Regiment]. After his enlistment was up he enlisted for one year in the same company and regiment. He was frequently out on scouting parties against the cowboys. When his enlistment was up he again enlisted and served until the remainder of the war.

After the death of Captain Flint, Primus was under the command of Captain Samuel Frazier. Primus said he was at the Battles of Saratoga, Monmouth, and Stony Point. His claim for a pension was rejected, because he could not prove 6 months of service. Also Colonel Tarleton was not on any army rolls.

Sources: 1. National Archives Pension Application R10795. **2.** Grundset, *Forgotten Patriots, National Society of the D.A.R.*, page 134.

Luke Valentine

Luke Valentine was born c. 1754 in Bedford County, Virginia. He received a yearly pension of $38.33 for his service. Luke stated in his pension application dated November 13, 1832,

> That about the middle of May 1780, I was drafted into a Malitia Company in the service of the United States, commanded by Captain Thomas Leftwitch and met together at New London in Bedford County in Virginia, Augustine Leftwich was the Lieutenant. I marched to Hillsborough in North Carolina, where all the Virginia Malitia rendavouzed in that campaign; and where they were organized into regiments forming a brigade, commanded by General Stevens; The regiment to which Captain Leftwitch's company was attached was commanded by Colo.Stubblefield & Spencer; at which place (Hillsborough) the Brigade was stationed five or six weeks, and from thence marched to South Carolina, and joined the regular army at Rugeley's mills about two days before General Gates' defeat near Camden and I was in said battle The company to which I belonged was so scattered that they were not got together again so far as I know, and I joined a new company under Captain Daniel Mitchell of Bedford County and marched to Hillsborough in North Carolina early in the month of September 1781 [the correct year is 1780] I think the battle at Camden was in August before. Captain Daniel Mitchell's Company was attached to a Company of Malitia in the United States service at Hillsborough N.C. & commanded by Captain Phillip Webber of Goochland County Virginia, Lieutenant John Towns, and Ensign John Grissom which company was attached to a regiment commanded by Colo. Lucas and Major Glen; from Hillsborough we were marched to the Cheraw Hills in South Carolina, and from thence marched to Pittsylvania old Court in the State of Virginia and I, with the rest of the regiment, was discharged about the first of Febuary 1781, making eight months and a half that I served.
>
> About the first of May 1781 I was again drafted from the said County of Bedford and

entered the service of the United States in a Company of malitia commanded by Captain Adam Clement, Lieutenant Robert Cobbs, and Ensign Edmund Tate and marched from the County of Bedford to Salisbury in North Carolina, and was attached to a regiment commanded by Colo. Alexander Rose with Major John Ward; From thence we marched to Fort 96 in South Carolina where the regiment joined the Southern Army under General Nathaniel Green during the seige of that fort which continued 15 or 20 days after the arrival of Colo. Rose's regiment. From thence we marched to Broad River, and from thence to Wanesborough, from thence to Camden, from thence back to Salisbury where the Virginia Malitia took charge of a number of British prisoners and marched them into Virginia in the County of Pittsylvania where I was discharged by Major John Ward about the first of August 1781.

Sources: **1.** National Archives Pension Application S6299. **2.** Grundset, *Forgotten Patriots, National Society of the D.A.R.,* page 528.

Prince Vaughn

Prince Vaughn was born c. 1763 in Rhode Island, and he died on November 25, 1820, in New York City. He applied for a pension on June 23, 1820,

He enlisted in the black Regiment [1st Rhode Island Regiment] commanded by Colonel Greene in the company commanded by Captain Elijah Lewis as a private in the month of March 1778. He enlisted for and during the war. Deponent was in the Battles of New Port, White Plains, and at the Siege of Little York in Virginia at the time Lord Cornwallis surrendered.

Deponent was in the Oswego expedition under the command of Colonel Willett where he had all his toes frozen on his right foot, and his left partially frozen, and was honorably discharge at Albany in the year 1783.

The first engagement of the Black Regiment was at the Battle of Rhode Island, also called the Siege of Newport, which took place on August 29, 1778. Prince stated that he enlisted in 1778, so he could not, as he stated, have fought at the Battle of White Plains on October 28, 1776.

In February of 1783 General Washington sent Colonel Willett and 500 troops to capture the British fortification of Oswego in New York. Prince Vaughn and the rest of the Americans arrived at Oswego Falls about two in the afternoon on February 10th. Prince may have been one of the men sent into the woods to make eight ladders that would be used to scale the walls of the fort. By 10 o'clock that night the troops were about four miles from the fort.

Colonel Willett got a young Oneida Indian by the name of Captain Jack and two of his friends to act as guides for the Americans. The night was very cold, and the Americans had to march to the fort in deep snow. Unfortunately, the guides became lost, and they had led the men into a swamp. Some of the men including Prince had begun to have their feet frozen in the cold icy water.

The element of surprise was lost, and Colonel Willett decided to abandon the mission and return back home. During this time one soldier had frozen to death, and two others nearly frozen left the army and went on to the fort and surrendered to the British. Many of the American soldiers were lame from the cold conditions and had to be attended to. The Americans left their scaling ladders behind, which the British later gathered and brought into the fort. One of the American prisoners in the fort said the British placed the ladders against the walls, and they only reached two-thirds of the way to the top.

When Prince Vaughn left the army he was very poor and had moved to New York City. In his pension application he had to give the worth of his property and explain why he was deserving of assistance. He wrote in his pension letter that the value of his personal property came to $1.82.

> He is a shoe black by occupation [shines shoes and boots] and keeps an oyster stand when he is able. He has been sick for four years & subject to rheumatism and able to do very little. He has no family and cannot support himself without private and public charity.

He received a monthly pension of $8 for his five years and three months of service. He was also able to write his name on some of the pension documents. He died a free man in 1820.

Sources: 1. National Archives Pension Application S42603. **2.** Willett, *A Narrative of the Actions of Colonel Marinus Willett*, pages 30–33. **3.** Glatthaar & Martin, *Forgotten Allies: The Oneida Indians and the American Revolution*, page 268.

Drury Walden

Drury Walden was born in 1762 in Surry County, Virginia, and he died on December 22, 1834. He received a yearly pension of $38.33 for his eleven months of service. He stated in his pension application of September 4, 1832,

> That in the spring of the year of 1779 he was drafted for 5 months in Bute County North Carolina (since divided into Franklin & Warren) a musician in Capt Charles Allen's Company Lt. Wm Allen 4th Reg North Carolina Militia commanded by Col Thomas Pugh with his company he marched to Georgia crossed the Savannah River at Augusta, went down the River to Brier Creek where we had an engagement. Our Troops were commanded by General Ashe, of the Militia, Gen'l Elbert of the Regulars. Only about 300 Regulars there. Lord Cornwallis and Col Hamilton commanded the British. The Americans retreated about 300 men & 12 officers were taken, also Col Phil Alston. The company rendevoused at Pughsbury So. Ca. where he staid until his term expired. He was discharged & his discharge signed by the Col. Eaton.

The Battle of Brier Creek was a British victory that took place on March 3, 1779. Lord Cornwallis was not at this battle as reported in the pension statement of Drury. Cornwallis had left for England in November 1778 to be with his sick wife Jemima. She died in February 1779, and Cornwallis returned to the colonies in July of 1779.

The American troops were taken by complete surprise by the British and their Tory allies. American General Thomas Eaton fled from his tent in such a hurry that he left his boots behind. Eaton had a small foot and wore boots of unusual finish and neatness. The Tory leader Colonel Hamilton knew Eaton and recognized the boots. He purchased the boots from the soldier that had taken them.

After the war Colonel Hamilton and General Eaton were at a dinner party given by Willie Jones in 1809. Hamilton returned Eaton's riding boots that he had taken from Eaton's tent during the battle. Eaton, it was reported, became enraged and threw the boots across the table at Hamilton's head.

> This applicant again enlisted for a tour of three months under Col Long who was Commissary General of North Carolina Militia stationed at Halifax; here he served at his occupation making gun carriages for the cannon, canteens for the soldiers, building barracks &c &c. After his term of service expired he was discharged by Col Long.
>
> He was in 1781 a substitute for Edward Jackson a private in Capt Kid's company in Halifax County No Ca Reg't NoCa Mil'a In this company he was employed as a Guard for the Jail in Halifax which was filled with Tories. While here Cornwallis was taken at Little York.

William Hardie wrote a letter to the pension bureau supporting Drury, "Drury Walden was for years a preacher of the Gospel of Jesus Christ, and that in his will he acknowledged Elizabeth Walden as his beloved wife."

Roberson Kee also wrote a letter on November 27, 1844, "No man, no, not Jas. K. Polk himself is of better moral character than was the said Drury Walden." On May 20, 1846, Mrs. Winifred Holly made a statement that said,

> She was an eye witness to the marriage of Drury Walden to his wife Elizabeth, whose maiden name was Elizabeth Harris; That they ran away, and was married some time in the year (1780) seventeen hundred and eighty (she well remembers) in an old field a little from the Road, in the County of Northampton North Carolina by Herbert Harris, who was at that time, an acting Magistrate in the said County of Northampton; and that the said Drury and wife (after their intermarriage) took supper that evening at her Winifred Holley's Mothers House. That she well recollects, that at the time of the aforesaid marriage (To Wit) in the year (1780) her husband Jesse Holley was then a soldier in the army.

The son of Elizabeth, Armstead Walden, was denied his mother's widow's pension because in 1838 she was not a widow as required by law. Drury is listed as a "free colored person" in the 1830 Federal Census.

Sources: 1. Schenck, *North Carolina 1780–81 being a History of the Invasion of the Carolinas by the British Army under Lord Cornwallis*, pages 306–7. **2.** National Archives Pension Application R11014.

Caesar Wallace

Caesar Wallace was born c. 1738 in Africa, and he was brought to the colonies as a slave at the age of five. He married Katy Duce on March 25, 1783, in

Exeter, New Hampshire. Caesar died on November 18, 1821, in Rye, New Hampshire. He received a monthly pension of $8 for his five years of service. He stated in his pension application dated April 23, 1818,

> That he the said Caesar Wallace sometime in the year 1777 enlisted and entered the aforesaid service in Newbury, State of Massachusetts for during the war in the company commanded by Captain Caleb Robinson and regiment commanded by Col. George Reed, New Hampshire line that he continued to serve in said service of the United States in the war aforesaid on the continental establishment from the 1777 until June the 7th 1783 when was discharged at New Windsor in the State of New York. That we was in the battle of Monmouth and at Horseneck and at Newtown and that he is in reduced circumstances and stands in need of the assistance of his country for support.

Caesar joined the 2nd New Hampshire Regiment under the command of Colonel George Reed and he spent the cold winter of 1777–8 at Valley Forge. At the Battle of Monmouth Caesar was on the right wing of the main army under the command of General Greene.

Sources: 1. Grundset, *Forgotten Patriots, National Society of the D.A.R.*, page 56. **2.** National Archives Pension Application S43250. **3.** *Collections of the New Hampshire Historical Society*, Vol. 7, page 313. **4.** Parsons, *History of the Town of Rye, New Hampshire*, page 268–9.

Cuff Wells

Cuff Wells was a slave belonging to Israel Wells. Cuff served in the army from the winter of 1777 until the fall of 1783. He took the last name of Saunders when he gained his freedom after the war. Many of his friends called him Doctor Cuff.

Phillis Hinkley wrote that Cuff would come home on furlough occasionally and would call on her. He proposed marriage, but her mistress Mrs. Elizabeth Hinkley would not consent to the marriage. In April 1783 Phillis got John Shapley, a clerk of her master Charles Hinkley, to write to Cuff that her mistress finally gave permission for them to marry. Cuff got a furlough and the couple were married in May of 1783.

After Cuff died in 1788, Phyllis married Anthony Tatton who died in June of 1806. Phyllis never married again and later received a widow's pension of $80 a year. She applied for a widow's pension on November 3, 1837, and stated,

> Cuff Wells who was a slave of Israel Wells of S. Colchester and that in order to obtain his freedom enlisted into the Army of the United States in the winter of 1777 as a private soldier for the term of during the war and was placed in a Reg. commanded by Cols. John Durkee & Benjamin Shroop who was a brother to my old mistress Mrs. Elizabeth Hinkley. He did duty as a private army waiter to the Surgeon of said Regt. and it having been discovered by the officers of said Reg. that the said Cuff possessed considerable Medical skill by having some years been a slave of Doctor Langsel of Hartford who was a Physician and

kept an apothecary store where said cuff learnt the art of preparing & mixing medicine, he was accordingly placed in a Hospital as a waiter assistant to the Surgeon and part of the time as an assistant in the apothecary store belonging to the Continental Army at Danbury in said state where he continued till late in the fall of 1783.

That we had agreed to marry each other before he went into the army, that he returned home in the month of May 1783 on a furlough dressed in uniform with said __?__ and the letters U.S.A. on his buttons at which time she married to the said Cuff in the month of May 1783 at the house of my master Charles Hinkley by the Rev. Timothy Stone.

The said Cuff soon after returned to the army at said Danbury where he combined until the fall of 1783. He returned home and purchased about three acres of land [from Jonathan Webster] & built a small house in S. Lebanon where we lived together until Dec. 1788 and that her husband died in the month of Dec. 1788 after a severe sickness with the Influenza. Doctor Coleman who likewise belong to the Revolutionary Army and a neighbor, attended my husband as Physician in his last sickness.

Sources: **1.** National Archives Pension Application W18103. **2.** Grundset, *Forgotten Patriots, National Society of the D.A.R.,* page 294.

Prince Whipple

Prince Whipple was born in Amabou, Africa, to fairly wealthy parents. When he was about ten years old he and his cousin Cuff were sent to America to be educated. Prince had an older brother who had returned from America several years earlier. The ship's captain proved to be dishonest, and when the two boys were taken to Baltimore he sold them as slaves. Prince was purchased by William Whipple a future signer of the Declaration of Independence. Cuff was purchased by William's brother Joseph Whipple. Prince said that his first name was his actual name, because it reflected his status in Africa. Usually a slave's real name was taken away in order to strip away their African identity.

When the American Revolution began William Whipple became a Brigadier General in the New Hampshire militia. The American troops were gathered at Saratoga, and General Whipple took Prince along as a waiter. Prince told General Whipple that his owner was going to fight for his freedom but he had none to fight for. The General promised Prince his freedom if he did his duty in the army. Prince accompanied General Whipple on military campaigns to Saratoga, New York, and Rhode Island.

According to legend Prince Whipple accompanied George Washington at the crossing of the Delaware River, and he is portrayed fending off ice with an oar in the famous painting *Washington Crossing the Delaware.* It is very unlikely there is any truth to this legend. At the time of the crossing William Whipple was serving in the Continental Congress, and his servant Prince Whipple would have been with him.

In 1779 Prince was one of twenty African petitioners who said they were taken from their native lands while children, and they were now pleading to the New Hampshire legislature for the abolition of slavery in the state. No action was taken on the petition, and slavery would not be abolished in New Hampshire until 1857.

After the war Prince was given freedom in gradual stages by William Whipple. When Prince married Dinah Chase on February 22, 1781, William wrote a special document that gave Prince the rights of a freeman.

William had great trust in Prince. On one occasion he gave Prince a large sum of money to carry from Salem to Portsmouth. Prince was attacked by two robbers on the road near Newburyport. Prince struck one robber with a whip, the other one he shot, and he arrived home safely with the money. William finally gave Prince his freedom in 1784, and when William died the next year his widow honored the General's promise to provide a lifetime home for Prince and his family. Prince moved to a house on the property of the General, and he and his wife Dinah raised seven children.

Prince died in 1796, and in Dinah's obituary in 1846 Prince was described as, "A large, well proportioned, fine looking man, and of Gentlemanly manners and deportment. His death was much regretted both by white and colored inhabitants of the town, by the latter of whom he was always regarded as their prince."

Sources: 1. Nell, *The Colored Patriots of the American Revolution*, pages 198–9. **2.** Grundset, *Forgotten Patriots, National Society of the D.A.R.*, page 56.

Cuff Whittemore

Cuff Whittemore was born c. 1751 and was the servant of William Whittemore. Captain Thompson of the Menotomy Light Horse related this story about the battle of April 19, 1775,

> Cuff was on the hill with the Memotomy militia, of which Solomon Bowman was Lieutenant, and on the opening of the fight at that point, which was evidently near the house of Jason Russell of Arlington, the negro acted cowardly, and in his alarm turned to run down the hill. But the Lieutenant threatened to shoot him with a horse pistol, and pricked him in the leg with the point of the sword. This brought Cuff to his senses, and the negro "about facing" fought through the contest, as the colonel said, like a wounded elephant, making two cuss'd Britishers bite the dust.

He enlisted for eight months on June 4, 1775, in Captain Benjamin Locke's Company in the Regiment of Colonel Thomas Gardner. The Regiment took part in the Battle of Bunker Hill on June 17, 1775. The Colonel was the second highest ranking officer killed in that battle. It was reported that Cuff fought bravely in the redoubt and had a ball pass through his hat. He also seized the sword of a slain British officer and left the redoubt with it, which he later sold.

In 1776 he served a year in Colonel William Bond's Regiment at Fort

Ticonderoga. On May 15, 1777, he had enlisted in Colonel William Shepard's 4th Massachusetts Regiment and fought at the Battle of Saratoga. During the battle he was captured and taken to the camp of British General Burgoyne. The British were apparently not worried about Cuff, for one morning he was ordered to take the favorite horse of the General to the creek and water it. Cuff knew that the Americans were somewhere on the other side of the creek, so when he saw his chance he jumped on the back of the horse and took off across the creek. The surprised British troops took several shots at Cuff, but he made it back to the American army unharmed.

After the war he returned home a free man and received a pension of $8 a month for his service. On January 26, 1826, he died a pauper and with no family. He was one of a few men of color that received an obituary notice. It was published in the *Columbian Sentinel* January 28, 1826, "In Charlestown, Mr. Cuff Whittemore, a soldier of the revolutionary war, and a man of color."

Sources: 1. National Archives Pension Application S33896. **2.** Swett, *History of Bunker Hill Battle*, pages 25–6. **3.** Parker, *Town of Arlington Past and Present*, page 197. **4.** Cutter, *History of the Town of Arlington, Massachusetts formerly the Second Precinct in Cambridge or District of Menotomy, Afterward the Town of West Cambridge 1635–1879*, page 202.

Benjamin Wilkins

Benjamin Wilkins was born c. 1761 and probably in North Carolina. His pension was rejected because he provided no proof of dates of service. He stated in his pension application on August 28, 1832, that he was a freeman of color,

> That he enlisted in the Army of the United States, in the year he cannot recollect—it was in the autumn however, with Colonel John Branch who, at that time was recruiting in the Town of Halifax. He thinks he served in the 2nd Regiment of the North Carolina line under the following officers. The company was commanded by Captain Levi Lane and William Perkins was Lieutenant. He recollects Major Read and the whole under the general direction of General Caswell. He enlisted for 18 months— and after serving his term out left the Army in the month of February or March. From Halifax he went to Hillsboro—Salisbury— thence to Augusta Georgia and after beating up and down the country he was discharged at Lynchs' Creek in S. C. During this time he was in the battle at Brier Creek and at Pine Tree upon the Wateree. He recollects to have encountered many at the latter place and was wounded in the arm and thigh.
>
> The same deponent further says that soon after his discharge at Lynchs' Creek he was hired as a substitute for Jno Glover, and was put in a company commanded by Captain White—of which company Ben. Faircloth was Lieutenant. The Regiment was under command of Major Read still belonging to the Brigade of General Caswell. He remained for 9 months and was employed on a regular duty in South Carolina—during which time he was in several skirmishes with Tories. He was discharged at the White House in South Carolina and came home.
>
> After remaining at home about 4 months he was again hired as a substitute by Saml

Foreman and put in a company commanded by Griscom Cofield with Francis Williamson as his Lieutenant. This company was placed in the Regiment of Colonel Read—and having organized at Tarboro' marched to South Carolina passing through Fayetteville—Lumberton & to Pine Tree where he met General Caswell. He remained in South Carolina & Georgia performing such duties as were imposed upon him—and was discharged at Rutledge's Mill on Lynches Creek and came home. The British soon passed through the country and soon after Cornwallis surrendered. He thinks he has killed at least fifty British and Tories.

Source: **1.** National Archives Pension Application R11545.

Henry Williams

Henry Williams served in the 5th Maryland Regiment driving wagons. He was born c. 1750, and he died on January 5, 1850, in Baltimore City, Maryland. He married Easter Giles on August 11, 1785, and a Methodist minister, Charles Dorsey, performed the ceremony. His wife applied for a widow's pension, and she received a yearly pension of $80 for the service of her husband. She stated in her application dated April 28, 1857,

> She is the widow of Henry Williams deceased (colored) who was A Soldier in the Maryland line in the revolutionary War and that he also drove the waggons and made himself Generally useful have often heard him related the horros of war and how he has waded in Blood and walked over dead Bodies after battle in said war to the best of her Knowledge & Belief from what she has heard her aforesaid husband speak of his services that he served during said war under the Following Officers. John Kilty, Beal Smith, Norwood Ford and John Wayman or Wyming that he served in all about six years always heard him say that he entered the service at Anne Arundle County and that her husband the aforesaid Henry Williams was born in Anne Arundle County and that she was not married prior to the Termination of her said husband services but prior to 1794 that she has no record proof of her aforesaid husbands services but heard him relate many Incidents & exposures that he encountered during his services in said war.
>
> She further states that she dose not know that her said husband did ever apply for a Pension have often heard him say that he was Entitled to one she further says that she has had several children by her said husband who are now all dead the last one died in Eighteen hundred and Fifty four her only dependence She is now in Necessitious circumstances and applies for relief for the serviceses of her deceased husband Henry Williams.

Sources: **1.** National Archives Pension Application W3638. **2.** Grundset, *Forgotten Patriots, National Society of the D.A.R.*, page 463.

Matthew Williams

Matthew Williams was born free c. 1755 probably in Virginia, and he died on July 29, 1833. He received a yearly pension of $60 for his eighteen months of service. In his pension statement of September 17, 1832, he stated,

> That he served in the [blank] Regiment of [blank] Enlisted in cabin Pointin the year [blank] under colonel Dabney, was under the command of Col. Dabney & a Lieutenant Slaughter marched from cabbin Point to HillsBorough in N. Carolina thence to Saulsbury & was in

the battle of Guilford where he was wounded in the knee by a musket Ball That he was at the Siege of YorkTown in Virginia under the command of Col. Merrywether Major Dick & capt Ewel That under the command of capt. Ewel they attacked the Pidion Hill Fort and Drove the English from it. After the Battle of Guilford he marched to the Hanging Rocks under the command of Thomas Ewel.

When the Battle of Gilford Court House was fought on March 15, 1781, Matthew belonged to the 2nd Virginia State Militia. The battle lasted only ninety minutes and the British were outnumbered two to one, and yet they defeated the Americans.

William was also at the battle that took place at Pigeon Hill near Yorktown. The Siege of Yorktown took place between September 29 and October 19, 1781. Pigeon Hill was taken on September 28, 1781. The following is an account of the battle written by Ebenezer Denny of Pennsylvania and a Major in the Continental Army,

> September 28—The whole army moved in three divisions toward the enemy, who were strongly posted at York, about twelve miles distance. Their pickets and light troops retire. We encamped about three miles off—change ground and take a position within one mile of York; rising ground (covered with tall handsome pines) called Pigeon Hill, separates us from a view of the town. Enemy keep possession of Pigeon Hill. York on a high, sandy plain, on a deep navigable ricer of the same name. Americans on the right, French on the left, extending on both sides of the river; preparing for a siege. Our regiment, when on this duty, were under cover, and secured from the shot by Pigeon Hill; now and then a heavy shot from the enemy's works reached our camp. Our patrols, and those of the British, met occasionally in the dark, sometimes a few shot were exchanged—would generally retire. Possession taken of Pigeon Hill, and temporary work erected. Generals and engineers, viewing and surveying the ground, are always fired upon and sometimes pursued.
>
> **Sources: 1.** Ebenezer, *History of the U.S. from the Colonial Period until Modern Times, Ebenezer Denny 1781 Describing the Surrender of Cornwallis at Yorktown.* **2.** American History from Revolution to Reconstruction and Beyond website. **3.** National Archives Pension Application S6414. **4.** *Register of Free Negroes* 1794–1832, No. 589.

John Womble

John Womble was born c. 1756 in Edgecombe County, North Carolina, and he died there in October of 1820. He and his wife Catherine were married c. 1798 and had eleven children. He is listed in the 1820 Federal Census as a "Free Colored person." He received a monthly pension of $8 for his service.

> That on or about the first of June in the year of our Lord one thousand seven hundred & seventy nine, at the town of Halifax in the County of Halifax, State aforesaid, he enlisted as a private soldier under Major Hogg of the 10 Regiment of the North Carolina Line belonging & being attached to the Southern Department of the Continental army of the United States of America. From Halifax he marched with Major Hogg's recruits to Kinston (N.C.); at which place he was put under the command of Capt Quinn of the s'd 10 Regiment

commanded by the field officers Col. Robt. Mebane & Major Hogg—From Kinston he marched to Cross Creek (now Fayetteville N.C.) as a place of Rendezvouz, thence he marched in the summer of the said year to Charleston S.C. where soon after his arrival he was transferred to the company under the command of Capt Campbell of the said 10 Regiment commanded by the aforesaid Field officers. He remained in Charleston under the same officers till some time in August in the year of our Lord one thousand seven hundred & seventy nine when the American Forces under the command of Gen'l. Lincoln were called to make an attack on Savannah he then left Charleston & marched to assist in the said attack; but Gen'l. Lincoln being unsuccessful in his attempt on Savannah, the army returned to Charleston—soon after his return to Charleston he was placed under the command of Capt. Maun of the said 10 Regiment commanded by the aforesaid Field officers Col. Robert th Mebane & Major Hogg. He further maketh oath that sometime in May in the year of our Lord one thousand seven hundred & eighty, he assisted in the defence of Charleston, when attacked by the British Forces under Sir Henry Clinton; & in the unfortunate capture of that City he was taken prisoner & sent to Haddrell's Point. He further maketh oath that he well recollects that Capt Singles, then acting Brigade Major & Doctor Lumus Surgeon were among the captured & paroled officers. The battle, he remembers from circumstances that will never be effaced from his memory—according to the articles of capitulation, the officers & their servants were to be paroled & their persons & property held sacred; he embraced the opportunity as to avoid going on board the Prison Ships, immediately became Doctor Lumus servant & was with the Doctor dismissed on parole. He attended the Doctor to Washington (N.C.) & there remained some time, the residue of the time till the end of the War, he passed on the Banks of the Tar River on his Parole having never been exchanged & therefore not regularly discharged.

Sources: 1. National Archives Pension Application S42083. **2.** Sons of the American Revolution Application.

Dan Woodman

Dan Woodman was approached by a neighbor, Joseph Coe, who offered to handle his pension application. Dan consented and gave Joseph all the necessary papers. Joseph apparently filed for the pension and kept the money, a total of $288 from 1818 until 1821. In 1821 a new pension act required a person applying for a pension to show their income and worth, in order to prove need to keep getting their pension.

Dan realized that he was being cheated and requested that Joseph return all the papers he took from him, and also he forbid Joseph from drawing any more money. Joseph refused to do this, so Dan wrote to the pension bureau requesting a new pension certificate. His pension certificate of 1818 was canceled.

Dan made a new statement to the pension bureau and listed his worth at $9.83. He also stated that he and his wife Nancy were unable to work due to poor health. Dan received a monthly pension of $8 and the money was sent to him. He died on December 3, 1838.

He enlisted on June 24, 1777, and served in Captain William Rowell's Company in Colonel George Reid's 2nd New Hampshire Regiment. Dan fought in the Battles of Stillwater, Monmouth, and Newtown, and he was discharged in June of 1780.

Sources: **1.** National Archives Pension Papers S44103. **2.** Grundset, *Forgotten Patriots*, National Society of the D.A.R., page 56.

Asahel Woods

Asahel Woods was born c. 1749, and he was a servant to Captain Elisha Allis of Hatfield, Massachusetts. He enlisted for eight months on May 8, 1775, and the following June he fought at the Battle of Bunker Hill. On March 27, 1781, he enlisted for three years in the Continental Army at the age of 32, and he is listed as a farmer and 5 feet 5 inches tall.

Primus Hall, also in this book, stated in a letter in Asahel's pension application that Woods served as a wagoner, and the two men served together. "The said Asahel Wood was in the service as a waggoner in the Staff Department and taken out of the Line in which he previously was. The said Wood continued in that service with me until April following."

Asahel stated in his application dated April 20, 1818, "He was a soldier in the year 1775 in Col. Woodbridge's Regiment and was in the Battle at Bunker Hill. And in the year 1781 enlisted into Capt. Thomas Pritchard's Company in Col. Greaton's Regiment. He served until the close of the war."

In 1782 he returned to his regiment and served until late 1783. He married Tylea Job in 1802, and they had at least three children. Asahel died on December 27, 1822.

Source: **1.** National Archives Pension Application S33947.

Pompey Woodward

Pompey Woodward was born in June 1762 in Shrewsbury, Massachusetts, and he died January 13, 1843, in Sullivan, New Hampshire. He received a yearly pension of $56.66 for his service. He stated in his pension application dated August 21, 1832,

> In the year 1776 he thinks in June, at Crown Point when the army arrived there under General Arnold from Canada he volunteered and entered the service as a private. Was immediately placed in the hospital and inoculated with small pox, had the disease and as soon as he was removed from it was taken as a waiter by Col. or Capt. Edward Raymond who was then or soon after, and most of the time while he, Woodward, was in the service a commissary.
>
> That he went from Crown Point with the troop to Ticonderoga—was employed in repairing fort at Ti.— nd at Mount Independence, was back and forth stationed on the Ti

side—continued there in the service until Burgoyne came down in the spring of 1777. That Burgoyne landed above Ticonderoga across the neck of Lake George and took possession of Mount Defiance and that our troops then abandon Ticonderoga. That he was then marched off on Mount Independence side and went towards Bennington through Hubbardston—was in the advance at the time of the Hubbardston battle.

General Burgoyne marched his 8,000 British troops near Fort Ticonderoga on July 1, 1777. The Americans abandoned the Fort on the 5th of July, when they discovered that the British had placed cannons on a position overlooking the fort. As the Americans retreated, a British force caught up with the Americans' rear guard and a battle was fought near Hubbardton on July 7, 1777. The battle was a draw.

Went from there to Castleton and afterwards from there to Bennington was at Bennington at the time of the battle saw the prisoners taken in the battle __?__ into Bennington and put into the meeting house—recollects that there was a disturbance among the prisoners in the night and that they were fired upon by the sentries while in the meeting house and that some of them were killed. That after the Battle of Bennington he remained there until Burgoyne surrendered at Saratoga. That he then went with Capt. or Col. Raymond to Castleton that Capt. Or Col. Raymond then proceeded upon to the neighbor of Ticonderoga and left him at Castleton—waiting his return, for the purpose of looking after some property which said Raymond had in the vicinity of Ticonderoga. That said Raymond as he afterwards understands from him, was taken prisoner there—carried to Canada and afterwards to Halifax & exchanged in about two years & __?__ into Boston. That said Woodward when he learned said Raymond was taken which was soon after said Raymond left him at Castleton __?__ no further duty does not know that he engaged for any definite term—but __?__ as above stated from June 1776 to sometime in Nov. 1777 making as he believes 7 months.

After the war Pompey married Rosanna Hendley on April 15, 1788. After her death he married Polly (Mary) Harry in 1804, and they moved to Sullivan, New Hampshire. Mary was considered a "character" of the town.

On the first Sunday after her arrival in town, Mary and Pompey approached the meetinghouse. They were sitting on the same horse and Mary was heard to say, "Hold up your head Pomp, they will all look at us." When the pews of the second meetinghouse were sold, she insisted on Pompey buying a pew on the lower floor, "where the respectable people sat."

Mary wanted a house which would be the equal of any in town. She had Pompey take down an old house and erect a two-story house. They got the frame raised, and then the work stopped. Finally they boarded off a little room in one corner, in which they lived as best they could. She later told a neighbor, "Only three men in our neighbor have upright houses [two story] Deacon Steward, Captain Seward, and Mr. Woodward." Mary was not aware that Pompey had to borrow a large sum of money from Mr. Seward, in order to keep creditors from taking the home of Pompey. Mr. Seward took over the note himself and assured Pompey that any income from the property would go to Pompey and his wife.

The neighbors saw that with winter approaching Pompey and Mary would not survive in the little room they built. So, all the neighbors got together a build a small cottage for them. Mary was not happy with it, because it was not a two story house. Anytime someone would pass her house, she would raise the window and ask where they were going and what they were going to do when they got there.

Mary was well liked by others in town, and children enjoyed calling on her because of her very quaint observations. On one occasion some young ladies called on Mary and she told them, "I never drink tea because it unravels my nerves."

Pompey suffered for many years from the "shaking palsy" and he died in 1843. In the newspaper *Sentinel* on February 1, 1843, was the following obituary, "In Sullivan, Pompey Woodward, a colored man aged 77. He had been a professor of religion for a great number of years, and died a Revolutionary pensioner, always maintaining a character for strict integrity, and was highly respected by his neighbors."

Mary continued to live in the cottage until it burned in the winter of 1844. She was granted a widow's pension, and she died July 28, 1856.

Sources: 1. National Archives Pension Application W4867. **2.** *The Granite Monthly,* Vol. LIII, 1921, page 286. **3.** Seward, *A History of the Town of Sullivan New Hampshire 1777–1917 Vol. 1.*

Part II
Native American Soldiers

INTRODUCTION

> "In my Youth I bled, that you might be independent, let not my heart in my old age, bleed, for the want of your Commiseration."—*Peter Harris a Catawba Indian asking for a pension.*

The Declaration of Independence stated that King George III, "endeavored to bring on the inhabitants of our frontiers, the merciless Indian Savages, whose known rule of warfare is an undistinguished destruction of all ages, sexes and conditions." Thomas Jefferson's words had placed the Indians on the wrong side of the Revolution at the beginning of the war.

In July of 1776 the British had not begun to send their Indian allies against the Americans. The first group of Indians that fought in the revolution were the Stockbridge Indians of Western Massachusetts, when they joined Washington's Army against the British. Most Indians saw the war as a civil war, and they did not want to get involved in a "family dispute."

The Mohegan Preacher Samuel Occom wished that the whites "would let the poor Indians alone, what have they to do with your Quarrels?" The Seneca chief Kayashuta agreed, saying, "We must be Fools indeed to imagine that they regard us or our Interest who want to bring us into an unnecessary War."

Soon both warring sides began to lobby for the support of the various Indian tribes. The British, Americans, and other Indians demanded to know who friends were and who were not. The tribes eventually realized that they were going to have to support one of the sides.

The majority of the Indian tribes sided with the British. It was the colonists that for years had been expanding into Indian Territory and setting up settlements. The British government passed the Royal Proclamation of 1763 that provided Indian lands some protection against colonial expansion. The Indians realized the best way to keep their lands secure was to support the British.

The Americans were also guilty of blunders in seeking Indian support. The Shawnee Chief Cornstalk visited the American Fort Randolph seeking a way for his people to remain neutral. A militiaman from the fort was killed by unknown Indians, so the soldiers arrested and executed Cornstalk, his son, and several other Shawnees.

Another time White Eyes the chief of the Delaware people agreed to join an American expedition as a guide and negotiator. The Americans claimed that the Indian died from smallpox, but it was later discovered he was murdered by a militia officer.

The Praying Indians of New England had felt a close personal relationship with the colonists, due to many years of religious interactions. The Oneidas in

New York also had close friendships with frontier settlements. When it became apparent they could not remain neutral, and being influenced by Christian missionaries like Samuel Kirkland, the Indians in those areas supported the American cause.

Massachusetts and Connecticut exempted Indians from their drafts, along with blacks, mulattoes, schoolteachers, and students at Harvard and Yale. Some Indians rallied to the American cause and served and suffered great losses. A small Indian town of Mashpee on Cape Cod had twenty six men enlist, and only one returned home. Half the Pequots who enlisted did not return home. So many Indian women were widowed by the war, that they were forced to go outside their communities for husbands. Many chose to intermarry with European and African American neighbors.

One interesting story did take place during the war. It was noted in the book *America: Through Revolution to Empire* by Francis Jennings. American Captain John Wood was taken prisoner by the Mohawk Chief Thayandanegea, who was also called Captain Joseph Brant. Wood gave the Mohawk Chief's hand the Master Mason's grip by accident. The chief had been made a Mason while visiting England and thought Wood was a lodge brother, so he ordered his men to spare the prisoner. Wood was not a Mason, but later felt compelled to join.

After the surrender of Cornwallis in 1781, some of the Indians on the frontier continued fighting to protect their land. For example, in 1782 Shawnee warriors ambushed and defeated Daniel Boone and his Kentuckians at the Battle of Blue Licks.

At the Peace of Paris in 1783 the Indians were not present and not mentioned in the terms. They were extremely angry to later learn that the British had given to the Americans all the land between the Atlantic and Mississippi, as well as the Great Lakes and Florida. The British had sold out their Indian allies and given away their land. The end of the war signaled the beginning of the assault on the Native American lands and their culture.

* * *

Akiatonhartonkwen (Louis Cook)

Louis Cook was a Mohawk Chief born c. 1740 in Saratoga, New York, and he died in October 1814 on the Niagara frontier. He was born to an African father and his mother was of the Abenaki tribe in Quebec. All three family members were captured when the French attacked Saratoga around 1745. His father became a servant in Montreal, while mother and son were taken to a Mohawk village in New York. There Louis was influenced by the Jesuit missionary Jean-Baptiste Tournois.

Louis later converted to Roman Catholicism and became fluent in Mohawk, French, and English. Although he was illiterate, he had a sharp mind and took an interest in the tribe's council. He distinguished himself as a fighter for the French during the French and Indian War. He was wounded during a skirmish against the British in the spring of 1756. His bravery in battle earned him a command of a party of Indians.

Louis was never able to accept being ruled by the British, which resulted in his becoming sympathetic to the American cause. Although most of the Indian tribes including the Mohawks joined the British side, Louis offered his services to General Washington in 1775. When Louis visited Washington again in 1776, he offered to raise 400 to 500 men. By 1777 Louis was in command of the Indian Rangers company which was attached to the 1st New York Regiment.

Washington later wrote, "On Sunday evening, thirteen of the [Mohawk] Indians arrived here on a visit. I shall take care that they be so entertained during their stay that they may return impressed with sentiments of friendship for us, and also of our great strength. One of them is Colonel Lewis Cook, who honored me with a visit once before."

Louis went with Benedict Arnold on his expedition to capture Quebec, and he was already referred to as "Colonel Louis." On June 15, 1779, he was awarded a Lieutenant Colonel's commission by the Second Continental Congress, and this made him the highest ranking Native American in the American Army. Louis fought in the American victory at the Battle of Oriskany on August 6, 1777. It was a bloody fight between American troops, and a large group of Oneida warriors against British troops, and Indians mainly from the Mohawk and Seneca tribes.

The memory of hand-to-hand fighting haunted Seneca Chief Blacksnake into his old age, "There I have seen the most dead bodies all it over that I never did see and never will again. I thought at the time the Blood Shed a Stream Running Down on the descending ground during the afternoon."

The Mohawk Indians were led by their Chief, the hated Joseph Brant (Thayendanegea). Some people falsely claimed that the Indians under Brant tortured and ate some of their prisoners. Louis began to develop a hatred for Joseph Brant. When each returned to their homes after the war, their hatred for each other divided the Mohawk nation and brought their tribes to the brink of war.

Louis Cook spent the winter of 1777–78 at Valley Forge. On October 19, 1780, the two enemies faced each other again at the Battle of Stone Arabia. A larger American force defeated the force of British troops, Brant's Indians, and Walter Butler's Tories. Louis was with Lieutenant Colonel Marinus Willett at the Battle of Johnstown in 1781, which was one off the last North American battles of the Revolution.

On October 25 a British raiding party, Tories led by Walter Butler, and Mohawk Indians marched into the Mohawk Valley to raid Johnstown. Willett although outnumbered stopped the enemy and chased them off. The Americans pursued the Tories under Butler, and despite a snowstorm caught up with them on October 31, 1781. Under the command of Colonel Willet was Joseph and sixty Oneida, Tuscarora, and Mohawk warriors.

A Mohawk warrior named Anthony and a white soldier shot at Walter Butler who was across the creek from them. Anthony ran across the creek and killed the wounded Butler with his tomahawk. When Louis rode up Anthony asked permission to scalp Butler. Louis turned to Willett and asked if he should be scalped. Willett replied, "He belongs to your party, Colonel." Walter Butler was relieved of his hair.

After the war Louis settled in the area of Sterling, New York, and became an adviser to the Oneida tribe. He married Marguerite Thewanihattaha, and they had several children. The Oneidas were the first Indians to suffer from the land greed of New York State. Governor George Clinton, the legislature, and land speculators pressured their loyal friends to sell off much of their tribal lands. The tribe lost nearly five million acres of land, and they ended up with a small reservation that could not support the Oneida population. Louis, who was probably too trusting, encouraged the tribe to make the land deals. For this modern historians have criticized him for making these bad deals.

When the War of 1812 began he encouraged the Indians tribes in his area to remain neutral. Louis, who had fought many years with the Continental Army was detained at Fort Niagara. The Americans had forgotten his service, and he was finally released when he showed his commission in the Continental Army and letters from George Washington. Louis followed the army into Canada, and he was present at one of the bloodiest battles of the war, The Battle of Niagara Falls on July 25, 1814. He was involved in a skirmish, fell from his horse, and died from injuries in October 1814.

Sources: 1. *Dictionary of Canadian Biography.* **2.** Shujaa & Shujaa, *The SAGE Encyclopedia of African Heritage in North America.* **3.** Watt, *Rebellion in the Mohawk Valley: The St. Leger Expedition of 1777,* pages 166–167. **4.** Donaldson, *Indians: the Six Nations of New York,* pages 39–40. **5.** Oberg, *Professional Indian: The American Odyssey of Eleazer Williams,* pages 19–21. **6.** Campisi & Hauptman, *The Oneida Indian Experience: Two Perspectives* edited, pages 39–40. **7.** Bonvillain & Deer, *The Mohawk,* page 63.

John, Robert, Joseph, and Samuel Ashbow

John Ashbow was one of four brothers who fought in the early days of the Revolution. The brothers were Mohegan Native Americans whose tribe was historically based in central southern Connecticut. John was born c. 1753 in Norwich, Samuel was born c. 1746, Robert was born c. 1725, and Joseph was born c. 1722. Robert died in the army during the retreat from New York in 1776.

John and Samuel enlisted in May 1775 in the company commanded by Captain John Durkee in Colonel Israel Putnam's Regiment. On June 16, 1775, they joined other regiments on Breed's Hill. The Connecticut troops were assigned to guard the rail fence on the north side of the hill. The troops held against two British attacks, but they were overtaken in the third attack. It was probably during the last attack that Samuel was killed, and he became the first Native American to be killed in the Revolution. John survived the battle and was discharged on December 16, 1775.

Sources: 1. *Yale Indian Papers Project.* **2.** *Biographies of Patriots of Color at the Battle of Bunker Hill* from National Park Service, page 10. **3.** Quintal, *Patriots of Color*, page 51.

Colonel Andrew Jackson Brown

Andrew Brown was born in 1730 in Spartanburg County, South Carolina, and he died of illness in 1783 in Elberton, Georgia. During the Revolutionary War John served with his father Colonel Andrew Jackson Brown. Colonel Brown, a full blooded Cherokee Indian, served with his twelve-year-old son nicknamed "Cherokee" John Brown. Andrew was an Indian spy under Colonel Pickens and Colonel Roebuck.

Sources: 1. *D.A.R. Lineage Book,* Vol. 39, page 297. **2.** *Roster of South Carolina Patriots in the American Revolution.*

Henry Cato

Henry Cato was born on March 25, 1756, or 1757 within five miles of Newark, New Jersey. His father was a Catawba Indian, and his mother was of mixed heritage.

In Henry's pension application dated April 29, 1834, he states that he is afraid that his name may not be found on any army rolls, so he makes out his statement as if he had been a militia soldier. He believed that he enlisted in Newark, New Jersey, about four weeks before the British first came into Long Island Sound. Since the British first arrived at Long Island around June 29, 1776, Henry must have enlisted at the end of May or first of June.

At this time Henry was stationed for several weeks at a fort on Staten Island. He describes the landing of the British troops, "Whilst at this Fort, the time I cannot state, the Asia a very large British vessel, under the command of Lord Howe or Cornwallis (which I cannot say particularly) when she came into sight, she ran aground, the tide having left her—she then hoisted a white Flag. But when the tide rose she hoisted a "Bloody Flag," and then fired upon the Fort. There were only one hundred & Five men at that time in the Fort. We did not fire at all, but were ordered to retreat. We retreated to Newark, where the whole army was then stationed under General Leigh or Lee. The British landed at New York."

Henry and the other Americans retreated from the fort on July 2, 1776. As the British troops began landing at Staten Island, the Americans took a few shots at them before they retreated to Newark and joined the army under General Charles Lee. One group of citizens' militia switched over to the British side when the Continental regulars retreated.

Henry stated in his pension,

> They [the British] also landed at Elizabeth Town Point. A short time after they landed we went and repulsed them at White Plains, under General Green or Sullivan. General Lee had been taken at Newark by the British.

He refers to the Battle of White Plains fought on October 28, 1776, which was a British victory. General George Washington was in command that day not Greene or Sullivan.

Henry also mentions the capture of General Lee. Lee was captured near his own camp by the British on December 13, 1776, at White's Tavern in Basking Ridge, New Jersey. The previous night Lee and a dozen of his guards stopped at the tavern for the night, even though they were just several miles from their camp. In the morning Lee was in his dressing gown writing letters, when he was captured by a British patrol that had stopped at the tavern. They let the General throw a blanket over his dressing gown, tied him on a spare horse, and sent him to the British camp about 80 miles away.

General Lee was not fond of his commander General Washington, because he thought he should have been appointed the commander of the American Army and not Washington. Lee once said of Washington, "He is not fit enough to command a Sergeant's Guard." It should be noted here that General Washington was never captured by the British. General Lee returned to serve several years later, after he was exchanged for British General Prescott.

Henry spent the winter months of 1777 in Morristown under the command of General George Washington. Henry stated in his pension,

> During this winter quarter I was with General Washington, where he took 500 Hessians on Christmas day without firing a gun. I think the Hessians were taken on Staten Island. They were in a Drunken frolic when taken. At this time, which I think was in December 1776, all New Jersey was overrun by the British. I was present at the battle of Trenton and there fought, under General Washington.

Henry was at the Battle of Trenton on December 26, 1776. Most reports claim that the Hessians were not drunk at the time of their capture. Henry said they captured the Hessians without firing a shot, which is incorrect. The Hessians had twenty-two killed and nearly ninety men wounded. The Americans had five wounded, and two men died of exposure during the march. The Battle of Princeton occurred on January 3, 1777.

> After the battle at Princeton a detachment was ordered by Washington consisting I think of 700—to guard Springfield then invaded by the British. In this detachment I marched. When we arrived at Springfield, the houses were on fire. The British fled—we pursued to Elizabeth Town Point firing on them as long as they could reach them. The British then crossed over to Long Island. 20 or 30 of the British were killed & wounded. 10 or 12 were taken prisoners. The army then came together. After this I was at the Battle of Monmouth

The above statement made by Henry is out of chronological order. The Battle of Monmouth took place on June 28, 1777, after Washington's army spent the winter at Valley Forge.

After the Battle of Princeton the army went into winter quarters. Henry probably described the Battle of Springfield, an American victory which took place on June 23, 1780. There were New Jersey Continental troops under the command of Brigadier General William Maxwell at this battle.

Henry states in his pension application dated October 24, 1834, that he acted as a waiting servant to General Washington for three years and he performed this service at the Siege of Yorktown in the fall of 1781. He also states that he bore arms in actual military service for four years, which gave him a total of seven years' service.

> The date at which I was transferred to this regiment [to serve as a waiter] must have been February 1778. In Ogden's Regiment I remained untill I became a waiter to Gen Washington. At the end of this term of Four years my father, who was a Regular in the United States troops (and who was a Friendly Indian) interceded on account of met, being unable to bear Arms, by reason of the Ravages of the Small Pox. and I became a waiter to Washington, in place of a man with whom Washington was dissatisfied on account of his habit of drinking—and who took my place in the Line under Ogden. Washington promised me that I should receive the same wages as a soldier. When my broke the Small Pox it was supposed the Contagion was brought into the army by a Ship load of clothing for the soldiers. It committed great ravages, and the men died 'like rotten sheep.'
>
> I was in the battle when Gen Burgoyne surrendered his army to Gen. Gates at Saratoga. This was about the middle of October in the second year of his enlistment [17 Oct 1777] and whilst I was in Darke's company and Henley's Regiment. After this Surrender, a Hogshead of rum was rolled out of the British stores, upon the Green, and each soldier was to fill his Canteen. I tied two Canteens together, and dipped them into the Rum and filled both. the only piece of roguery I will confess. The quarter master of the troops to which I then belonged at the time of this defeat, was named Swales, as I now believe, and was very hard upon the soldiers.

When Gen. Morgan (commonly called the "Black Waggoner" was taken prisoner by the British, he was bound under an oath never to raise arms against Britain again. He was released (or escaped) which I cannot say and came to Washington, whilst I was waiter to him, and got permission to raise a company. I was in the door of Washington's markee, when the application was made. Washington asked him, what about his oath, he had taken to the British? Morgan replied "By God Sir, he had let it run down the wrong side"! Washington smiled and told him, that if the British would take him again, they would quarter him. Gen Morgan a short time afterward went to the South, and fought there till the close of the War.

General Morgan was a big man, six feet tall, and brawny. Before the war he was a wagoner and drove his wagon loaded with supplies across hard and dangerous terrain to settlers. During the French and Indian War he used his wagon to help the British and earned the nickname "Old Wagoner," and not the Black Wagoner as suggested by Henry Cato.

General Morgan shared command with General Benedict Arnold during the Battle of Quebec on December 13, 1775. The two men at times did not get along, and one time they nearly got into a fight. During the battle Morgan and his troops were surrounded and had to surrender. Morgan, who had a deep hatred for the British, refused to surrender his sword.

He put his back to the wall, and with his sword in his hand he dared them to take it from him. The British threatened to shoot him, but the General would not hand over his sword. His men finally convinced him to hand over his sword to a priest that was present. Morgan said to the priest, "Then I give my sword to you; but not a scoundrel of those cowards shall take it out of my hands."

While a prisoner Morgan was offered the rank of Colonel in the British army, which he refused. He was exchanged in January of 1777 and he rejoined the American Army.

The pension application for Henry was rejected because his service as waiter to Washington was not believed. He had some people write to the pension bureau in his support, but to no avail. Later Henry Cato served in the Indian wars from April 18 to November 20, 1791, under Captain Zebulon Pike, Sr. His son, Zebulon Pike, Jr., was a famous explorer and had Pikes Peak named for him.

Sources: 1. Grundset, *Forgotten Patriots*, National Society of the D.A.R., page 382. **2.** Lengel, *General George Washington: A Military Life*, page 135. **3.** Lee, *Dictionary of National Biography*, 1885–1900, Vol. 32, pages 343–346. **4.** National Archives Pension Applications R1815. **5.** Graham, *The Life of General Daniel Morgan of the Virginia Line of the Army of the United States*, pages 103–104.

John Chowen

John Chowen was a mulatto who called himself an Indian. He was a minuteman from Lancaster, Massachusetts, who marched on the alarm of April

19, 1775, in the Company of Captain Benjamin Houghton in the Regiment commanded by Colonel John Whetcomb. On April 26, 1775, he enlisted for eight months service in Captain Benjamin Hastings Company in the Regiment of Colonel Asa Whitcomb. He was on the rolls dated October 6, 1775, at Prospect Hill, when he deserted. A newspaper printed a wanted description:

> Deserted from Prospect Hill, late of Bolton, in the county of Worcester.... John Chewen, of Capt. Hill's company, in Col. Phinney's regiment, in the new establishment, but of Capt. Hasting's company, in Col. Whitcomb's regiment, in the old.... John Chewen is a molatto, but calls himself Indian, about 5 feet 5 inches high, had on a dark coloured-coat, and a pair of breeches something lighter, has a wife at Holden, a proper Indian squaw, he loves a good deal of rum...

As many as one out of four American soldiers, especially in the militia, deserted during the Revolutionary War. Very few men ran away because they feared getting shot or killed. Men deserted because of the harsh military life, it was time for spring planting or fall harvesting, or they wanted to enlist in another unit and get an addition bounty for enlisting. Since John left in early October, it may have been to harvest his crops for fall so that his family would not starve.

In 1776 John served at Hull, Massachusetts, and probably as a coastal observer or guard in Captain William Warner's Company under the command of Colonel Josiah Whitney. In 1777 he served in the militia and later he transferred into the Continental Army for three years in Colonel Samuel Brewer's Regiment.

Sources: 1. Nourse, *The Military Annals of Lancaster, Massachusetts 1740–1865*, page 107. **2.** Quintal, *Patriots of Color*, page 81. **3.** Grundset, *Forgotten Patriots*, National Society of the D.A.R., page 105.

Nicholas (Kaghnatsho) Cusick

Nicholas Cusick was born c. 1756 in New York, and he died October 29, 1840, in Niagara, New York. He was a Tuscarora Indian Chief who recruited both Tuscarora and Oneida warriors to fight for the patriots. He served at the Battle of Saratoga and also served as an interpreter and bodyguard to General Lafayette. In his later years Nicholas served as an interpreter for the United Foreign Missionary Society of New York. Nicholas received a pension, which very few Indians received from the United States.

During the Revolutionary War Nicholas formed a band of Indian Rangers and offered their service to General Washington. Nicholas was commissioned a Lieutenant by General Washington. The Indian Rangers served in a regiment under the command of Colonel Van Schaick's Regiment and General Lafayette.

Nicholas is credited with saving Lafayette's life, and the two men became very good friends.

Many years after the war ended the chief was passing through Washington, when he accidently heard the name of Lafayette spoken. His eyes brightened and he asked, "Is he yet alive?" "Yes," was the reply, "he is alive and looking well and hearty." Nicholas answered, "I am glad to hear it." "Then you knew Lafayette, Mr. Cusick?" "Oh, yes," Nicholas answered. "I knew him well, and many time in battle threw myself between him and the bullets, for I loved him."

In 1825 Lafayette made a triumphant tour of the United States. On June 6, 1825, the group stopped at the Tuscarora Reservation and were greeted by a large number of Native Americans. According to newspaper accounts Lafayette asked at once for Chief Nicholas his old friend. The newspaper said, "The old chief appeared and was embraced by the general and invited to ride in the carriage and talk over old times."

After the war friends of Nicholas suggested that he was probably entitled to a pension, which he later received for several years. Congress later passed a law making it necessary that each pensioner should swear that he could not live without the pension. When the old chief was asked to do this he said, "Now, here is my little log cabin, and it is my own; here is my patch of ground, where I raise my corn and beans, and there is lake Oneida, where I catch fish, with these I can make out to live without the pension, and to say that I could not, would be to lie to the Great *Spirit*."

Nicholas could speak the English language very well, but when he said grace at his table he used his native tongue. "When I speak English, I am often at a loss for a word; when, therefore, I speak to the Great Spirit, I do not like to be perplexed, or have my mind distracted to look after a word, when I use my own language, it is like my breath, I am composed."

During the War of 1812 Nicholas again came to the aid of the United States. During the British and Mohawk Indian "scorched earth" raids from Fort Niagara on December 19, 1813, Cusick helped save fleeing refugees. His tribe fought off the raiders, which give the refugees ample time to escape.

He received a monthly pension of $20, 1,000 acres of land from New York, and 200 acres of land from the United States for his service. He stated in his pension application: "The said Nicholas Cusick entered as a Lieutenant in the year 1779 about the 1st of June and served under Colonel Louis of the 1st Indian tribe of Indians until the close of the Revolutionary War." On October 8, 1850, the son of Nicholas wrote to President Fillmore:

> My father Nicholas Cusick were services for the American independence in revolutionary war, though he was claimant some land lying in Seneca county five hundred acres

of land which he got cheated of it and loss of that land, we had once, to endeavoring to get recover it of the said land, but we could not recover.

Another thing I want to get my money, which is now in the treasury of the United States $125, the congress has been made approbations for my relief when I was at the west in 1848.

After the War of 1812 there was a period of rapid migration of white settlers into Niagara County. The government decided to solve the "Indian problem" and made the land available to the whites and encouraged the eastern Native Americans to move westward. The Indian land was wanted by two land speculators, Thomas Ogden and Joseph Fellows. The Tuscarora's agreed to sell the land to them for $9,000, but fortunately there was a federal government provision that would void the transaction if less than 250 Tuscaroras migrated west. Only about forty did move west in 1846. Most of them died, and no more ventured west.

Sources: 1. Johnson, *Legends, Traditions, and Laws of the Iroquois, or Six Nations and History of the Tuscarora Indians*, pages 165–6, 1881. **2.** Hauptman, *The Iroquois in the Civil War: from Battlefield to Reservation*, page 40. **3.** Grundset, *Forgotten Patriots*, National Society of the D.A.R., page 332. **4.** National Archives Pension Application S18788. **5.** Sons of the American Revolution Application. **6.** Kostoff, *Nuggets of Niagara County History*, pages 14–17.

Peter Harris

Peter Harris was a Catawba Indian born c. 1756. Both of his parents died in one of the major smallpox epidemics in 1759 that reduced the Catawba population to small numbers. Thomas Spratt, an early settler, came to the area c. 1761 and raised the young Indian boy in his family.

When the Revolution began the Catawba Indians of South Carolina debated which side they would be loyal to and fight for. The tribe talked with some of the South Carolina leaders, and they were promised ten shillings a day for each warrior that would fight for the Americans. Members of their tribe had fought with the British under the command of George Washington in the 1750s, so they agreed to join with the patriots.

They fought in most of the engagements that took place in the south, and because they could read the land they were often used as scouts. To distinguish themselves from the local Cherokee Indians, who had sided with the British, they wore deer tails in their hair.

Peter Harris was the only Catawba to serve in the regular Continental Army. He served as a private in a Battalion of Georgia Minutemen from June 3, 1777, until March 1, 1778. Peter joined the Third South Carolina Regiment commanded by Colonel William Thompson in February 1779 for one year.

Peter was wounded at the Battle of Soto Ferry on June 20, 1779. The Americans attacked a force of British and Hessian troops and were on the verge of victory when British reinforcements arrived. Running low on ammunition the Americans retreated.

After the war Peter applied for a pension, and he dictated the following statement to Senator Crafts of the Charleston District,

> I'm one of the lingering embers of an almost extinguished race, Our graves will soon be our only habitations, I am one of the few stalks; that still remain in the field, where the tempest of the revolution passed, I fought against the British for your sake, The British have Disappeared, and you are free, Yet from me the British took nothing, nor have I gained anything by their defeat. I pursued the deer for my subsistence, the deer are disappearing, & I must starve God ordained me for the forest, and my ambition is the shade, but the strength of my arm decays, and my feet fail in the chase, the hand which fought for your liberties is now open for your relief. In my Youth I bled in battle, that you might be independent, let not my heart in my old age, bleed, for the want of your Commiseration.

South Carolina awarded Peter a pension of $60 a year and later gave him 200 acres of land for his service.

Around 1783 Peter and two other Catawbas traveled to England with three white men. The white men made money from the Catawbas by taking them to show off in London and Ireland. After the tour was completed the white men disappeared with the money and left leaving the three Catawbas with just enough money to get home. On the return voyage two of the Indians jumped overboard, and Peter returned home alone. In 1795 a musical was written about the experiences of the three Catawbas in England entitled *The Catawba Travelers*. It was first performed at London's Sadler's Wells Theater.

In 1823 Peter made a death bed confession to a friend James Spratt. He said that he regretted killing a British soldier, who had set aside his gun to get a drink of water at a spring. Peter said that it was the act of, "a coward, rather than of a brave man, in which category he had always hoped his fellow-man would place him."

Sources: 1. Scoggins, *The Catawba Indian Company in Sumter's Brigade*. **2.** Nell, *The Colored Patriots of the* American Revolution, page 384. **3.** Blumer, *Catawba Nation: Treasures in History*. **4.** *The Historical Magazine and Notes and Queries Vol. V*, page 46. **5.** National Archives Pension Application SC18.

Nicholas Hawwawas

Nicholas was a leader of the Passamaquoddy Indians along the St. John River in Maine. He applied for a pension and received a yearly amount of $320. He claimed to own a sword presented to him by George Washington. He stated in his pension application,

On January 4, 1778 he was commissioned by the Council of Massachusetts Bay as Lieutenant of a body of Indians, under the command of Col. John Allan & served as such until the close of the War of the revolution, during which time he had fifty Indians under his command. They staid at Machias, in different places as at Indian so called, at the Lake Satagwagum, now Hadley's Lake, where they could be called in by alarm guns. Previous to getting his commission he was faithfully serving the United States, & helped drive off the English vessel commanded by one Dawson & also taking a vessel called the Neshquoit & also in taking their prisoners out of eight persons who were observed on shore from a British Ship near Cross Island gathering water, & of whom he & his men killed four more as they were pulling off in their boat to the to the vessel, the name of which vessel he does not know. He was not in any battle after he was commissioned as aforesaid, but once started on an expedition to Penobscot, now Castine, & went as far as Naskway where they heard the fleet at Penobscot was destroyed & it became useless to proceed & all came back.

The Penobscot Expedition was a 4,000 man American naval expedition consisting of nineteen warships and twenty-four transport ships. The purpose was to capture a 750 man British garrison at Castine on the Penobscot Peninsula in Maine. The expedition arrived July 25, 1779, and lasted until the middle of August. The Americans were defeated and lost 470 men compared to a loss of thirteen men by the British.

Sources: 1. National Archives Pension Application S17997. **2.** Grundset, *Forgotten Patriots, National Society of the D.A.R.*, page 22.

Joseph Burd Jaquoi

Joseph Jaquoi, a Mohegan Indian was born c. 1736 and probably in Connecticut. He served in the French and Indian War in the spring of 1758 in the Provincial Troops in Connecticut. After the war he accepted a Lieutenant's Commission in the Rangers under Major Rogers. He was at the taking of Montreal in 1760.

Joseph was in England on a Lieutenant's half pay when the Revolution began. He was offered a Captain's commission in the British Army, but refused it saying he, "refused to serve in that unnatural contest." He gave up his rank and pay in the British Army, and he returned to the colonies and settled in North Carolina. When the British invaded North Carolina he joined the American Army and served under Generals Lincoln and Greene. After the war he returned to his tribe after an absence of forty-eight years.

Sources: 1. Calloway, *The American Revolution in Indian Country*, page 28. **2.** *The Yale Indian Papers Project.* **3.** Grundset, *Forgotten Patriots, National Society of the D.A.R.*, page 281.

Anthony Jeremiah

Anthony Jeremiah was a Nantucket Indian that fought in the Continental Navy. He was called "Red Jerry" or "Red Cherry," and he served as a gunner under Captain John Paul Jones in the *Alfred,* the *Ranger,* and the *Bon Homme Richard*. In 1779 Jeremiah survived the battle off the English coast between the *Bon Homme Richard* and the British ship *Serapis*. With his tomahawk in hand, Jeremiah joined the boarding party that captured the *Serapis*.

A book written about John Paul Jones describes the action, "From the first broadside till the gun-deck was abandoned nineteen different men on this gun, and at the end but one of her original crew remained, That was our little Indian, Anthony Jeremiah, or as his messmates' nicknamed was 'Red Jerry,' generally pronounced by the crew 'Red Cherry.' He was 'port-fire' throughout. When the gun-deck was abandoned and we went above Jerry joined Mayrant's boarding party and was among the first over the enemy's hammock netting in the final rush. He seemed to bear a charmed life."

Sources: 1. Crawford, *The Sailor Whom England Feared: Being the Story of Paul Jones, Scotch Naval Adventurer and Admiral in the American and Russian Fleets,* page 240. **2.** D.A.R. magazine, Vol. LIV #1, January 1920, page 96.

James Keeter

James Keeter was born c. 1755 and he and his wife Mercy belonged to the Mashpee Indian Tribe in Massachusetts. The Mashpee Indians were given a district or "plantation" and the right to elect their own officials to maintain order. The white lawmakers appointed white overseers, because they believed that the native people were not capable of running their own affairs. For years the Indians asked for self-government but were turned down each time.

During the Revolutionary War many of the Mashpee enlisted in 1777 in a Regiment in the Massachusetts Line. The war took a heavy toll on the Mashpee enlisted men. After the war one source stated, "After the war our fathers had sixty widows left on the plantation whose husbands had died or been slain." Some of the women in the tribe were forced to look outside the tribe for husbands. James Keeter received a monthly pension of $8 for his service, and he stated in his pension application,

> I was a soldier in the war of the Revolution and enlisted into Capt. Smart's Company and Col. Smith's Regiment of the Massachusetts line for during the war and served faithfully therein to the close of it which was nearly four years.
>
> I was at the Battle of Kingsbridge and at the taking of Cornwallis. During my service I was often transferred from one Regt. to another and was finally discharged from my own company and Regt. in which I first enlisted.

Sources: 1. National Archives Pension Application S32942. **2.** Simmons, *Spirit of the New England Tribes: Indian History and Folklore, 1620–1984,* page 19–21. **3.** Freeman, *The History of Cape Cod: The Annals of Barnstable County, Vol. 1,* page 692.

John (Canada) Kenneda and Tall William

John Kenneda was born c. 1754 and was a member of the Oneida Tribe. Even though he had several soldiers write letters stating he was in the army and at different battles, his pension was rejected. The reason was that names of the officers under whom John served were not given. John stated in his pension application,

> That he was a member of the Oneida Tribe of Indians in the state of New York and entered and served in the Revolutionary War with the white men under Col. Willett on the Mohawk River—was at the battle at Canada Creek where Col. Butler was shot in the breast and killed—was at Osnyo [Battle of Oriskany], Sandy Creek, Johnstown and all along the Mohawk region.—was in the battle of Burgoyne. He served as much as three years, for the Americans and served them faithfully—has been Gen. Washington and many other American officers. There is no Indian now living at Oneida who was with Kemmeda except one about 100 years old and who has both his reasons. Kenneda acted often with the Indians as Spy Scouts.

Colonel Marinus Willett was the commander of the 2nd Albany County Militia Regiment and the Tryon County Militia in the Mohawk Valley. John Kenneda was in this regiment when the Tory officer Walter Butler was killed on October 30, 1781. In 1778 Butler and a Mohawk chief, Joseph Brant had led a company of Tories and Indians on a raid at Cherry Valley. They killed many women and children at the Cherry Valley Massacre.

When the hated Butler was killed at the Battle of Canada Creek on October 30, John Kenneda was there and witnessed it. Several men who were present described the event in their pension applications.

Henry Shaver stated, "That he" [Butler] "cried out to his pursuers to 'Shoot and be damned' which he had no sooner done than he was struck by a Ball from one Louis [the words "An Oneida" are crossed out] The Indian [the word "swam": is crossed out here] waded over [the words "and tomahawked" are crossed out] and scalped him."

Richard Casler wrote in his application, "When Willett's men came upon the enemy they were drying their cloaths by fires & were surprised at that place Walter Butler was killed by an indian (he believes) an Oneida indian. He [Casler] was there & saw the indian who killed Butler & who had Butlers Coat and scalp The indian shot Butler from across the Creek Butlers Sergeant was also killed at this place." John Kenneda wrote a letter to support the service of another Oneida Indian Tall William and in the letter he described the death of Butler,

> That he was together with the said Tall William engaged in a battle at West Canada Creek in which Col. Butler was shot through the head and killed and in which the enemy were defeated and after the battle was over I took from the pocket of Col. Butler a half guinea

and Black William took the shoe Buckles from his feet and saucy Nick another member of our Tribe & the one who shot Col. Butler took his Clothing and occasionally after that wore the same.

He, Canada [Kenneda], took a half guinea [equal to about one-half British Pound] from the body of Butler; *Black William* of the Oneida Nation took Butler's shoe buckles to wear around his neck; and while another Oneida and Laucy Nic:, who John states shot Butler, took Butler's clothing and occasionally wore it thereafter. Canada states Butler was shot through the head.

Tall William was born c. 1740, and he died on October 15, 1833, in New York. He served with John Kenneda through much of the war. His wife Betsey applied for a widow's pension and like John Kenneda's, it was rejected. The reason given was that Tall William did not belong to a regular military unit. In 1833 Congressman Barnitz presented a petition to Congress that the widow and children of Tall William of the Oneida tribe of Indians be given a pension for service rendered in the war. It was referred to the committee on Revolutionary War Pensions.

Sources: 1. National Archives Pension Applications for Henry Shaver S113710, Richard Casler W6637, and Tall William R5866. **2.** *Journal of the House of Representatives of the United States, December 2, 1833*, page 333. **3.** Grundset, *Forgotten Patriots*, National Society of the D.A.R., pages 334 & 338.

Robert Mursh

Robert Mursh was born c. 1758 in Virginia, and he died on December 7, 1837, in South Carolina. He graduated from the Indian School at the College of William and Mary in 1769. Robert belonged to the Pamunkey Indian tribe, and he married Elizabeth in an Indian marriage ceremony in August of 1783. About twelve years later he and Elizabeth decided to become Christians, so they were married in the Baptist Church. Robert became a preacher and was the pastor of Hopewell Baptist Church. He stated in his pension application,

> The declaration of Robert Mursh a native of Virginia and one of the Pamunky Tribe of Indians, and now a Citizen of & resident in York District in the state of South Carolina. The Declarer saith that he enlisted as a common soldier in the army of the United States in the War of the Revolution in the latter part of the year 1776 and in the Early part of the year following he joined the 15 Virginia Reg't of Continental Troops Col. Mason attached to a company commanded by Capt James Gray at Walliamsburgh & shortly after joined the main army at Middlebrook in New Jersey. That shortly after he joined the Reg't the Command of it devolved on Col. James Ennis and under his command he fought at the battles of Brandywine & Germantown in the Brigade commanded by Genl. Woodford.

Robert enlisted in the 15th Virginia Regiment and served in the 3rd Company under Captain James Gray. He later served in the 9th Virginia Regiment. At the Battle of Germantown the Regiment became separated from the remainder of General Greene's division, and many were taken prisoner, including Colonel Ennis.

> The Declarer further saith that having served in this Regiment for something more than two years he reinlisted in the Continental army in the service of the United States during the war, and was attached to a Regiment from out of the remnants of the 7 & 15 commanded by Col. Russell, Lieut Col. Burgess Ball denominated the __?__ Reg't. of the Virginia Continental line, Capt. William Mosely and that with this Regiment he marched to Charleston were he remained untill that place was surrendered to the British and was among the prisoners of war and remained in that situation about fourteen months when he was carried to Jamestown and exchanged and then joined a Regiment commanded by Col. Phebecca Capt. Kirkpatrick the number of which Regement is not now recollected. The command of this Regement was afterwards asigned to Col. Posey and with this Reg't. he marched to Ebeneezer in Georgia where they joined the Army of Gen'l. Wayne, and that he continued with this army until after the peace when he was regularly discharged from the service.

After Robert was exchanged, he joined a new eighteen month battalion under the command of Colonel Posey. They marched to Georgia and served under General Wayne against the British in Savannah.

When Robert died he had been receiving a yearly pension of $96. His wife Elizabeth applied for a widow's pension, which was rejected because their Christian marriage had taken place after the cutoff date for a marriage. To receive a widow's pension you had to be married to the soldier by 1794. After twelve years the pension bureau finally accepted her Indian marriage to Robert, which was before 1794. The pension bureau wrote,

> If at the time of the first marriage, the parties belonged to a tribe of Indians, over whom the law of Virginia, in regard to marriages, had not been in fact extended and enforced, & if they were married according to the usages & customs of their tribe, and lived together, and sustained the relations of husband and wife, by virtue of said marriage, among their tribe—such marriage would be valid in any country to which the parties might emigrate—and could not be rendered invalid by a subsemnization by other forms, induced by a change of religion.

Elizabeth received a yearly widow's pension of $80.

Sources: 1. National Archives Pension Application W8416. **2.** Roundtree, *Pocahontas's People: The Powhatan Indians of Virginia through Four Centuries*, page 335. **3.** Watson, *Catawba Indian Genealogy*, pages 70–2.

Jonathan Occum

Jonathan Occum was a Mohegan Indian born c. 1725 in Connecticut. The majority of Connecticut Indian soldiers were from the Mohegan tribe, which lived in New London County. Jonathan's brother was the famous Sampson Occum, who was the Christian missionary of all the tribes of southern New England.

Jonathan was fifty years old when he enlisted on May 10, 1775, in the Regiment under Colonel Israel Putnam. The Regiment fought at the Battle of Bunker Hill on June 17, 1775. Jonathan and other men from Connecticut were positioned behind a rail fence that had been constructed. Jonathan and the men stuffed the space between the rails with hay and dirt. The men repelled the British attacks but were forced to retreat when their ammunition was about gone.

Jonathan continued to fight during the war, and when it was over he returned to New London. He received twenty acres of land that was given to veterans in 1790. There is a record of him living in New London in 1804.

Sources: 1. Love, *Sampson Occum the Christian Indians of New England*, pages 204 & 354. **2.** Cutter, *The Life of Israel Putnam, Major-General in the Army of the American Revolution*, page 170. **3.** Grundset, *Forgotten Patriots, National Society of the D.A.R.*, page 285.

John Pin (Pinn), Robert Pin, Billy Pin, James Pin and Rawley Pin

John Pin was born c. 1760 in Virginia, and he married Anne Cassady on September 12, 1785. After the death of Anne he married Nancy Coffin in 1801. The Pins were Native Americans who originated from Indian Town in Lancaster County, Virginia. John served at Yorktown with his father, two brothers, and uncle. His pension was rejected for lack of proof of service. He stated in his pension application on October 8, 1842,

> That he the said John Pin together with his late Father Robert Pin and brothers Billy & James or Jim Pin, were Soldiers in the army of the Revolutionary War and that his Father Robert Pin aforesaid & himself served together in Captain William Yerby's Company of Virginia Artillery, and of the Regiment commanded by Col Williams. That himself was a Powder Boy, and attached to Gun No 3, under the command of said Captain Yearby. During which service he was at the siege of Yorktown in Virginia, when Lord Cornwallis surrendered his army to Genl Washington, that during the cannonade on that occasion he said John received two several wounds—one from an enemies spent cannon ball, which injured his right ancle—the other from a Musquet shot thro the left Legg.

James and his father Robert served in the Virginia Artillery. There were usually two gunners and six soldiers for each cannon. It took several men to load the cannon, and then after it was fired several men had to clean the piece. James, being a powder boy, had the responsibility to bring powder wherever it was stored to the cannon. This job required strength and quickness, because a good gun crew could fire four times or more per minute.

At Yorktown there were a total of fourteen American guns. On October 9, 1781, the American guns were placed, and at five in the evening they opened fire on the British. General Washington fired the first cannon. The guns fired all night, and soon British troops began to desert. It was the actions of these cannons that played a large part in forcing the British to surrender ten days later.

> The declarant further states that he is a descendant of the Aboriginies of America—that his Father was a Mustee (mixed) [probably part African and part Indian] & his Mother a Cherokee, & were inhabitants of Lancaster County Virginia at a place called Indian Town near Carters Creek in said County. that he is a Seaman by Ocupation in which employment he has been engaged ever since the termination of the Revolutionary War which calling he still follows. He also states that he has sailed out of most of the principle ports in the United States more particularly from Boston & Salem in this state. In the former place he married as his wife Nancy Coffin, some Forty years since, who died 22 years ago, and that he has been an Inhabitant of Massachusetts upwards of Fifty years, residing occasionally at Boston—Salem & Danvers in said state. At Salem he formerly owned a small House and Lot of Ground which House was thro' some accident burned down, and that he has more recently lost upwards of Five hundred and Ninety Dollars in money by the failure of Mr Aaron Ordway—a Merchant of Salem, in whose hands he had left the proceeds of his wages for many a voyage in the Merchant service, Intending thereby to have a sum of money in store to help himself in old age, but is now deprived of the same and is in indigent circumstances & stands in need of the assistance of his country. The declarant further states that soon after the termination of the Revolutionary War, his Father Robert Pin, obtained from the United States the quantity of Bounty Lands due on account of the services of himself & his three sons in the army—amongst it whose was the declarant & his brothers Jim & Billy Pin, who as he believes served in the Rifle Corps under Colonel Morgan—the former of whom was killed while in said service.
>
> That according to the best of my recollection the Troops to which I belonged were stationed at Gloucester some twelve months before the siege of York Town commenced. That my Father & myself were in Captain William Yarby's company of Artillery, that during the siege of Yorktown I was placed under Captain Moses Hawkins in whose company myself & Father served through the whole of the siege aforesaid I further testify and say that I have but a very limited knowledge of the terms of our enlistment or of its duration as my Father Robert Pinn aforesaid, transacted all the business relating thereto, and afterward in procuring Bounty Lands for himself and his three sons including myself. Which Bounty Land was sold to a Gentleman, called Captain John McTier of Lancaster, I received one Crown as the proceeds of the sale of my Bounty Land.

Rawley Pinn marched with his unit under the command of Major William Cabell in Colonel John Pope's Militia Battalion from Amherst, Virginia. At Yorktown the Battalion was merged with the main army commanded by Lafayette.

Sources: 1. National Archives Pension Application R8264. **2.** Grundset, *Forgotten Patriots, National Society of the D.A.R.*, page 525.

John Redcross

John Redcross, a Monacan Indian, was born in 1740 in Amherst County, Virginia. His daughter Nancy married James Pin, the son of Rawley Pin, who is in the Native American section of this book.

John enlisted in February 1779 in Captain William Long's Company of the 2nd Virginia State Regiment commanded by Colonel William Brent. The Regiment was called back to Virginia in late 1779. He probably served until the spring of 1780, when most of the Regiment was discharged.

In 1781 John was a member of the 2nd Virginia Cavalry and left Amherst on June 21, 1781, under the command of Major William Cabell, Jr. He joined with the troops under the command of Lafayette at Yorktown. John was discharged on April 25, 1783, and he returned to Amherst County.

Sources: 1. McLeRoy & McLeRoy, *Strangers in Their Midst: the Free Black Population of Amherst County Virginia*. **2.** Grundset, *Forgotten Patriots*, National Society of the D.A.R., page 525.

Cyrus Shelly

Cyrus Shelly was an Eastern Pequot Indian born in 1763 and probably in Connecticut. At the age of ten he was bound out to John Denison III of Stonington, Connecticut. A child might be an orphan or the parents too poor to take care of him, so the child would be "bound out." This meant that the child would work for their master for a certain number of years, usually until the age of twenty-one. In return the master would feed, shelter, and in some cases educate or teach a trade to the child.

In 1781 Cyrus enlisted in the 1st Regiment of the New York Line as stated in his pension application, "The first of March 1781 he enlisted as a soldier in the company commanded by Captain James Gregg, Colonel Van Schaick's Regiment for the duration of the war." He gave up his discharge to Nehemiah Fulmer to whom he sold his land to." Cyrus probably took part in the Siege at Yorktown.

After the war he returned home to the reservation and married Hannah Sowas December 19, 1784. When he applied for a pension he had to describe the property he owned and declare its value. He wrote on June 26, 1820, "I have 1 old decayed & miserable hovel for a house standing on Indian land worth about $15." The rest of his property had a value of $5.00. Cyrus received a monthly pension of $8.

In 1788 he signed a petition with other Eastern Pequots and sought the appointment of new overseers for the tribe. The overseers acted as guardians for the tribe. They established rules for managing the interest and concerns of the tribe. They controlled the property, contracts, and wages of the Indians. They also took care of the poor and bound out their children to suitable families. The Indians submitted a petition, because they were unhappy about the inconsistent distributions of profits from the rental of tribal lands.

By 1810 the marriage to Hannah had ended, either due to divorce or death.

Cyrus married Betsy Rogers on April 8, 1822, in North Stonington. Cyrus died on December 5, 1830, due to weakness and poor health, after he had fallen into a stream near his home. Some of the locals said that he had bought his usual quart of alcohol at the Squire's grocery in the morning, and he was drunk all day. The next morning he was found dead in water not more than six inches deep.

Sources: 1. DeForest, *History of the Indians of Connecticut*, pages 442–3. **2.** *Non Mohawk Valley Pensioners N–Z*. **3.** Yale Indian Papers Project. **4.** Pension Application S36312. **5.** Report of the National Society of the D.A.R., Vol. 17, page 601.

Amos Tanner and Joseph Tanner

Amos and Joseph Tanner were brothers and sons of Rebecca Tanner. According to the census of the Mohegan tribe taken in 1782, nine of the tribe members were killed in the Revolutionary War, and five of them were sons of the widow Rebecca Tanner.

Amos enlisted on May 3, 1775, in Captain John Durkee's Company in Colonel Israel Putman's Regiment, and Joseph did the same five days later. Both brothers marched from Norwich, Connecticut, and at the Battle of Bunker Hill they were assigned to the rail fence. Both probably died in the service during the war.

Sources: 1. Needham Historical Society. **2.** Grundset, *Forgotten Patriots*, National Society of the D.A.R., page 69.

Han Yerry Tewahangarahken and Tyonajanegen (Tyona)

Han Yerry Tewahangarahken ("He Who Takes Up the Snow Shoe") was born sometime in the 1720s or 1730s. His father was a German settler and his mother a Mohawk. Han grew up in New York's Mohawk Valley region that was close to Oneida territory. This explains why Han, before the French and Indian War, was identified as a member of the Oneida tribe. During his teenage years Han was taught by the Oneidas to hunt and train for combat. Sometime in the 1750s Han married a woman named Tyonajanegen, or "Two Kettles Together."

During the French and Indian War in 1759 a British official, Sir William Johnson, encouraged Mohawk and Oneida warriors to go with him to capture Fort Niagara. During this expedition Han gained a reputation for his fighting skills.

During the mid–1760s Han and his wife, Tyona, joined with other tribal members, and they founded the settlement of Oriska a few miles from Fort Stanwix. Han became the village leader and chief warrior of the Wolf clan. Han's family adopted the European way of life by living in a farmhouse and raising a variety of farm animals. Slowly the British began taking territory away from the various Indian tribes, and this included the land owned by Han.

When the Revolutionary War began, Han and the other Oneida people tried to stay neutral. In 1777, however, British Lt. Colonel Barry St. Leger led a force of 1,800 men and invaded the Oneida homeland. With the British were Mohawk and other Indians under the command of Joseph Brant.

Han and his wife fought at the Battle of Oriskany. Han along with Colonel Louis Cook (also in this book) led the 100 Oneida warriors against the British and their allies. One of the Oneida warriors, Blatcop Tonyentagoyon, rushed into the battle with only his tomahawk. He passed through the fighting three times, and each time "knocking right and left" as he went. He came upon a pro–British Indian and as he tomahawked the man Blatcop broke his own arm.

During the battle Han was sitting atop his horse with his sword dangling at his side, and on one side was his wife with two pistols, and on the other side was his son Cornelius. The three family members rode into the thick of the battle. Han killed at least nine pro–British soldiers that day with his gun, tomahawk, and sword. At one point he was shot in the wrist, but he continued fighting with his good arm. His wife would reload his musket while he fought.

An article in the September 3, 1777, *Pennsylvania Journal and Weekly Advertiser* described the incident. "…a friendly Indian, with his wife and son, who distinguished themselves remarkably on the occasion. The Indian killed nine of the enemy, when having received a ball through his wrist that disabled him from using his gun, he then fought with his tomahawk. His son killed two, and his wife on horseback, fought by his side, with pistols during the whole action, which lasted six hours."

A family friend later referred to Han as "Too old for the service" during the Revolutionary War, and yet he still went fearlessly into the fights. The Americans and their Indian allies defeated the British, and they rode on to defend Fort Schuyler. After the battle Tyona left on horseback to take news of the outcome of the battle to local rebels and Indians.

During the Saratoga campaign in the fall of 1777, Tyona carried messages between the rebel troops. When the campaign ended General Horatio Gates ordered Colonel Peter Gansevoort to "deliver to her three gallons of rum, for a winter's supply for her family" as a reward for her services. Han was killed in an Indian attack and was buried in a mass grave along with other members of a scouting party. He was the Oneida guide for the party.

Sources: 1. Young, Nash, & Raphael, *Revolutionary Founders: Rebels, Radicals, and Reformers in the Making of the Nation*, pages 199–206. **2.** *Oneida Indian Nation Annual report 1012*, pages 43–5. **3.** Lender, *The War for American Independence: A Reference Guide*, page 266. **4.** Glattharr & Martin, *Forgotten Allies: The Oneida Indians and the American Revolution.* **5.** Frank, *An Encyclopedia of American Women at War Vol. 1*, page 541.

Honyere Tewahangarahken (Captain Honyere Doxtator)

Honyere was born c. 1745, and he died on July 4, 1838. He married Dolly Cobus August 20, 1774, and they had four children. He was half-brother to Han Yerry Tewahangarahken through their mother. In their culture the indemnity of one's father is largely immaterial since clan structure is maternal.

Honyere's pension file is very large consisting of 131 pages. Honyere did not apply for a pension, and his wife Dolly did not apply for a widow's pension because they did not know that a pension was available. In the 1850s their surviving son, Peter, applied for a pension as their child and heir. Peter had to submit many letters from himself and people that knew his parents. These letters had to prove his father's service, his parents' marriage and death, and that they were his parents.

To complicate matters there was a letter dated July 22, 1854. In this letter several chiefs of the Oneida Nation had George Wood, probably a lawyer, write to the Commissioner of Pensioners. In the letter Mr. Wood stated that James B. Jenkins had filed for the pension due Honyere without his knowledge. Jenkins had been receiving $30.00 a year from March 4, 1831, to July 4, 1839, since the death of Honyere. Mr. Wood also stated in the letter that Jenkins was currently in the penitentiary serving a five year prison term of pension fraud. Mr. Wood was asking the Commissioner of Pensions to advise them on how to proceed.

On December 22, 1822, Jenny Doxtator, age 92, dictated a letter to be sent in support of the pension application of Peter Doxtator. Jenny knew the family and the service of Honyere.

> In the year 1775 she resided in the village of Oriskany Oneida County and was then well acquainted with Captain Honyere Tewahangarhken an Indian of the Oneida Tribe who then enlisted or volunteered into the military service of the Revolutionary War at Oriskany. He continued to serve as a Captain of a company of Indians to the close thereof. She believes he was at one time in the Regiment commanded by General Herkimer and at another under Col. Jacob Klock.
>
> Captain Honyere was soon after said war called Doxtator a name given him by one Stephen Parkhurst of Oneida Castle, he told said Captain Honyere that it was the English name of Tewahangarhken and he was always Captain *thereafter known and called Captain Honyere Doxtator* until he died.
>
> The said Captain was married to Dolly a person also known to this deponent, also a member of the First Christian Party of the Oneida Indians by one Rev. Abraham Johnson a Methodist Minister of Oriskany sometime in the year 1774. That soon after he entered the service aforesaid his wife had a child which she named Jacob Doxtator.

After Jacob was born they had Dolly, Cornelius, and Peter. When Peter applied for his father's pension he was the only surviving child.

Jenny said that after the war Captain Honyere received about 1,800 acres of land for his service. In the town of Jennings he received Lot 30 with 600 acres and also Lot 81 with 600 acres. In the town of Pompey he received Lot 97 with 600 acres.

Captain Honyere was at the bloody Battle at Oriskany and the Siege of Fort Stanwix in 1777. Dolly, the Captain's wife, was also at a skirmish at Fort Timmerman in 1780. In a letter written to the pension bureau by David Welsh on August 22, 1858, he describes the skirmish that involved his mother and Dolly, the mother of Peter.

> That said Capt. Doxtator in 1780 was at Fort Timmerman on the Mohawk Flats. The Indians who served at Fort Timmerman had their wives there & said Peter's mother & this deponent's mother among other Indian women were there. At said Fort Col. Klock ordered his regiment to go to Fort Nellis to aid Col. Bellinger against an anticipated attack on that fort by British & Indians. All the officers & soldiers left for Fort Nellis & left the Indians at Fort T. After the troops all left the unfriendly Mohawk Indians attacked said Fort and it was protected by the women by their through the port holes. That his mother & Peter's mother fought bravely to defend the fort. This deponent was there but a small boy at that time.

Sources: 1. Glattharr & Martin, *Forgotten Allies: The Oneida Indians and the American Revolution*. **2.** Grundset, *Forgotten Patriots, National Society of the D.A.R.* page 337. **3.** Campisi, *The Oneida Indian Experience: Two Perspectives*, pages 34–8.

Honyost Tewahangarahken (Doxtator)

Honyost was the brother of Honyere Tewahangarahken (Captain Honyere Doxtator). They served in the same regiment, the 2nd regiment of the Tryon County Militia, and were in the same battles. Honyost was a Lieutenant under Colonel Jacob Klock. He married Jenny on January 16, 1778. For his service he received 1,200 acres of land on July 12, 1792. Honyost died on March 29, 1838.

Honyost's wife Jenny did not know she was entitled to a widow's pension until 1852. Her nephew Peter probably told her she could file for it. She wrote a letter in support of Peter's claim for his father's pension, and on December 22, 1852, she filed her own claim.

> She is the widow of Honyost Tewahangarahken who was a Lieutenant in the Revolutionary War. Her husband in the year 1775 sometimes in the spring he volunteered or enlisted into a company of Indians as a Lieutenant under captain Honyere Tewahangarhken an Indian chief and captain & who was brother to the husband of this deponent at one time in the Regiment of Continental troops commanded by General Jacob Klock. He was in the battle of Oriskany, the battle of Fort Stanwix and other battles. Her husband was stationed at Oneida with his company for about 11 months in the year 1777.

Jenny was also one of the female defenders of Fort Timmerman, as described in a letter from Peter. Jenny's claim for a pension was rejected.

Source: 1. National Archives Pension Application R3065. **2.** Grundset, *Forgotten Patriots, National Society of the D.A.R.* page 337.

The Praying Indians

The Praying Indians refer to Native Americans in the New England area, New York, Ontario, and Quebec who converted to Christianity. Their villages were known as praying towns and were established by the Puritan leader John Eliot in mid–1600. In the Praying towns Indians renounced their native language, ceremonies, beliefs, traditional dress, and customs. Young Indian men were trained as missionaries and sent out to other tribes hoping to convert them.

John Eliot's Rules of Conduct for the Praying Indians:

1. If any man shall be idle a week, or at most a fortnight, he shall be fined five shillings.
2. If any unmarried man shall lie with a young woman unmarried, he shall be fined five shillings.
3. If any man shall beat his wife, his hands shall be tied behind him, and he shall be carried to the place of justice to be punished severely.
4. Every young man, if not another's servant, and if unmarried shall be compelled to set up a wigwam, and plant for himself, and not shift up and down in other wigwams.
5. If any woman shall not have her hair tied up, but hang lose, or be cut as a man's hair, she shall pay five shillings.
6. If any woman shall go with naked breasts, she shall pay two shillings.
7. All men that shall wear long locks, shall pay five shillings.
8. If any shall crack lice between their teeth, they shall pay five shillings.

Over a hundred of the Praying Indians fought for the Americans in the Revolutionary War. They fought in integrated units, and they received equal pay and treatment from the white soldiers. Many of them fought at Bunker Hill, Battle Road after Lexington and Concord, Trenton, and Saratoga. The Indians below were members of the Praying Indians.

James Anthony

James Anthony enlisted for eight months in the Company of Captain James Mellen, Colonel Jonathan Ward's 21st Continental Regiment. The Regiment was raised on April 23, 1775, and was at Bunker Hill and the Siege of Boston.

When British General Burgoyne threatened northern New York, James joined the 4th Massachusetts Regiment under the command of Colonel William Shepard. He enlisted on March 14, 1777, for three years and was at the Battle of Saratoga. In the winter of 1777 he went with the army to winter quarters at Valley Forge, and the January 1778 roll listed him as sick at home. He served out his time at Providence and West Point. He may have participated in the Battle of Rhode Island.

Sources: 1. *Massachusetts Soldiers and Sailors of the Revolutionary War,* Vol. 1, page 278. **2.** Grundset, *Forgotten Patriots, National Society of the D.A.R.* page 100.

Isaac and Samuel Comecho

Isaac and Samuel were brothers, and both were born in Natick, Massachusetts. Isaac was baptized on October 27, 1745, and Samuel was baptized on November 9, 1735.

Isaac marched on the alarm of April 19, 1775, and served for nine days in Captain William Ellis's Company, in Colonel William Heath's 3rd Massachusetts Regiment. On May 4, 1775, Isaac enlisted in Captain Joseph Guild's Company in Heath's 3rd Regiment.

Isaac Comecho marched with his Regiment to Bunker Hill. His Regiment joined with New Hampshire and Connecticut troops on the left flank on Breed's Hill. They quickly formed a line of defense composed of rails and other materials found nearby.

The Americans held their fire until the British troops were near, and then they opened fire. The sudden volleys broke the British line, but the British charged again and again. Finally, the Americans began to retreat, because they were almost out of ammunition. Isaac was discharged from the army on October 5, 1775.

Samuel Comecho enlisted for eight months on May 24, 1775, and he served in the Company commanded by Captain Benjamin Bullard, of the 13th Massachusetts Regiment commanded by Colonel Jonathan Brewer. The 13th Regiment was comprised of 180 men as they marched to the Battle of Bunker Hill.

Samuel and the rest of the men took a position on the left of the redoubt in an open field during the battle. He was stationed not too far from his brother Isaac. Samuel and the rest of the 13th Regiment retreated when they ran out of ammunition.

After the battle the 13th Regiment was stationed at Prospect Hill where Samuel remained until his enlistment was up in the fall of 1775. On January 1, 1776, he enlisted in the Company commanded by Captain William Hudson

Ballard of the 13th Regiment commanded by Colonel Asa Whitcomb. In August Samuel and the Regiment were sent to northern New York to oppose the British counteroffensive in Canada, and the Regiment never rejoined the main army. Samuel died on March 14, 1776, and probably of smallpox. There was an outbreak of the disease in the army at this time.

Sources: 1. *Memoirs of Major-General William Heath by Himself,* 1901, page 15. **2.** *Massachusetts Town and Vital Records, 1620–1988,* page 28. **3.** *Massachusetts Soldier and Sailors in the Revolutionary War,* Vol. 3, page 851, 857, & 863.

Caesar Ferrit and His Sons John and Thomas

Caesar Ferrit was born on one of the West India Islands c. 1720. He was raised in an English family in Milton and later moved to Boston. Due to the high unemployment and the cost of living in the city, he purchased land at Natick in 1751.

Caesar had been a coachman for a wealthy man in Boston. A ward of this man, by the name of Naomi, had fallen in love with Caesar. Another man had been chosen for Naomi, and the wedding day had been established when the secret romance was discovered. She was given a choice of wealth with the man of her guardian's choosing, or poverty with a mulatto husband. Naomi chose to marry Caesar and live in Natick. They had at least seven children.

When the Lexington alarm was given on April 19, 1775, Caesar and his youngest son John, born c. 1753, joined Captain Joseph Morse's Company in Colonel Samuel Bullard's Regiment. The older son Thomas born c. 1751 joined Captain Ebenezer Battle's Company. Caesar and John arrived at a house near Lexington meeting house, which was a short time before the British soldiers arrived on their retreat from Concord. Both men fired their muskets at the British troops from the door of the house, and then they hid under the cellar stairs as the British searched for them in the house. Thomas was reported to have joined the two men on Battle Road, as the British were marching back to Boston.

Caesar and John enlisted for eight months service on April 24, 1775, in Captain Joseph Morse's Company in Colonel John Paterson's Regiment. On December 20, 1776, they were drafted into Captain Sabin Mann's Company of Medfield Militia in order to reinforce the Continental Army at or near New York. Both were paid fifteen pounds for their service.

Caesar and John enlisted on March 10, 1781, in Captain Staples Chamberlain's Company in Colonel Dean's Regiment, and they marched to Rhode Island on a forty day expedition. They were discharged on March 14, 1781.

Sources: 1. Quintal, *Patriots of Color,* pages 102–4. **2.** *Massachusetts Soldier and Sailors in the Revolutionary War,* Vol. 5, page 632. **3.** Biglow, *History of Natick Massachusetts,* page 44. **4.** Drake, *Middlesex County, Massachusetts,* page 444.

Joseph Paugenit

Joseph Paugenit was born in 1754 in Natick, Massachusetts. His father fought in the French and Indian War and received serious wounds. Five days after the Battle of Lexington and Concord, Joseph joined the Company commanded by Captain Thomas Drury in Colonel John Nixon's 6th Massachusetts Regiment. Joseph was one of sixteen Indians who fought at the Battle of Bunker Hill in 1775. Nixon's Regiment was one of the last units to leave the field.

In 1776 he fought in the New York Campaign in Colonel Thomas Nixon's (the brother of John) 6th Regiment. Joseph fought at the Battle of Harlem Heights and Saratoga. He died in a military hospital near Albany, either from wounds or disease.

Sources: 1. *Massachusetts Soldier and Sailors in the Revolutionary War*, Vol. 12, page 499. **2.** Hall, *Praying Indian in the American Revolution* lecture transcript, February 8, 2004.

Alexander Quapish

Alexander was born c. 1741 in Yarmouth, Massachusetts, and he died March 23, 1776. He married Sarah David in 1767, and they moved to Dedham. Sarah died in 1774, and Alexander enlisted from Dedham on May 8, 1775, into the Company commanded by Captain Daniel Whiting in Colonel Jonathan Brewer's 13th Massachusetts Regiment. The Regiment marched to Bunker Hill and were positioned on the left of the redoubt in an open field.

On July 3, 1775, he served in the 26th Continental Regiment, which was later designated the 9th Massachusetts Regiment, under Lt. Colonel Loammi Baldwin. The Regiment remained in the Boston area until April of 1776.

Alexander became ill near Cambridge on November 15, 1775, and taken to the home of Michael Bacon. Michael was a drummer boy, and he served with Alexander. Michael may have been part Indian and his parents lived around the Praying Indians. Alexander died at the Bacon home on March 23, 1776. Michael Bacon, Sr., saw to it that his son's army buddy was buried.

Michael Bacon, Sr., later sought compensation for boarding and burying Alexander. The petition for payment was passed on May 10, 1776,

> Resolved that there be allowed & paid out of the Publick Treasury to Michael Brown the Sum of Six pounds Eight Shillings in full discharge of the within acc and that the Sum of Two pounds fourteen Shillings & Seven pence of S'Sum which was due to Said Alexander Quapish on Capt. Daniel Whitings Muster Role in Col. Jonathan Brewers Regt. Shall be paid to said Bacon as part of S'Sum and the Treasurer is directed to pay the same accordingly.

The payment to Michael included eight shillings for a coffin, and three shillings for digging a grave. Alexander was buried in the 100 acre Indian Burial

Ground in Needham along with seventeen Indian Veterans of the Revolutionary War.

Sources: 1. Adams, *Genealogical and Personal Memoirs Relating to the Families of the State of Massachusetts, Vol. 1,* page 576. **2.** Clifford, *The Acts and Resolves, Public and Private, of the Massachusetts Bay,* page 945. **3.** *Massachusetts Soldier and Sailors in the Revolutionary War,* Vol. 12, page 886. **4.** Dedham Historical Society.

Bibliography

Publications

Acts of the Legislature of the State of New Jersey. Trenton, NJ: Phillips and Boswell, 1847.
Adams, William. *Genealogical and Personal Memoirs Relating to the Families of the State of Massachusetts, Vol. 1*. New York: Lewis Historical Publishing Co., 1910.
Alexander, Rudolph, Jr. *Racism, African Americans, and Social Justice*. Lanham, MD: Rowman & Littlefield, 2005.
Alexander, William T. *History of the Colored Race in America*. Kansas City: Palmetto Publishing Company, 1888.
Anderson, William J. *Life and Narrative of William J. Anderson Twenty-four Years a Slave*. Chicago: Daily Tribune and Job Printing Office, 1857.
Arnold, James N., ed. *The Narragansett Historical Register A Magazine, Vol. 1, April, 1883, No. 4—A List of Slaves Enlisted in to the Continental Army*. Hamilton, RI: The Narragansett Historical Publishing Company, 1883–1884.
Bailey, Sarah Loring. *Historical Sketches of Andover*. Boston: Houghton, Mifflin and Company, 1880.
Bancroft, Charles, and George Munsor Curtis. *An Historical and Pictorial Description of the Town of Meriden*. Meriden, CT: Journal Publishing, 1906.
Barry, William. *A History of Framingham, Massachusetts*. Carlisle, MA: Applewood Books, 1847.
Bell, Charles Henry. *History of the Town of Exeter, New Hampshire*. Boston: J.E. Farwell & Company, 1888.
Beveridge, Albert Jeremiah. *The Life of John Marshall*. Boston: Houghton, Mifflin, 1916.
Biglow, William. *History of Natick Massachusetts*. Boston: Marsh, Capen, & Lyon, 1830.
Biographies of Patriots of Color at the Battle of Bunker Hill. Boston: National Park Service.
Bittinger, Cynthia D. *Vermont Women, Native Americans & African Americans: Out of the Shadows of History*. Charleston, SC: The History Press, 2012.
Blumer, Thomas J. *Catawba Nation: Treasures in History*. Charleston, SC: The History Press. 2007.
Bonvillain, Nancy, and Ada Elizabeth Deer. *The Mohawk*. Philadelphia: Chelsea House, 2005.
Bouton, Nathaniel. *Collections of the New Hampshire Historical Society, Vol. 7*. Concord, MA: G. Parker Lyon, 1863.
Brace, Jeffery. *For the Blind African Slave, or Memoirs of Boyrereau Brinch, Nick-Named Jeffery Brace*. St. Albans, VT: Harry Whitney, 1810.
Burgan, Michael. *The Untold Story of the Black Regiment: Fighting in the Revolutionary War*. North Mankato, MN: Capstone, 2015.
Burney, Charles M. *Kidnapping the Enemy: The Special Operations to Capture Generals Charles Lee and Richard Prescott*. Yardley, PA: Westholme Publishing, 2014.
Burns, Annie Walker. *Record of Abstracts of Pension Papers Concerning Soldiers of the Revolutionary War, War of 1812 and Indian Wars Who Settled in Wayne County, Kentucky*. Washington, D.C., 1936.
Campisi, Jack, and Laurence M. Hauptman, eds. *The Oneida Indian Experience: Two Perspectives*. Syracuse: Syracuse University Press, 1988.
Cannon, Richard. *Historical Record of the 17th Regiment of Light Dragoons; Lancers: Containing an

Account of the Formation of the Regiment in 1759 and Its Subsequent Service to 1841. London: John W. Parker, 1841.
Carpenter, William Wilton. *The History of the Town of Amherst, Massachusetts.* Amherst, MA: Carpenter & Morehouse, 1896.
Carrington, Henry Beebee. *Battles of the American Revolution, 1775–1781.* New York: A.S. Barnes & Company, 1876.
Clifford, John Henry. *The Acts and Resolves, Public and Private, of the Massachusetts Bay.* Boston: Wright & Potter, 1918.
Coburn, Silas R. *History of Dracut, Massachusetts.* Lowell, MA: Press of the Courier-Citizen Co., 1922.
The Connecticut Magazine 15, 1899. Hartford, CT.
Contee, Clarence G. *The Crisis* 83, no. 2, Feb. 1976.
Crawford, M. MacDermot. *The Sailor Whom England Feared: Being the Story of Paul Jones, Scotch Naval Adventurer and Admiral in the American and Russian Fleets.* London: Eveleigh Nash, 1913.
Crow, Jeffery J. *The Black Experience in Revolutionary North Carolina.* Raleigh: North Carolina Dept. of Cultural Resources, Division of Archives and History, 1977.
Cutter, William. *The Life of Israel Putnam, Major-General in the Army of the American Revolution.* New York: Derby & Jackson, 1859.
Cutter, William Richard. *History of the Town of Arlington, Massachusetts Formerly the Second Precinct in Cambridge or District of Menotomy, Afterward the Town of West Cambridge 1635–1879.* Boston: David Clapp & Son, 1880.
Cutter, William Richard, ed. *Historic Homes and Places and Genealogical and Personal Memoirs, Vol. 4.* New York: Lewis Historical Publishing, 1907.
Dann, John C. *The Revolution Remembered: Eyewitness Accounts of the War for Independence.* Chicago: University of Chicago Press, 1980.
Daughters of the American Revolution. *D.A.R. Magazine* LIV, no. 1, Jan. 1920. Washington, D.C.
Daughters of the American Revolution. *Lineage Books.* Washington, D.C., 1921.
Daughters of the American Revolution. *Proceedings of the 21st Continental Congress of the D.A.R.* 21 Apr. 1912.
Daughters of the American Revolution. *Report of the National Society of the D.A.R.* 17. Washington, D.C.
Davis, Burke. *Black Heroes of the American Revolution.* New York: Harcourt, 1976.
Davis, Damani. "The Rejection of Elizabeth Mason." *Prologue* 43, no. 2, Summer 2011.
DeForest, John W. *History of the Indians of Connecticut.* Hartford, CT: William Jas. Hamersley, 1853.
Denny, Ebenezer. *History of the U.S. from the Colonial Period Until Modern Times, Ebenezer Denny 1781 Describing the Surrender of Cornwallis at Yorktown.* American History from Revolution to Reconstruction and Beyond website.
Dictionary of Canadian Biography. Toronto: University of Toronto Press, 1990.
Dictionary of National Biography, 1885–1900, Vol. 32. Online Book Service, Charles Lee pages, 1900.
Dixon, David D. "Freedom Earned, Equality Denied: Evolving Race Relations in Exeter and Vicinity, 1776–1876." New Hampshire Historical Society 61, 2007.
Dohla, Johann Conrad. *A Hessian Diary of the American Revolution.* Norman: University of Oklahoma Press.
Donaldson, Thomas. *Indians: The Six Nations of New York.* Ithaca: Cornell University Press, 1995.
Drake, Samuel Adams. *History of Middlesex County, Massachusetts.* Boston: Estes and Lauriat, 1880.
Duffy, John J., Samuel B. Hand, and Ralph H. Orth, eds. *The Vermont Encyclopedia.* Burlington: University of Vermont Press, 2003.
Ervin, Anthony, and Constantine Markides. *Chasing Water: Elegy of an Olympian.* Brooklyn: Akashic Books, 2016.
Falkner, Leonard. "Captor of the Barefoot General." *American Heritage* II, no. 5, August 1960.
Finekelman, Paul, ed. *Encyclopedia of African American History, 1619–1895.* New York: Oxford University Press, 2006.
Flexner, James Thomas. *Washington: The Indispensable Man.* New York: New American Library, 1979.
Franco, Janis Leach. *Meriden.* Charleston, SC: Arcadia Publishing, 2010.
Frank, Andrew, ed. *American Revolution: People and Perspectives.* Santa Barbara: ABC-CLIO, 2008.
Frank, Lisa Tendrich. *An Encyclopedia of American Women at War, Vol. 1.* Santa Barbara: ABC-CLIO, 2013.

Freeman, Frederick. *The History of Cape Cod: The Annals of Barnstable County, Vol. 1.* Boston: George C. Rand & Avery, 1858.
Frothingham, Richard, Jr. *History of the Siege of Boston and of the Battles of Lexington, Concord and Bunker Hill.* Boston: Charles C. Little and James Brown, 1851.
Garrison, William Lloyd. *The Loyalty and Devotion of Colored Americans in the Revolution and War of 1812.* Boston: R.F. Wallcut, 1861.
Gilbert, Alan. *Black Patriots and Loyalist: Fighting for Emancipation in the War for Independence.* Chicago: University of Chicago Press, 2012.
Glattharr, Joseph T., and James Kirby Martin. *Forgotten Allies: The Oneida Indians and the American Revolution.* New York: Hill & Wang, 2006.
Graham, James. *The Life of General Daniel Morgan of the Virginia Line of the Army of the United States.* New York: Derby and Jackson, 1856.
Graham, William Alexander. *General Joseph Graham and His Papers on North Carolina Revolutionary History.* Edwards, Broughton, & Raleigh, 1904.
Greene, Jack P., and J.R. Pole, eds. *A Companion to the American Revolution.* Hoboken, NJ: Wiley, 2003.
Greene, Jerome. *The Guns of Independence: The Siege of Yorktown, 1781.* New York: Savas Beatie, 2005.
Greene, Robert Ewell. *Black Courage, 1775–1783.* Washington, D.C.: National Society of the Daughters of the American Revolution, 1984.
Greene, Robert Ewell. *Black Defenders of America, 1775–1973.* Chicago: Johnson Publishing Co., 1974.
Gregg, Gary L., and Mark David Hall, eds. *America's Forgotten Founders, 2nd Edition.* Wilmington, DE: ISI Books, 2012.
Grundset, Eric G., ed. *African American and American Indian Patriots in the Revolutionary War.* Washington, D.C.: National Society of the Daughters of the American Revolution, 2008.
Grundset, Eric G., ed. *Forgotten Patriots, National Society of the D.A.R.* Washington, D.C.: National Society of the Daughters of the American Revolution, 2008.
Guthrie, James M. *Camp-fires of the Afro-American: Or, the Colored Man as a Patriot.* Philadelphia: Afro-American Publishing, 1899.
Hall, Robert D. "Praying Indian in the American Revolution." Lecture delivered by Robert D. Hall, Jr,. for a joint meeting of the Col. William McIntosh Chapter of the Daughters of the American Revolution, and the Needham Historical Society, February 8, 2004.
Hamilton, Duane, ed. *History of Bristol County, Massachusetts, Part 2.* Philadelphia: J.W. Lewis, 1883.
Harper's Encyclopedia of the United States, Vol. IV. New York: Harper and Brothers, 1901.
Harvey, Oscar Jewell, and Ernest Fray Smith. *A History of Wilkes-Barre, Luzerne County, Pennsylvania, Vol. 2.* Wilkes-Barre, 1909.
Hauptman, Lawrence M. *The Iroquois in the Civil War: From Battlefield to Reservation.* Syracuse: Syracuse University Press, 1993.
Hay, Gertrude May, ed. *Roster of Soldiers from North Carolina in the American Revolution.* Durham: North Carolina Daughters of the American Revolution, 1932.
Heath William. *Memoirs of Major-General William Heath by Himself.* New York: William Abbatt, 1901.
Heinegg Paul. *Free African Americans of North Carolina, Virginia, and South Carolina Vol 1.* Baltimore: Clearfield, 1992.
Heyl, the Rev. Francis. *Battle of Germantown.* Philadelphia: Horace McCann, 1908.
Hicks, George W. *Revolutionary War Amid Southern Chaos.* Baltimore: Publishamerica, 2008.
Hine, Darlene Clark, and Earnestine Jenkins, eds. *A Question of Manhood: A Reader in U.S. Black Men's History and Masculinity.* Volume 1,"Manhood Rights": The Construction of Black Male History and Manhood, 1750–1870. Bloomington: Indiana University Press, 1999.
Hinkle, Alice M. *Prince Estabrook: Slave and Soldier.* New York: Pleasant Mountain Press, 2001.
The Historical Magazine and Notes and Queries, Vol. V. Morrisania, NY: Henry B. Dawson, 1872.
History of the Connecticut Valley in Massachusetts. Philadelphia: Louis Everts, 1879.
Hodges, Graham Russell Gao. *Root and Branch: African Americans in New York and East Jersey, 1613–1863.* Chapel Hill: University of North Carolina Press, 1999.
Hodgman, the Rev. Edwin R. *History of the Town of Westford 1659–1883.* Lowell, MA: Westford Town History Association, 1883.

Horton, James Oliver, and Lois E. Oliver. *In Hope of Liberty: Culture, Community and Protest Among Northern Free Blacks.* New York: Oxford University Press, 1998.
Hudson, Charles. *History of Lexington.* Cambridge, MA: The Riverside Press, 1913.
Hunt, Freeman. *American Anecdotes: Original and Select, Vol. 1.* Boston: Putnam & Hunt, 1830.
Huntoon, Daniel Thomas Vose. *History of the Town of Canton, Norfolk County, Massachusetts.* Cambridge: Cambridge University Press, 1893.
Hurd, Duane Hamilton. *History of Middlesex County, Massachusetts.* Philadelphia: J.W. Lewis & Company, 1890.
Hurd, Duane Hamilton. *History of Rockingham and Strafford Counties, New Hampshire.* Dover, NH: J.W. Lewis & Company, 1882.
Ireland, Corydon. "Harvard's Year of Exile." *Harvard Gazette,* October 13, 2011.
Johnson, Elias. *Legends, Traditions, and Laws of the Iroquois, or Six Nations and History of the Tuscarora Indians.* Lockport, NY: Union Printing & Publishing, 1881.
Johnson, George D. *Profiles in Hue.* Harrisburg, PA: Trafford Publishing, 2011.
Johnston, Henry Phelps. *The Yorktown Campaign and the Surrender of Cornwallis, 1781.* New York: Harper & Brothers, 1881.
Jones-Wilson, Faustine Childress, et al. *Encyclopedia of African-American Education,* Westport, CT: Greenwood Press, 1996.
The Journal of Negro History XXVII, no. 3, July 1942. Association for the Study of Negro Life and History.
Journal of the House of Representatives of the United States, December 2, 1833. Washington, D.C.: Gales & Seaton, 1843.
Kaplan, Sidney, and Emma Nogrady Kaplan. *The Black Presence in the Era of the American Revolution.* Amherst: University of Massachusetts Press, 1989.
Kennedy, David M., and David Bailey. *The American Spirit: United States History as Seen by Contemporaries, Vol. 1.* Boston: Wadsworth, 2009.
Ketchum, Richard, M. *The Battle of Bunker Hill.* Papamoa Press, 2017.
Knight, Lucian Lamar. *Georgia's Landmarks, Memorials and Legends, Vol. II.* Gretna, LA: Pelican Publishing, 2006.
Knoblock, Glenn A. *African American Historic Burial Grounds and Gravesites of New England.* Jefferson, NC: McFarland, 2015.
Kostoff, Robert. *Nuggets of Niagara County History.* New York: iUniverse, 2003.
Landers, Howard Lee. *The Virginia Campaign and the Blockade and Siege of Yorktown.* Washington, D.C.: U.S. Government Printing Office, 1931.
Lanning, Michael. *African-Americans in the Revolutionary War.* New York: Citadel Press, 2000.
Lanning, Michael Lee. *The African-American Soldier: From Crispus Attucks to Colin Powell.* New York: Kensington Publishing, 2004.
Lender, Mark Edward. *The War for American Independence: A Reference Guide.* Santa Barbara: ABC-CLIO, 2016.
Lengel, Edward G. *General George Washington: A Military Life.* New York: Random House, 2007.
Lippitt, Charles Warren. *The Battle of Rhode Island.* Newport, RI: Mercury Publishing Co., 1915.
Lossing, Benjamin J. *Lossing's Field Book of the Revolution.* New York: Harper Brothers, 1850.
Love, DeLoss. *Sampson Occum the Christian Indians of New England.* Boston: Pilgrim Press, 1899.
Mahoney, Harry Thayer, and Marjorie Locke Mahoney. *Gallantry in Action: A Biographic Dictionary of Espionage in the American Revolutionary War.* Lanham, MD: University Press of America, 1999.
Marable, Manning, and Leith Mullings, eds. *Let Nobody Turn Us Around: An African American Anthology.* Lanham, MD: Rowman & Littlefield, 2009.
Martin, James Kirby. *Forgotten Allies: The Oneida Indians and the American Revolution.* New York: Hill and Wang, 2006.
Mayo, Martha. *Profiles in Courage: African-Americans in Lowell.* An Exhibit by Martha Mayo, University of Massachusetts Lowell, the Center for Lowell History.
Mays, Terry M. *Historical Dictionary of the American Revolution.* Lanham, MD: Scarecrow Press, 2010.
McAllister, Joseph Thompson. *Virginia Militia in the Revolutionary War.* Hot Springs, VA: McAllister Publishing, 1913.
McLeroy, Sherrie, and William McLeroy. *Strangers in Their Midst: The Free Black Population of Amherst County Virginia.* Berwyn Heights, MD: Heritage, 2007.

Meltsner, Heli. *The Poorhouses of Massachusetts: A Cultural and Architectural History.* Jefferson, NC: McFarland, 2012.
Messler, Abraham. *History of Somerset County* [New Jersey]. Somerville, NJ: C.M. Jameson, 1888.
Metcalf, Henry Harrison, and John Norris McClintock. *The Granite Monthly* LIII, 1921. Concord, NH: Harland C. Pearson, 1921.
Metz, Elizabeth Ryan. *I Was a Teenager in the American Revolution.* Jefferson, NC: McFarland, 2006.
Minardi, Margot. *Making Slavery History: Abolitionism and the Politics of Memory in Massachusetts.* New York: Oxford Press, 2010.
"Minutes of the Court of Pleas and Quarter Sessions of Craven County, March 1811." *North Carolina Historical Review* XIX, no. 3, July 1942. State Department of History and Archives.
Mitnick, Barbara J., ed. *New Jersey in the American Revolution.* New Brunswick, NJ: Rivergate Books, 2005.
Morgan, Robert. *On This Day: 365 Amazing and Inspiring Stories About Saints, Martyrs, and Heroes.* Nashville: Thomas Nelson, 1997.
Morrison, Leonard A. *The History of Windham.* Boston: Cupples, Upham & Co., 1883.
Moss, Bobby Gilmer, and Michael C. Scoggins. *African-American Patriots in the Southern Campaign of the American Revolution.* Blacksburg, SC: Scotia-Hibernia Press, 2004.
Moultrie, William. *Memoirs of the American Revolution.* New York: David Longworth: 1802.
Muraskin, William A. *Middle-Class Blacks in a White Society: Prince Hall Freemasonry in America.* Berkeley: University of California Press, 1975.
Murry, Thomas Hamilton. *General John Sullivan and the Battle of Rhode Island.* Providence, RI: The American-Irish Historical Society, 1902.
Needham Historical Society website.
Neimeyer, Charles Patrick. *America Goes to War: A Social History of the Continental Army.* New York: New York University Press, 1996.
Nell, William C. *The Colored Patriots of the American Revolution.* Boston: Robert F. Wallcut, 1855.
New York History: Quarterly Journal of the New York State Historical Association. New York: New York State Historical Society, 1920.
Nourse, Henry Stedman. *The Military Annals of Lancaster, Massachusetts, 1740–1865.* Clinton, MA: W.J. Coulter, 1889.
Obereg, Michael Leroy. *Professional Indian: The American Odyssey of Eleazer Williams.* Philadelphia: University of Pennsylvania Press, 2015.
Official Register of the Officers and Men of New Jersey in the Revolutionary War, 1842. Trenton, NJ: William T. Nicholson, 1872.
Ogden, J.W. *The History of Champaign County, Ohio, 1881.* Chicago: W.H. Beers & Co. 1881.
Othow, Helen Chavis. *John Chavis: African American Patriot, Teacher, and Mentor.* Jefferson, NC: McFarland, 2001.
Parker, Charles S. *Town of Arlington Past and Present.* Arlington, MA: C.S. Parker 7 Son, 1907.
Parsons, Langton Brown. *History of the Town of Rye, New Hampshire.* Concord, NH: Rumford Printing Co., 1905.
Patrakis, Joan. *Andover Stories.* Andover Historical Society website, February 17, 2011.
Pennsylvania Journal; and the Weekly Advertiser, May 24, 1775. New York Public Library Digital Collections.
Phinney, Elias. *History of the Battle of Lexington: on the Morning of the 19th April, 1775.* Boston: Phelps and Farnham, 1825.
"Praying Towns" Nipmuc Indian Association of Connecticut, Historical Series, Number 2, Second Edition, 1995.
Pulsifer, David, and John Burgoyne. *Battle of Bunker Hill, Comp. from Authentic Sources.* Boston: A. William and Company, 1872.
Putney, Martha S. *Blacks in the United States Army: Portraits through History.* Jefferson, NC: McFarland, 2003.
Quarles, Benjamin. *The Negro in the American Revolution.* Chapel Hill: University of North Carolina Press, 1961.
Quarles, Benjamin. *The Negro in the Making of American Revolution.* New York: Touchstone, 1996.
Quintal, George, Jr. *Patriots of Color.* Boston: Division of Cultural Resources Boston Natural Historical Park, 2004.
Raphael, Ray. *A People's History of the American Revolution.* New York: The New Press, 2001.

Reef, Catherine. *African Americans in the Military.* New York: Facts on File, 2004.
Report of the Committee Appointed to Revise the Soldier's Record. Salem, MA: Newcome & Gauss, 1895.
Rimkunas, Barbara. *Hidden History of Exeter.* Charleston, SC: The History Press, 2014.
Rosenburg, John. *First in War: George Washington in the American Revolution.* Minneapolis: Millbrook Press, 1998.
Roundtree, Helen C. *Pocahontas's People: The Powhatan Indians of Virginia through Four Centuries.* Norman: University of Oklahoma, 1990.
Saffell, W. T. R. *Records of the Revolutionary War: Containing the Military and Financial Correspondence.* Baltimore: Charles C. Saffell, 1894.
Salter, Krewasky A. *Combat Multipliers: African-American Soldiers in Four Wars.* Fort Leavenworth, KS: Combat Studies Institute Press, 2003.
Sanders, Nancy. *America's Black Founders: Revolutionary Heroes & Early Leaders.* Chicago: Chicago Review Press, 2011.
Savas, Theodore P., and David Dameron. *A Guide to the Battles of the American Revolution.* New York: Savas-Beatie, 2006.
Schenck, David. *North Carolina 1780–81 Being a History of the Invasion of the Carolinas by the British Army Under Lord Cornwallis.* Raleigh: Edwards & Broughton Publishers, 1889.
Schmidt, Ethan A. *Native Americans in the American Revolution: How the War Divided, Devastated and Transformed the Early American Indian World.* Santa Barbara: Praeger, 2014.
Scoggins, Michael, transcriber. *The Catawba Indian Company in Sumter's Brigade.* Southern Revolutionary War Institute website, 2009.
Seward, the Rev. Josiah Lafayette. *A History of the Town of Sullivan New Hampshire, 1777–1917, Vol. I.* Sullivan, NH: Keene, 1921.
Shaw, Henry I., and Ralph W. Donnelly. *Blacks in the Marine Corps.* History and Museums Division, Headquarters, U.S. Marine Corps, Diane Publishing Company, 1976.
Shujaa, Mwalimu, and Kenya J. Shujaa, eds. *The SAGE Encyclopedia of African Heritage in North America.* Thousand Oaks, CA: Sage, 2015.
Sidbury, James. *Becoming African in America: Race and Nation in the Early Black Atlantic.* New York: Oxford University Press, 2007.
Simmons, Martha. *Preaching with Sacred Fire: An Anthology of African American Sermons, 1750 to the Present.* New York: W.W. Norton & Company, 2010.
Simmons, William Scranton. *Spirit of the New England Tribes: Indian History and Folklore, 1620–1984.* Hanover: University Press of New England, 1986.
Smith, Jean Edward. *John Marshal: Definer of a Nation.* New York: Henry Holt & Company, 1996.
Smith, Jessie Carney. *Notable Black Men, Book II.* Detroit: Thomas Gale, 2007.
Smith, Samuel Abbot. *West Cambridge 1775.* Cambridge: Arlington Historical Society, 1974.
The Southern Review 1, 1828. Forgotten Books, 2017 (first published 1828).
Stearns, Ezra S. *History of the Town of Rindge, New Hampshire.* Boston: George H. Ellis, 1875.
Stevenson, Kris Coffin. *God's Might Champions: Daily Devotions for Juniors.* Hagerstown, MD: Review and Herald Press, 2004.
Summers, William. *Obituary Notices of Pennsylvania Soldiers, from the Pennsylvania Magazine of History and Biography, Vol. XXXVIII.* Philadelphia: Historical Society of Philadelphia, 1914.
Sutherland, Jonathan, D. *African Americans at War: An Encyclopedia, Vol. 2.* Santa Barbara: ABC-CLIO, 2003.
Swanton, John Reed. *The Indian Tribes of North America.* Washington, D.C.: Government Printing Office, 1952.
Swett, Colonel Samuel. *History of Bunker Hill Battle.* Boston: Munroe and Francis, 1907.
Taunton, Massachusetts, Historical Society. *A Catalogue of the Portraits and Other Objects of Historical Value Belonging to the Old Colony.* Taunton, MA: Garhom Printer, 1907.
Temple, J.H. *History of Framingham, Massachusetts, Early Known as Danforth's Farms, 1640–1880.* Framingham, MA: Published by a Committee in the Town, 1887.
Tomes, Robert. *Battles of America by Sea and Land, Vol. 1.* New York: James F. Virtue, 1878.
Vallar, Cindy, ed. and rev. "Pirates and Privateers." The History of Maritime Piracy website.
Von Daacke, Kirt. *Freedom Has a Face: Race, Identity, and Community in Jefferson's Virginia.* Charlottesville: University of Virginia Press, 2012.
Walker, Alice Morehouse. *Historic Hadley, A Story of the Making of a Famous Massachusetts Town.* New York: Grafton Press, 1906.

Watson, Ian. *Catawba Indian Genealogy.* Geneseo, IL: Geneseo Foundation, 1996.
Watt, Gavin K. *Rebellion in the Mohawk Valley: The St. Leger Expedition of 1777.* Toronto: Dundurn Press, 2002.
Willett, William Marinus. *A Narrative of the Actions of Colonel Marinus Willett.* New York: G. & C. & H. Carvill, 1831.
Willis, Anita. *Notes and Documents of Free Persons of Color Four Hundred Years of an American Family's History.* Morrisville, NC: Lulu Press, 2013.
Wilson, Joseph T. *The Black Phalanx African American Soldiers in the American Revolution.* Hartford, CT: American Publishing Company, 1880.
Woodson, Carter G. *The Journal of Negro History* XXVII, July 1942. Washington, D.C.: Association for the Study of Negro Life and History, 1922.
Writer's Program. Urbana and Champaign County, OH. Gaumer Publishers, 1942.
Yale Indian Papers Project. Website of Yale University.
Yazawa, James Henretta, and Kevin J. Fernlund. *Documents for America's History, Volume 1: To 1877.* Boston: Bedford/St. Martin's, 2000.
Young, Alfred F., Gary B. Nash, and Ray Raphael, eds. *Revolutionary Founders: Rebels, Radicals, and Reformers in the Making of the Nation.* New York: Vintage Books, 2012.

Government Records

American Revolution. Virginia Navy datasheet 1775–1782. Ancestry.com database.
Bounty Land Warrants. Ancestry.com database.
Census Records. Ancestry.com database.
Connecticut Town Birth Records. Ancestry.com database.
The History of Virginia's Navy of the Revolution, Roster Rolls. Ancestry.com database.
Massachusetts Soldiers & Sailors in the War of Revolution. Ancestry.com database.
Massachusetts Town & Vital Records 1620–1988. Ancestry.com database.
New Hampshire, Death & Burial Records 1654–1949. Ancestry.com database.
Minutes of the Court of Pleas and Quarter Sessions of Craven County, March 1811. North Carolina Historical Review, Vol XIX, No. 3, July 1942. State Department of History and Archives.
Non Mohawk Valley Pensioners N–Z. Ancestry.com database.
Pension List of 1792–1795. Ancestry.com database.
Roster of South Carolina Patriots in the American Revolution. Ancestry.com database.
Service of Connecticut Men in the War of the Revolution. Ancestry.com database.
U.S. Pension Records. Ancestry.com database.
U.S. Pensioners 1818–1872. Ancestry.com database.
U.S. Revolutionary War Rolls 1775–1783. Ancestry.com database.

Index

Abbot, Philip 9
Accomack 116
Adams, Adam 9
Addams, Thomas 10
Ailstock, Absalom 10–11
Akiatonhartonkwen (Louis Cook) 169–172, 189
Albany African Temperance Society 98
Albany's School for People of Color 98
Alexander, Gen. William 17, 63, 97, 143
Alfred 181
Alliance 99
amputation 42–43
Anderson, William 11–12
Andre, Major John: capture 19; execution 42, 44
Anthony, James 12
Anthony, James (Indian) 192–193
Arabus, Jack 12–13
Archer, Evans 13–14
Arcules, James 14
Armistead, James 14–15
Arnold, Gen. Benedict 33, 60, 97, 102, 119–120, 170, 175; escape 19–20
Ashbow, John 171–172
Ashbow, Joseph 171–172
Ashbow, Robert 171–172
Ashe, Gen. John 148
Asher, Gad 15
Atis, London 15–16

Babcock, Caesar 16–17
Bailey, Caesar 17
Bailey, Prince 17–18
Banks, Jacob 18–19
Banks, John 19
Barber, William 19–20
Barnett, Charles 20
Barracks, Albemarle 18, 19
Bartlett, Scipio 20–21
Bason, Caesar 21

Basset, Caesar 21
Bates, Benoni 21–22
Batherick, Mother 94
Battle Road 36, 192, 194
battles: Bemis Heights 74, 78, 102; Bennington 164; Blue Licks 169; Brandywine 9, 12, 22, 40, 44, 63, 65, 82, 88, 116, 119; Brass Town 126; Breed's Hill 9, 41, 72, 172, 193; Briar Creek 148, 154; Bunker Hill 9, 14, 17, 21, 36–37, 42, 71, 81, 84–85, 90, 100, 118, 120, 133, 158; Camden 9, 39, 40, 90, 101, 103, 109, 112–113, 137, 152, 163, 188, 192–194; Canada Creek 182; Chestnut Hill 68; Concord 17, 36, 41, 93; Cowan's Ford 149; Eutaw Springs 13, 39–40, 117; Fort Griswold 60–61; Fort Mifflin 29; Fort Slongo 85; Freeman's Farm 78; Froggs Point 29; Germantown 9, 22, 40, 63 65, 68, 88, 116, 119, 129, 134; Grassy Valley 126; Great Bridge 53–54; Groton Heights *see* Fort Griswold; Guilford Court House 9, 40, 51, 68, 91–92, 104, 149, 161; Harlem Heights 9, 64, 194; Horse Neck 29, 135, 156; Hubbardton 21, 164; Johnstown 171; Kettle Creek 47; Kings Mountain 51; Kingsbridge 181; Lexington 9, 17, 35–37, 41, 93, 133, 192, 194; Long Island 56, 138, 143–144; Millstone 141, 144; Monmouth 9, 12, 14, 17, 21–22 26, 29, 35, 40,44, 62–63, 65, 68, 71, 116, 119, 127, 133–134, 140, 152, 156, 163; Morrisania 42, 64; Newark 29; Newport 151, 153; Newtown 98, 156, 163; Niagara Falls 171; Ninety-Six 40; Oriskany 170, 189–191; Princeton 9, 27, 29 44, 73, 88, 141–142, 144–145, 174; Quebec 170, 174; Red Bank 122, 134; Rhode Island 6, 12, 14, 33, 82, 122, 128, 153, 157, 193–194; Saratoga 12, 14, 17, 21, 27, 35, 72, 78, 84, 118, 133, 152, 157, 164, 174, 176, 189, 192, 194; Savannah 39, 162; Short Hill 44; Soto Ferry 179; Springfield 44; Stillwater 32, 163; Stone

205

206 Index

Arabia 170; Stony Point 23–24, 35, 62, 92, 133, 152; Trenton 9, 27, 44, 55, 71, 86, 88, 174; White Marsh 35, 68, 103; White Plains 29, 40, 65, 82, 118, 133–134, 153, 173
Battles, Shadrach 22–23
Bibby, Solomon 23–24
Biddie, John 24–25
Blacksnake, Chief 170
The Blind African Slave 28–37
Bon Homme 181
Boone, Daniel 169
Boston 61
Boston, Siege of 102, 193
bound out 187
Bowles, Charles 26–27
Brace, Jeffrey 28–32
Brant, Joseph, 169–170, 182, 189
Brown, Col. Andrew Jackson 172
Brown, Joseph 32
Brown, Marlin (Roorback) 32–33
Brown, Scipio 33–34
Browne, John 34
Bucks of America 6
Budd, Bristol 34–35
Burdoo, Silas 35–37
Burgoyne, Gen. John 73–74, 78, 102, 126, 159, 164, 174
Burr, Seymour (Simo) 38
Butler, General 112, 150
Butler, Walter 170–171, 182

Caldwell, Hannah 44
Caldwell, the Rev. James 44
Capers, Jim 39
Carney, Thomas 39–40
Cato, Henry, 172–175
Chambers, Cuff 41–42
Charleston, Siege of 7, 26, 39, 41, 63, 91, 115–116, 162
Charlestown 61
Chavis, John 41
Chowen, John 175–176
Clinton, Gen. George 21, 171
Clinton, Gen. Henry 95–96, 98, 162
Clinton, Gen. James 95, 97, 122
coats, bounty 42
Coburn, Sampson 6, 42
Colburn, Primus 42–43
Comecho, Isaac 193–194
Comecho, Samuel 193–194
Confederacy 108
Congress 5, 8, 157, 177, 183
Continental Navy 50
Cook, Abraham 43–44
Cooper, James Fennimore 97
Cornstalk, Chief 168

Cornwallis, General 14–15, 23–26, 51–52 60, 63, 80, 88, 169, 172, 181, 185; defeat 10, 13, 20, 39, 59, 89, 110, 141, 154
Cromwell, Oliver 44–45
Cunningham, William "Bloody Bill" 51
Cusick, Nicholas (Kaghnatsho) 176–178
Cutler, Tobias 45

Dabney, Austin 46–48
Dart, Dolphin 48
Davidson, General 149
Dean, frigate 108
Declaration of Independence 157, 168
DeLancey's Cowboys 64, 135
desertion 176
Dewitt, Francis 49
Diligence 116
Dove 65
Dragon 101, 124
drummers 45, 52, 56, 65–66, 99, 116, 195; functions 33; killed 16, 39
Dunmore, Lord 4

Eastabrook, Prince 49–50
Eaton, Gen. Thomas 155
Eyes, Chief White 168

Ferguson, Andrew 50–53
Ferguson, Maj. Patrick 51
Ferrit, Caesar 194
Ferrit, John 194
Ferrit, Thomas 194
Fillmore, Pres. Millard 177
1st Rhode Island Regiment 5–6, 21–22, 34, 122, 127–128, 130, 133, 136, 151, 153
Fiske, Cato 52–53
Fleet, French 15
Flora, William "Billy" 53–54
Forge, Valley 12, 14, 17, 21–22, 26, 40, 62–63, 65, 71, 103, 118–119, 130, 133, 140, 156, 170, 174
Fort Clinton 65, 95
Fort Montgomery 65, 95–96
Fort Niagara 171, 177, 188
Fort Randolph 168
Fort Schuyler 189
Fort Stanwix 123, 188, 191
Fort Ticonderoga 50, 56, 119, 164
Fort Timmerman 191–192
Forten, James 54–55
Fox 61
Francis, Jacob 55–59
Franklin, privateer 130
Freeman, Chatham 59–60
Freeman, Jordan 60–61
Freeman, Sampson 61

Index 207

French and Indian War 93, 120, 170, 174, 188, 195
Fry, Nathan 62–63

Garnes, Anthony 63
Gates, Gen. Horatio 33, 112–113, 125, 137, 174, 189
Gates' Defeat *see* Camden, Battle of
George, Prince 65–66
Gilman, Anthony 63–64
Gilmore, Tobias 65
Grant, Jehu 66–67
Green, Jack 68
Green, Joseph 68–69
Greene, Gen. Nathanael 20, 23, 40 50–52, 92, 107, 112, 117, 129, 151, 156, 180, 184
Griffen, Ned 68
Guy, William 69–70

Hague 108
Hall, Jude 71–72
Hall, Pero 73
Hall, Primas (Trask) 73–80
Hall, Prince 73
Hancock 61
Harman, Edward 81–82
Harris, Peter 178–180
Hartwell, Jeffrey 81
Harvard 90, 93, 169
Hawwawas, Nicholas 179–180
Hector, Edward "Ned" 82
Hemenway, Jeffrey 82
Herkimer, General 190
Hessians 57–58, 73, 86–87, 135, 142, 145, 151, 173, 179
Hinton, Lewis 83
Howe, Gen. William 9, 39
Hull, Prince 83–84
Huzzey, James 84–85

Indian School 183
Indians: Abenaki 169; Catawba 172, 178–179; Cherokee 126; Delaware 168; Eastern Pequot 169, 187; Mashpee 181; Mohawk 170–171, 177, 187, 189, 191; Mohegan 171, 184, 187; Monacan 186; Nantucket 180; Oneidas 153, 168, 170–171, 182–183, 187, 189–190; Pamunkey 183; Passamaquoddy 179; Ponkapoag 38; Seneca 168, 170; Shawnee 168–169; Tuscarora 176, 178

Jackal 108
Jaquoi, Joseph Burd 180
Jefferson, Thomas 168

Jennings, Peter 85–89
Jeremiah, Anthony 180–181
Johonnot, Prince 89–90
Jones, Capt. John Paul 181
Jones, Tim 90–91

Kayashuta, Chief 168
Keeter, James 181
Kenneda, John (Canada) 182–183
Kirkland, Samuel 169
Knight, Moses 91–92

Lafayette, General 14, 20, 107, 176–177, 186–187
Lafayette, James *see* Armistead, James
Lamb, Pompey 92
Lambert, Plato 93
Lamson, David (Lampsom) 93–94
Latham, Lambert 60–61
Lattimore, Benjamin 95–98
Lee, Gen. Charles 57, 93, 127, 135
Leet, Richard 99
Lew, Barzillai 99–100
Lewis, Ambrose 100–101
Lincoln, Gen. Benjamin 20, 89, 162, 180
Lord Stirling *see* Alexander, Gen. William

Magus, Pomp 102
Marines 34, 103
Marion, Gen. Francis 39
Marshall, Chief Justice John 62
Martin, John (Keto) 103
Mason, Thomas 103–107
Masons 80, 169
Massacre, Cherry Valley 182
Matthews, Saul 107
Maxwell, General 174
McLellan, Prince 107–109
Mitchel, Oliver 109
Month, Ambrose 109–110
Moore, Abraham 110–111
Morgan, Gen. Daniel 50, 175; at Battle of Cowpens 24, 51
Murray, Mark 111–115
Mursh, Robert 183–184

Nash, Gen. Francis 88
Nash, Peter 115
New Jersey 54–55
New York Campaign 27, 48, 64, 82, 122, 133, 157

Occum, Jonathan 184–185
Occum, Sampson 184
Occom, Samuel 168
O'Hara, General 89

208 Index

Page 101
Paris, Peace of 169
Parker, Capt. John 33–34
Paugenit, Joseph 195
Penobscot Expedition 180
pensions 7–8
Percy, Gen. Hugh 93
Perkins, Isaac 115–116
Perkins, Nimrod 116
Peters, Jesse 117
Pin, Billy 185–186
Pin, James 185–186
Pin, John 185–186
Pin, Rawley 185–186
Pin, Robert 185–186
Poor, Salem 117–118
Pottage, Jabez 119–120
Praying Indians 168, 192–196
Prescott, General 173
Prutt, Caesar 120
Putnam, General 56

Quapish, Alexander 195–196

Ralls, Kenaz 120–122
Randall, Jack 122
Randall, Robert 122
Ranger 124, 181
Ranger, Joseph 124
Rangers, Indian 170, 176
Ray, Thomas 124–126
Redcross, John 186–187
Redman, William 126
Reprisal 130
Richard, Rhodes 126–127
Riley, Charles 127–128
Roberts, Reuben 128
Rochambeau, Count Comte de 89
Rodman, Mingo 128–129
Rodman, Prince 128–129
Rowland, Jack (Freeman) 129–130
Royal, Silas (Ryal Varnum) 130–132
Royal Lewis 54
Royal Proclamation of 1763 168
Runnels, Peleg 132

Salem, Peter 132–134
Salvador, Francis 126
Serapis 181
Shelly, Cyrus 187–188
Shelton, Caesar, 134–135
Simmon, Jack (Prince) 135–136
slaves: abolishment of slavery 4, 158; attitudes in New England 7; captured 7, 130–131; owners in the South 4–6; owners reimbursed 5, 123; serving with British 38;

sold 17
smallpox 25, 82, 168, 174, 178, 194
Sorrel, Edward 137–138
Spencer, Gen. Joseph 10, 125
Spencer's Expedition 10, 125
spies 14, 92
Stanhope, Richard 137–139
Steuben, Baron von 20
Stewart, Jordan 139
Stewart, William 139–140
Stockbridge Indians 168
Sullivan, General 37, 98, 145,151
Sullivan's Expedition 10, 71, 98, 145
Sumter, General 112
Sutphin, Samuel 140–147

Taborn, William 147–150
Tallmadge, Major Benjamin 120
Tann, Drewy 151
Tanner, Amos 188
Tanner, Joseph 188
Tanner, Quoum 151
Tarleton, Col. Banastre 24–25, 51, 149, 152, 163
Tewahangarahken, Han Yerry 188–190
Tewahangarahken, Honyere (Capt. Honyere Doxtator) 190, 191
Tewahangarahken, Honyost (Doxtator) 191–192
Thayandanegea, Chief *see* Joseph Brant
Tonyentagoyon, Blatcop 189
Tyng, Primus 152
Tyonajanegen (Tyona) 188

Underground Railroad 138

Valentine, Luke 152–153
Varnum, General 132
Vaughn, Prince 153–154
Vulture 20

wagons 18, 65, 148, 163, 175
Walden, Drury 154–155
Wallace, Caesar 155–156
War of 1812 111, 138, 171, 177
Washington, Gen. George 4–5, 20, 25–26, 29, 37–38, 44–45, 57, 60, 63, 70, 73, 78, 87–90, 97, 127, 137–138, 141, 143–144, 170–171, 174, 176–179, 185; crossing the Delaware 65, 86, 157
Weedon, Gen. George 22
Wells, Cuff 156–157
West Point 14, 20, 29, 42, 64–65, 86, 92, 140, 145–146, 192
Whipple, Prince 157–158
Whipple, Gen. William 157–158

Whittemore, Cuff 158–159
Wilkins, Benjamin 159–160
William, Tall 182
Williams, Henry 160
Williams, Matthew 160–161
Winthrop, sloop 16
Womble, John 161–162
Woodman, Dan 162–163

Woods, Asahel 163
Woodward, Polly (Mary) 162–163
Woodward, Pompey 163–165

"Yankee Doodle Dandy" 93, 100
Yorktown, Siege of 6, 9–11, 15, 33, 44–45, 54, 70, 85, 90–91, 117, 122–124, 127, 153, 174, 185–187

www.ingramcontent.com/pod-product-compliance
Ingram Content Group UK Ltd.
Pitfield, Milton Keynes, MK11 3LW, UK
UKHW042000140426
5217IPUK00015B/903